AF541797

BIO-TERRORISM AND BIO-DEFENCE

Bio-Terrorism and Bio-Defence

EDITED BY
P.R. CHARI
SUBA CHANDRAN

MANOHAR
2005

First published 2005

ISBN 81-7304-607-7

Published by
Ajay Kumar Jain for
Manohar Publishers & Distributors
4753/23 Ansari Road, Daryaganj
New Delhi 110 002

Printed at
Lordson Publishers Pvt Ltd
Delhi 110 007

Distributed in South Asia by
FOUNDATION
BOOKS
4381/4, Ansari Road
Daryaganj, New Delhi 110 002
and its branches at Mumbai, Hyderabad,
Bangalore, Chennai, Kolkata

Contents

Acknowledgements

We sincerely thank the Ministry of External Affairs (MEA), Government of India for its continued support to the Institute of Peace and Conflict Studies (IPCS) for this project. Third in the series, this study is undertaken by a generous grant provided by the MEA. Findings and conclusions are, however, the responsibility of individual authors who have contributed essays and do not reflect the views of either the MEA or the IPCS.

We also thank the research and administrative staff at the IPCS including Mallika Joseph, Vermani, Vishal, Surender, Sapna, Vijay and Prasenjit in organizing the conference.

Introduction

P.R. CHARI

The use of biological weapons (BW) for military purposes is as old as history itself. War is cruel and humanitarian or moral considerations have rarely inhibited the use of whatever means and instruments are available to defeat the enemy and attain the political or military objective. Hence, nations and war establishments have not been inhibited from using the 'deliberate spread of disease', which defines biological warfare, as a weapon in the past. Studies on biological warfare have noted that the ancient Persians poisoned wells to deny water to their enemies, a tactic that was common in medieval India as well. Catapulting disease infected corpses into besieged cities was practised by the Tartars, for example, during the siege of Kaffa in the Crimea in the fourteenth century bodies of plague victims were thrown into the city. The Black Death (bubonic plague), which wiped out one-third of the population of Europe, North Africa and parts of Asia and lasted over a century was, according to one theory, brought to Europe by Genoese traders trapped in Kaffa, who somehow survived and returned home when the Tartars lifted the siege. Their ships carried infected black rats, originally resident in India, that migrated to different parts of the Old World in the holds of trading ships—an early example, ironically, of the downside of globalization.[1] Historical accounts of biological warfare reveal that the British and French colonialists in North America supplied smallpox infected blankets to the native Indians. Since the New World population had no natural immunity against smallpox the effect was disastrous and exterminated large numbers of this native American population.[2]

What is new at the present juncture? Why should this arcane subject of biological weapons bestir more than casual interest? Why, more specifically, should India invest its limited resources to meet a remote contingency like bio-warfare and bio-terrorism? The reasons are fourfold.

- First, several countries including the United States, Russia, the United Kingdom, South Africa and Japan are known to have carried out research on BWs since the 1920s.[3] At present, nearly a dozen countries are suspected of pursuing a BW programme and possessing these weapons; some have not joined the BTWC. These investigations are proceeding under the rubric of bio-defence research in the United States and also in India. Clearly, the possibility of the use of biological weapons by state or non-state actors is not considered fanciful by their national security establishments; hence their investment in this area of research.
- Second, Japan is known to have conducted BW experiments with live human beings, and to have used biological weapons during its campaigns in Manchuria (1931) and China (1945).[4] A section of the Indian security establishment believes that BWs do not lend themselves ideally for use as weapons of mass destruction (WMD). But there is little appreciation of their being used to infect agricultural crops and livestock. For a country like India that derives a quarter to one-third of its national income from agriculture, which also provides employment to some 65–70 per cent of its people, BW use against these targets would spell an unparalleled disaster.
- Third, 9/11 has focused the attention of the security elite around the world on the wider possibilities of this innovative use of civil airliners to attack high value targets for, more generally, WMD or catastrophic terrorism. Terrorist organizations would find it hard to either steal or manufacture a credible nuclear weapon; hence, they could focus greater attention on acquiring chemical, biological and radiological weapons. An earlier (1995) WMD attack involved the use of sarin, a chemical agent, in the Tokyo subway. 9/11 was followed by several anthrax mail incidents in the United States, and copycat hoax attempts in India. It has been urged

that the threat of bio-terrorism is vastly exaggerated 'since the dissemination of anthrax caused a total of five deaths and a total of fewer than twenty cases of anthrax [in the United States]'.[5] This is true at the literal level, but fails to appreciate the massive disruption and panic caused in the wake of the anthrax mail attack. Some of the office rooms in the US Congress, where the anthrax mail was received and opened, are still not being used. There is an element of doubt about the aetiology of the plague outbreaks in Surat (1994) and Himachal Pradesh (2002), and whether they were a natural phenomenon or an induced occurrence.[6] The economic losses caused by an epidemic are incalculable, for example, the recent case of SARS in China. Hence, the possibility of BWs being employed for blackmail by threatening their use gains credibility from the recent cases of hostages being thus used.

- Fourth, epidemiologists are well aware that new diseases are constantly appearing while old diseases disappear from the world. They could infect not only human beings, but also animals, plants and bacteria. New diseases are believed to arise when changes occur in either the ecology or human behaviour. What is new in the current stage of human civilization is that these ecological and behavioural changes are occurring more rapidly and extensively than in the earlier periods of history; hence, the ubiquitous appearance of new diseases is a natural phenomenon. Compounding this development are the rapid advances being made in biotechnology, especially in genome sequencing and genetic mutation. New difficultly detectable and curable micro-organisms could be developed by state and non-state actors for use against their adversaries. This phenomenon is also obtaining in India; a new Hantavirus has been found in India, which is a mutant of this virus that originated in Korea, and causes HFRS (haemorrhagic fever with renal syndrome).[7]

It is worth noting that the earlier literature had emphasized the scientific, technological and financial difficulties, especially problems associated with delivery, that non-state actors would encounter in developing and using BWs for terrorist attacks. This assurance has not only been dispelled after the anthrax mail attacks and the discovery of ricin with a terrorist group in Britain, but also drawn attention to earlier attempts at using BWs for inimical purposes. An exhaustive study of bio-terrorism 'has chronicled 52 confirmed cases [in] this [20th] century in which terrorists, criminals or others expressed interest in biological agents . . . which resulted in 982 victims, including nine deaths, and were intended to achieve various ends: murder, extortion, incapacitation, mass murder, terror, making a political statement, and revenge.'[8] There are several other reasons to believe that bio-terrorist attacks are not fanciful and should, therefore, be taken into account in defence planning exercises:

- Groups like the Al Qaeda are known to have evinced an interest in acquiring both chemical and biological weapons,[9] as revealed by plans seized from its hideouts in Afghanistan. The Al Qaeda has established international networks in some 50-60 countries; this would make detection very difficult, given the ease with which a BW programme can be initiated and concealed, unless the willing cooperation of these countries is secured.
- Attempts to negotiate a Verification Protocol for the Biological and Toxin Weapons Convention (BTWC) received a setback in 2001 following the United States' decision to withdraw from these negotiations. The irony cannot be overemphasized that, while the dangers from BWs and bio-terrorism have enlarged manifold over the last decade, there is hesitation in the United States and the international community to proceed determinedly with non-proliferation measures. An inadequate modality of holding expert level meetings and annual conferences of the states parties had been envisaged at the Fifth BTWC Review Conference (November 2002) in lieu of a Verification Protocol. Their findings would be reviewed at the Sixth BTWC Review Conference scheduled for November 2006.[10] It is doubtful whether they will provide reassurance that the problem of bio-terrorism is being seriously addressed. Several alternative modalities have, of course,

been suggested,[11] but they have not received the attention they deserve.

- States suspected of pursuing offensive chem-bio programmes like Iran, Libya, North Korea and Syria are situated in zones of conflict. It is possible that these states may not use BWs directly, but form alliances with terrorist outfits to attack their adversaries. Past history has shown sub rosa organizations being used in this manner by these states, apart from those in South Asia, for achieving their political objectives. The possibility of a nexus being established between state actors and terrorist organizations to use BWs is, therefore, quite plausible. The ease of deniability and difficulty in tracing the source of a BW attack, especially between primary and secondary infections adds to this plausibility.

Bio-terrorism, therefore, presents a clear and present danger. The need for developing bio-defence measures is imperative, as also the need for international cooperation to meet this threat. Unfortunately, the last decade has been singularly bereft of any major arms control treaty or progress in the disarmament sphere. On the other hand, unthinking unilateralism has led to an impasse in efforts to secure arms control and disarmament. It is in this gloomy environment that national and international measures to seek bio-defence need consideration. Bio-defence remains an area of neglect in India as, indeed, much of the developing and developed world, with the sole exception of the United States that has invested heavily in its Homeland Security and related programmes for this purpose. The challenges in this regard are many, and attention may be briefly drawn to some of them.

- The basic infrastructure to handle the outbreak of disease—preventive and curative—is available in all countries, and is recognizable by their public health departments, hospitals, dispensaries, medical professionals, etc. They have practical experience in handling epidemics, but what a BW attack entails is dealing with a pandemic where the health infrastructure and personnel could get engulfed, but demands on their services would increase manifold. A surge effect needs to be catered for. Experience in dealing with large-scale natural disasters would be relevant here, especially of man-made disasters like the leakage of methyl-isocyanate in Bhopal (1984). Contingency planning, therefore, is of the essence for this purpose.

- A large stock of vaccines and antibiotics would have to be maintained in storage centres around the world for assisting countries that are attacked and to counter the pandemic. It is impossible to manufacture large quantities of these vital supplies within a short period of time. Hence, a global policy is required to ensure the turnover of time-expiry vaccines, drugs and medicines.
- An international research effort is required to improve the prophylactic and preventive measures available to deal with diseases, including those caused by genetic mutation, natural or induced, but also common diseases like anthrax and plague that could be the BWs of choice for terrorist groups and aberrant states. Second-generation vaccines can be quickly developed and manufactured. New and cheaper drug regimens are urgently required, and research programmes geared for this purpose need to be adequately funded.
- The most challenging problem facing the public health community in dealing with a bio-terrorist attack would be discovering how and where it had been launched, pointing to the need for better surveillance, reporting arrangements and scientific information management. Issues of unified command and coordination between civic and state authorities, apart from private medical facilities and practitioners is also required, both for detection and relief work. The role of the armed forces in these operations needs to be better defined, given their experience in dealing with disaster management under the rubric of 'aid-to-civil' functions. In short, a multi-pronged and holistic policy needs to be deliberated upon and formulated.

This volume addresses the issues embedded in the phenomenon of bio-terrorism and the problems of bio-defence to counter this threat. The essays included here have been grouped under three major heads relating to national and international efforts to combat bio-weapons, bio-terrorism and providing for bio-defence. A fourth section is devoted to investigations into SARS and bird flu, a chronology relating to biological weapons, and a bibliography of the important literature in this regard. The first draft of these essays was presented to a peer group at a conference held at the Institute of Peace and Conflict Studies, and an opportunity was provided to the contributors to revise their papers in the light of the criticisms made and the discussions held.

This study was made possible by the generous assistance received from the Policy Planning Division of the Ministry of External Affairs. The ministry is in no way responsible for the views expressed in these essays, which do not reflect the official policies adopted by the Government of India. It is hoped that these essays would pave the way for further work by the concerned academic communities in the country, particularly in the departments of international studies, more specifically disarmament studies. In the post-Cold War, post-9/11 world, the menace of WMDs in general, and biological weapons in particular, is likely to gain salience in the future.

NOTES

1. See the chapter entitled, 'The Flying Corpses of Kaffa', in Arno Karlen, *Plague's Progress: A Social History of Mankind and Disease*, London: Victor Gollancz, 1995, pp. 79–92.
2. Early attempts to use biological resources for military purposes are noted in Wendy Barnaby, *The Plague Makers: The Secret World of Biological Warfare*, London: Vision Paperbacks, 1999, p. 6.
3. Ibid., especially Chapters 5 and 6.
4. Ibid., pp. 106–12.
5. Victor W. Sidel, 'Defense against Biological Weapons: Can Immunization and Secondary Prevention Succeed?', in *Biological Warfare and Disarmament: New Problems, New Perspectives*, ed. Susan Wright, Lanham: Rowman & Littlefield Publishers, Inc., 2002, p. 82.
6. An analysis of these incidents is available in Animesh Roul, 'Plague Outbreaks in India: Surat and Himachal Pradesh', in *Biological Weapons: Issues and Threats*, ed. P.R. Chari and Arpit Rajain, New Delhi: India Research Press, 2003, pp. 115–28.
7. Arno Karlen, *Plague's Progress*, pp. 169–70.
8. This study was undertaken by Seth Carus of the National Defence University in Washington, but had excluded state-sponsored acts of

terrorism like the Bulgarian Secret Police assassinating the political leader, Georgi Markov, using ricin; cited in Wendy Barnaby, *The Plague Makers*, p. 36.

9. Official Text, 'New CIA Report Documents Global Weapons Proliferation Trends', 1 February 2002, http://www.usembassy.State.gov/delhi.html, p. 11.
10. These issues are discussed by P.R. Chari and Kalpana Chittaranjan in this volume.
11. Other approaches to the Verification Protocol are discussed in Kalpana Chittaranjan, 'Endgame in November 2002: US Position, Other Alternative Modalities to Protocol', in *Biological Weapons*, ed. P.R. Chari and Arpit Rajain.

CHAPTER 1

BTWC Verification: India's Position

P.R. CHARI

PROLOGUE

Biological and chemical weapons are linked to each other in the minds of people and governments. They were jointly addressed in the Geneva Protocol (1925), which prohibits the use in war of asphyxiating, poisonous or other gases, and bacteriological methods of warfare. The Geneva Protocol was primarily designed to outlaw the use of poisonous gases that had been extensively used in the First World War, it was on the suggestion of Poland that this prohibition was extended to bacteriological weapons.[1] Following the introduction of nuclear weapons, both chemical and biological weapons were collectively included within weapons of mass destruction (WMD) along with, more lately, radiological weapons.

This linkage of biological with chemical weapons hindered an agreement being reached on their elimination as part of a total scheme for general and complete disarmament. Opinion was sharply divided on this issue between the competing blocs during the Cold War. The UK favoured the separation of biological and chemical weapons and independent negotiations to discuss their elimination, but this was not acceptable to the Soviet Union and its allies that wanted these two classes of weapons to be considered together within a comprehensive agreement. Later, the Soviet Union and its allies changed their position and presented a revised draft to the Conference of the Committee on Disarmament restricted to biological weapons.[2] Thereafter, the Convention on the Prohibition of the Development, Production and Stockpiling of Bacteriological (Biological) and Toxin Weapons and on their Destruction (BTWC) was finalized, and it was presented for signature on 10 April 1972.

The operative provisions of the BTWC enjoin the parties not to develop, produce, stockpile, or acquire biological agents or toxins 'of types and in quantities that have no justification for prophylactic, protective, and other peaceful purposes', as well as weapons and means of delivery. All such materials, existing in the territory of the states parties, were to be destroyed within nine months of the BTWC's entry into force, which occurred in 1975. The BTWC is of unlimited duration, and envisages the exchange of information on peaceful uses of biological agents and toxins, amendment and review, accession and withdrawal from the Convention, but it does not absolve parties from continuing their obligations under the Geneva Protocol.

An engaging feature of the BTWC is its brevity, it has fifteen short Articles spread over four pages. Besides, it could be finalized after some three years of negotiations, which is a record of sorts for arms control agreements that usually drag on for several years. These two distinguishing features of the BTWC are due to the lack of verification measures in this Convention, which enabled its easy passage. It is not possible therefore to ensure that parties comply with its provisions. Article V of the BTWC enjoins its signatories 'to consult one another and to cooperate in solving any problems that may arise in relation to the objective of, or in the application of the provisions of, the Convention'. Article VI further allows the aggrieved parties to lodge a complaint with the Security Council, which is empowered to 'initiate, in accordance with the provisions of the Charter of the United Nations' an investigation into the complaint, and to 'inform the states Parties to the Convention of the results of the investigation'. These modalities are too feeble to deter proliferators or adjudicate upon complaints of non-compliance. Consequently, verification of the BTWC can only be accomplished by national technical means (satellite reconnaissance and electronic eavesdropping), but the confidence that parties are not infracting the prohibitions of the BTWC must largely rest on trust, which offends the principle voiced by late President Reagan 'Trust but Verify'.

Several reasons explain why, historically, the BTWC did not include any inbuilt verification measures to ensure its credibility.

- First, this enabled its early conclusion without entering the hugely contentious and time-consuming negotiations process to hammer out a Verification Protocol.[3]
- Second, it was then believed that such verification provisions were redundant since it was unlikely that these agents and toxins would find military applications.
- Third, several arms control treaties negotiated around this period (the early 1970s) also lacked provisions for their authentication and were premised on verification being undertaken by national technical means, since intrusive verification measures were politically infeasible, e.g. the Interim Agreement on Limitation of Strategic Offensive Arms (1972) and the ABM Treaty (1972).
- Fourth, the belief was strong then[4] that the BTWC is essentially unverifiable 'because the facilities to produce these agents are virtually the same as utilized to manufacture pharmaceuticals and agro-industrial products. Further, there is no prohibition on their development or production for curative or preventive medical purposes. Biological agents can be produced in a few weeks; therefore, the need for storing them may not arise.'[5] This situation persists to this day.

It is presumable that India was not unaware of these inadequacies; yet it was amongst the earliest entrants to the BTWC (15 January 1973), and ratified its entry on 15 July 1974. India's statement on signature declared:

> The Government of India would like to reiterate in particular its understanding that the objective of the convention is to eliminate biological and toxin weapons, thereby excluding completely the possibility of their use, and that the exemption with regard to biological agents and toxins, which would be permitted for prophylactic, protective or other peaceful purposes would not, in any way, create a loophole in regard to the production and retention of biological and toxin weapons. Also, any assistance which might be furnished under the terms of the convention would be of medical or humanitarian nature and in conformity with the Charter of the United Nations.[6]

The emphasis on the regulatory and disarmament aspects of the BTWC is unmistakeable in this long citation, but there was no particular anxiety at that time about its lack of verification provisions.

INDIAN PERCEPTIONS OF THE BW THREAT

What has highlighted this inadequacy in the Indian consciousness? These new perceptions were shaped by global developments like the explosive development of biotechnology in the 1980s, Iraq's clandestine WMD programme coming to light that included BWs, information about the extensive nature of the Soviet BW programme, efforts made by Aum Shinrikyo to develop and use BWs in Tokyo, and the anthrax mail attacks in the United States after 9/11. Further, the Chemical Weapons Convention (CWC) 1993/1997, which India has signed and ratified, contains stringent provisions to verify its compliance, which has added to angst regarding the absence of credible verification arrangements in the BTWC.

More specifically, three recent developments have influenced India's perceptions. First, India has been sensitized to anthrax mail attacks. Several such incidents after 9/11 were hoaxes, but they caused great alarm and disruption. Second, Osama bin Laden has identified India, apart from the United States and Israel, as being his chief enemy.[7] There is mounting evidence that he was contemplating the manufacture of biological, chemical and radiological weapons. Third, new technologies are maturing like the genetic manipulation of biological agents and toxins that would greatly complicate the control of induced diseases. The effect of all these developments has sharpened awareness of the BW threat within the Indian security establishment. The belief, however, also obtains that India's known adversaries will not use chemical and biological weapons in the 'weapons of mass destruction' mode, and the more realistic threat is believed to emanate from the likelihood of BWs being used by non-state actors.[8] Significantly, India moved a resolution at the 57th UN General Assembly entitled Measures to Prevent Terrorists from Acquiring Weapons of Mass Destruction, which sought collective action by the international community to address this threat, and was adopted by consensus.

This heightened sensitivity regarding terrorists gaining access to WMDs reflects India's recent experience of having been the victim of cross-border terrorism for some two decades in Punjab and now in Kashmir. Some part of this sensitivity derives from the vulnerability of its large population that lives in unhygienic conditions, and the possibility of its livestock and agricultural crops being targeted, which would be an unparalleled disaster for this large agricultural economy. These apprehensions found resonance in the recommendations made by the Group of Ministers set up by the Government of India to review national security after the Kargil conflict (May–July 1999). It assessed:

> Today's terrorists, be they religious extremists, Jehadis, international cults like Aum Shinrikyo or individual nihilists, may gain access to nuclear, biological, and chemical weapons or raw materials. NBC terrorism today has moved from the stage of far-fetched horror to a contingency that could happen tomorrow. The advances in IT and communications have made terrorism with Weapons/Materials of Mass Destruction easier to carry out.[9]

No terrorist group has yet used BWs in a WMD mode but,

> India's fears have been strongly influenced by those of the United States and further enhanced by the cooperative relationship the two countries have forged to meet the threat from terrorism after the September 11 attacks and heightened awareness of the WMD threat emanating from Afghanistan.[10]

Two further facts need mention to illustrate India's position on defensive measures against a possible BW attack. First, while acceding to the Geneva Convention in 1925 the colonial government had retained the right to use biological and chemical weapons against countries that were not parties to the Convention or might use such weapons against it. This reservation was not withdrawn by India on gaining independence in 1947. Second, the operative clause, Article I, of the Biological Weapons Convention does not prohibit the use of biological weapons.[11] Thus, in theory, India could use BWs if they were used against its territory. India has also proclaimed that, in the event of a major biological or chemical weapons attack, 'it will retain the option of retaliating with nuclear weapons'.[12]

ON VERIFYING THE BIOLOGICAL WEAPONS CONVENTION

A discussion of India's approaches to the controversial issues during the negotiations on the Verification Protocol to the Biological Weapons Convention is in order. Despite this discussion being largely historical in nature, they provide an insight into India's views on these issues. Moreover, these issues would surface again if the states parties decide to reinvigorate international efforts to devise effective arrangements to verify the BTWC, which is currently missing. Briefly India's position on these issues was as follows.[13]

THE PROBLEM OF DEFINITIONS

Opinion was divided between the negotiating states on whether terms like 'biological weapons' and 'hostile purposes' in Article I should be more precisely defined. The United States and Russia took diametrically opposite positions. The US argued that the discovery of new or genetically engineered biological agents would render the exercise of drawing up precise lists for definitional purposes futile. Russia was of the view that the absence of such precision would leave too much discretion for the inspectors to interpret facts whimsically. Via media solutions suggested that only such terms as were imperatively required for a verification regime be defined, or that only terms like 'biological weapons' and 'hostile purposes' be defined solely for the purpose of implementing the Verification Protocol.[14] India took no sides in this controversy, but it was inclined towards the US position. It urged that Article I 'cannot be constrained by the state of scientific and technological knowledge at a particular point of time and should be interpreted to take into account any further developments in science and technology'.[15] India also favoured Iran's proposal that the word 'use' be inserted into Article I to complete the list of prohibitions provided therein.

Organization for Implementing the Protocol

Differences arose regarding the structure of the organization proposed to ensure compliance with the Protocol. Russia favoured the Security Council, which did not garner much support on the suspicion that the veto available to the Permanent Council members would be used to thwart action against themselves and their allies. An alternative proposal envisaged a specialized organization being set up on the same lines as obtained to implement the Chemical Weapons Convention.[16] This question became linked with issues pertaining to the ambit of inspections to investigate complaints of non-compliance with the Protocol. India joined the non-aligned group in suggesting that all BTWC adherents be included in this organizing body, with a smaller group of representatives being selected to guide its actions and take urgent decisions.

On-site Inspections

This became the most contentious issue during the Protocol negotiations. Apart from declarations to provide information about BW capabilities, a system of 'challenge' inspections was envisaged to look over facilities and verify complaints of non-adherence to the BTWC's provisions, apart from investigating suspicious occurrences of disease. Opinion was divided among the negotiating parties on the merits of a 'red light' procedure wherein three-fourths of the BTWC adherents needed to vote to stop a challenge inspection from proceeding, and a 'green light' procedure in which three-fourths of the parties needed to approve a challenge inspection, which would have been very difficult to obtain. The United States wanted a 'green light' procedure, which was also favoured by India, with the caveat that inspections must not become instruments of harassment, and decisions must be reached within specified time frames. India was sceptical about the further need for 'non-challenge' or 'random' visits to check declarations or to familiarize inspectors with sensitive facilities, a view shared by the United States.

CONTROLS ON TECHNOLOGY TRANSFER

This issue revealed basic differences between the Indian and American positions. India joined the non-aligned and developing countries in decrying the need for the Australia Group, which was established to deny the transfer of chemical precursors and equipment for manufacturing chemical and biological agents. Instead, India favoured the multilateral monitoring of export controls, functioning within the ambit of a multilateral or universally accepted Treaty or Convention. India also suggested the use of declarations to monitor the export of dual-purpose materials and their regulation through multilateral guidelines.[17] Thereby, India opposed the subordination of Article X of the BWC, which envisages cooperation and peaceful development through the biological sciences, to the requirements of Article III, which commits states parties not to 'assist, encourage, or induce' any country or organization engaging in prohibited activities. By contrast, the United States supported the Australia Group, and argued that the goals of scientific cooperation and technology transfers enjoined by Article X were being fairly met. It was claimed that 'while the United States approved well over $ 250 million in export licence applications relevant to the Convention [in 1995]; we denied applications worth a grand total of $ 2,443'.[18]

ENDGAME AND INDIA'S ATTITUDES

India's negotiating position on the Protocol is important to appreciate its stand on verifying the BTWC. There were ominous presentiments, however, that these negotiations would come to naught after the US delegation declared in mid-2001 that it could not support the draft Protocol in the form that it had emerged. India expressed its support for the Rolling Text and the Chairman's Composite Text embodying the Protocol, pointing out specific areas that needed strengthening, but concluding that it had 'deliberately chosen to focus on specifics for two reasons. First, to emphasize that there are only limited issues that need to be "fixed", and secondly, that the "fix" can be found within the overall framework and thrust of the Composite Text.'[19] India's position on the Protocol was encapsulated in the statement:

The anthrax incidents of last year [2001], instead of prompting the world community to act collectively to challenge the threat of biological weapons, have instead led to a path that rejects the framework for multilateral action and may threaten the norm that has existed for thirty years. While national implementation measures and certain group efforts may be worth pursuing, they cannot substitute for meaningful multilateral efforts to strengthen the Convention.[20]

This critical and continuing role of multilateral negotiations was stressed again after the US finally rejected the draft of the Protocol and the entire approach underlying its negotiation. Recognizing the need to include the threat from bio-terrorism into these deliberations, India pointed out that:

The norm of prohibition of BW, embodied in the BWC, needs to be strengthened and this is where the Protocol, in accordance with the 1994 mandate, becomes a crucial input. Secondly, recent incidents have also highlighted the need for enhanced national controls on production, acquisition, storage, handling, transfer and use of dangerous pathogens. Some of these controls already exist in the form of international guidelines; what is needed is sensitization and widespread adherence. Finally, international cooperation and assistance is not only necessary for dealing with the use or threat of use of biological weapons, but reflects the political commitment of the international community to deal with such threats in a collective fashion.[21]

These official statements make clear that India was deeply committed to the finalization and promulgation of the Verification Protocol after overcoming the remaining difficulties and further refining its contents. However, these arguments and that of other members belonging to the Ad Hoc Group could not deflect the US from withdrawing its support, and nullifying the negotiations that had led to the drafting of the Verification Protocol.

The core of the US objections to the draft Protocol was that '[it] will not improve our ability to verify BWC compliance. It will not enhance our confidence in compliance and will do little to deter those countries seeking to develop biological weapons. In our assessment, the draft Protocol would put national security and confidential business information at risk.'[22] America's rejection of the draft Protocol was noted by India, while extolling its own role, since it had 'remained active in efforts to strengthen the Convention' and had 'played a central role in facilitating progress towards consensus on key elements with a view to recommending a programme of work for the future.'[23] Later, President Bush announced several steps for consideration by the state parties to devise a comprehensive strategy for combating the threat from BWs and bio-terrorism.[24] These steps envisaged all parties taking measures to:

1. Enact strict national criminal legislation against prohibited BW activities with strong extradition requirements.
2. Establish an effective United Nations procedure for investigating suspicious outbreaks or allegations of biological weapons use.
3. Establish procedures for addressing BWC compliance concerns.
4. Commit to improving international disease control and to enhance mechanisms for sending expert response teams to cope with outbreaks.
5. Establish sound national oversight mechanisms for the security and genetic engineering of pathogenic organisms.
6. Devise a solid framework for bioscientists in the form of a code of ethical conduct that would have universal recognition.
7. Promote responsible conduct in the study, use, modification and shipment of pathogenic organisms.

On the opening day of the resumed Fifth Review Conference (19 November 2001) the United States formally set out its reasons for rejecting the draft Verification Protocol, suggesting what could be done to verify the BTWC. Accommodating this demand, the Final Document adopted by the Conference[25] notes that it will 'hold three annual meetings of the States Parties of one week duration each year commencing in 2003. A two-week meeting of experts would precede the annual meetings. Items (i) and (ii) will be considered in 2003; items (iii) and (iv) in 2004, and item (v) in 2005. The Sixth Review Conference would be held no later than the end of 2006 to discuss and promote common understanding and effective action on:

(i) the adoption of necessary national measures to implement the prohibitions set forth in the Convention, including the enactment of penal legislation;

(ii) national mechanisms to establish and maintain the security and oversight of pathogenic microorganisms and toxins;

(iii) enhancing international capabilities for responding to, investigating and mitigating the effects of cases of alleged use of biological or toxin weapons or suspicious outbreaks of disease;

(iv) strengthening and broadening national and international institutional efforts and existing mechanisms for the surveillance, detection, diagnosis and combating of infectious diseases affecting humans, animals, and plants;

(v) the content, promulgation, and adoption of codes of conduct for scientists.'

This segmented approach tries to address the need for verifying the prohibitions of the BTWC in a holistic manner. There is little to suggest that any kind of international agreement or norms would be established by pursuing this agenda, which is primarily intended to 'discuss and promote common understanding' on these issues, although 'effective action' is gratuitously enjoined. Can this agenda realistically meet the threat from the dissemination of biological agents and toxins to state and non-state actors? The obvious answer is 'no'.

What is India's position on the drafting of this Conference Document to reflect American predilections? A sense of foreboding and resignation informed the Indian delegation even before the resumed Fifth Review Conference buried the Verification Protocol. India's Ambassador to the CD noted that the five points are a 'very modest step. What's important here is to see what the five points leave out? There is no concept of a review, even though this is meant to be a review conference. The word negotiation is conspicuously absent . . . as is the process of multilateralism, which is not mentioned.'[26] A less critical judgement of this Conference Document holds:

> The current state of multilateral response is woefully inadequate if not irresponsible. There are real political reasons why it has not been possible to achieve more but it simply is not good enough [but] . . . the series of

meetings over the coming three years does at least offer a way of keeping attention globally on the biological weapons problem and for generating greater public knowledge of and engagement with this issue area. It is vital that the most is made of this opportunity.[27]

It is noteworthy that there was no organized resistance by the states parties to the US forcing its views on the Review Conference; hence the harsh judgement that 'BWC states parties are in a position of their own making; they can neither wish away the problems brought about by the failure of their own efforts nor revise recent history that demonstrates they are *all*—collectively—responsible for the Convention's problems.'[28] This realization may explain why India, despite its protestations and reservations, decided to cooperate and participate in the expert level and annual meetings in the countdown to the Sixth Review Conference in 2006.

UNFOLDING MEASURES TO IMPLEMENT THE MANDATE

Fundamental doubts, however, plague the Government of India with respect to the approaches suggested by the Fifth Review Conference to address the BTWC's verification problems. As expressed before the CD:

> . . . developments in the bio-technology field remind us that Treaties cannot remain static in a world driven by technology. Treaties need to keep pace with changing reality, whether political or technological in order to retain validity. And in all of this, multilateral approaches are the only viable approaches. Even when we perceive inadequacies in multilateral agreements, the answer lies in pursuing solutions through the multilateral route rather than resorting to further ad hoc technology controls.[29]

The underlying sentiment against the technology control route to prevent proliferation is that this modality has only succeeded in penalizing responsible countries like India; its record in protecting sensitive transferred technology from getting lost or surreptitiously transferred is impeccable. On the other hand, countries known to be irresponsible and having proliferated such technology have not been penalized. The manner in which China and Pakistan have blatantly transferred nuclear and missile technology with fair impunity is too obvious to require elaboration.

The First Meeting of Experts to consider items (i) and (ii) mandated by the Final Document issued after the Fifth Review Conference was held in August 2003. Its findings were discussed at a meeting of states parties in November 2003, which agreed:

- To review, and where necessary, enact or update national legal, including regulatory and penal, measures which ensure effective implementation of the prohibition of the Convention, and which enhance effective security of pathogens and toxins.
- The positive effect of cooperation between states parties with differing legal and constitutional arrangements. States parties in a position to do so may wish to provide legal and technical assistance to others who request it in framing and/or expanding their own legislation and controls in the areas of national implementation and biosecurity.
- The need for comprehensive and concrete national measures to secure pathogen collections and the control of their use for peaceful purposes. There was a general recognition of the value of biosecurity measures and procedures, which would ensure that such dangerous materials are not accessible to persons who might or could misuse them for purposes contrary to the Convention.[30]

In compliance with the objectives of items (i) and (ii) India provided details of its legislation and rules and regulations concerning both national implementation and security and oversight procedures to the Meeting of Experts. The existing biosafety arrangements, in respect of laboratory research and industrial applications that involve recombinant DNA technologies, involves a three-tier structure that is in position.

Each institution involved in such work must have a biosafety committee that provides the first level of monitoring. Then a Review Committee on Genetic Modification (RCGM), functioning in the Department of Biotechnology, is expected to maintain oversight over all research activities in the country. Finally, any large-scale use must be cleared by the Genetic Engineering Approval Committee (GEAC) under the Ministry of Environment and Forests.[31]

These institutional arrangements provide for monitoring and regulating biotechnology in the areas of medicine, pharmaceuticals, agriculture and food technology. However, these measures do not amount to a national legislation to implement the BTWC, which requires serious consideration. This legislation, among other things, should have regulations to register pathologists in the same manner as doctors are registered by the Medical Council of India, and also to establish controls over the production and sale of pathogens.

The Meeting of Experts may be denigrated as being a factual information collection exercise that could, at best, identify the problem areas and national implementation efforts that have been introduced to overcome them. However, a positive development at this meeting was the submission of information by the states parties on their national implementation measures that had originally been sought in 1981 for the First Review Conference of the BTWC. However, India's basic scepticism continues on these new modalities, and is embodied in:

> The question that even if domestic legal constraints exist on a country's statute book how can the body of States Parties conclude that these are being fully implemented. Unsatisfactory compliance was identified as a principal concern, and inability to verify was the main reason [given] by many States Parties for rejecting the idea of negotiations on a legally binding instrument. But if a multilateral instrument does not exist how then can the collective body of States Parties obtain re-assurance that there is compliance? And if verification is not possible then how should compliance be ensured?.... For the same reason that we have domestic laws, we also need international treaties and conventions, to codify rights and obligations of members of the community of sovereign states.[32]

These arguments highlight the undercurrent of worldwide resentment against the unilateralism of the Bush administration in matters relating to arms control.

Items (iii) and (iv) would be considered at the Second Meeting of Experts that is to be held in August 2004, and its results would, no doubt, also be accepted by the meeting of states parties that would be held later in November 2004. But, it could be reasonably surmised that India would have no objection to establishing effective procedures for investigating suspicious outbreaks of disease and allegations of BW use, and establishing international mechanisms for this purpose, if this is done under credible international arrangements, respecting the compulsions of national security and confidentiality of commercial information. It could also accept a code of conduct being devised for bioscientists having universal applicability as envisaged under item (v) that is to be discussed at the Meeting of Experts coming up in August 2005.[33]

CONCLUSION

In retrospect, it is apparent that a frisson of doubt had always informed India's position on the negotiations to finalize the Verification Protocol on whether, even in its ideal form, it could have ensured satisfactory compliance of the BTWC, due to the intrinsic nature of BWs. Some of these difficulties are technical, others are political in nature. The same facilities can manufacture BWs and pharmaceutical or agro-industrial products, and no prohibition can be placed on manufacturing the latter for civilian purposes. Biological agents can be produced within weeks and there is no need for storing them. Distinguishing between permitted and prohibited activities, therefore, may not be possible unless on-site inspections are undertaken, and samples drawn for assay on a real-time basis. Such intrusive verification measures would be anathema to governments on national security considerations and to industry on grounds of their need to maintain commercial secrecy. The modality of 'managed access' to provide for targeted inspections may not be useful since evidence relating to the clandestine manufacture of BWs and toxins can be destroyed within hours by simple processes like passing steam through containers and connecting pipes.[34]

That said, India should have no difficulty in undertaking any further steps agreed upon by the states parties to strengthen measures for securing compliance with the BTWC like further tightening of export controls—end-use certificates could be made mandatory, apart from stockpiling vaccines and antibiotics in storage centres around the world for emergency use, undertaking international research programmes to develop new and cheaper drug regimes against common diseases, including those for biowarfare.[35]

A new dispensation is urgently required, however, to combat the menace of bio-terrorism, which should be framed within the larger context of international terrorism. BW manufacture is progressively becoming indigenized and less dependent on foreign suppliers for procuring materials, technology and equipment. Merely gating exports, therefore, is no longer relevant to prevent BW proliferation or bioterrorism. Besides, indigent scientists and engineers from the Republics of the erstwhile Soviet Union are available to help aspiring nations gain access to WMDs, including BWs. 'Osama bin Laden has professed the acquisition of "weapons of mass destruction" to be a "religious duty" and he has threatened to use such weapons. Reports that documents retrieved from Al-Qaeda facilities in Afghanistan contain information on CBRN materials underscore Bin Laden's rhetoric.'[36]

The Al-Qaeda organization is spread over 50 to 60 countries. Proceeding against this loosely networked organization will be ineffective unless these countries cooperate in the war against terrorism. Consequently, the unilateral approach pursued by the United States would prove counter-productive, since the US seeks international cooperation to wage its war against terrorism against Afghanistan and Iraq, while acting unilaterally to pursue its national self-interests in other directions. These include weakening the arms control regime by not ratifying the Comprehensive Test Ban Treaty, withdrawing from the ABM Treaty, weakening the Chemical Weapons Treaty and rejecting the draft Verification Protocol for the BTWC. Seeking to implement the Convention by threats of condign punishment against proliferators and devising a stricter export controls regime would not serve much purpose without securing the willing cooperation of the international community to identify and bring to justice terrorists and their organizations operating from their territories.

Hence, it is imperative to urge that a multilateral regime is established to prevent BW proliferation, especially to non-state actors. The overall intention should be 'to use the review process and other means to strengthen the BWC and to draw out the potential latent in its provisions, so as to steer it into a constructive evolution'.[37] Several innovative steps are possible such as:

- First, obtaining the cooperation of civil sector organizations and prominent NGOs that are already seized with the BW problem like the Pugwash Society and the International Committee of the Red Cross. A role for the WHO should also be envisaged and pressed for, especially with regard to investigating suspicious outbreaks of disease. A heartening fact is that the Chambers of Commerce and Industry in India, especially the Confederation of Indian Industry, has evinced interest in BW issues, due to the burgeoning biotech and pharmaceuticals industries, with agro-industries poised for an exponential growth in future. The Government of India should take steps to actively encourage these civil sector organizations to discuss their views on what needs to be done to strengthen the BTWC and promote steps in this direction.
- Second, the Government of India should take active steps to establish a core group of like-minded countries to draw up a draft agreement to detail the steps that could be realistically pursued to adequately verify compliance of the BTWC. It is arguable that India should not be too enthusiastic in taking the lead in this matter lest it finds itself abandoned and isolated by the non-aligned group and other like-minded nations. This cautionary note is well taken, but it would need acceptance that the BTWC remains an ineffective adjunct to the disarmament regime. For this reason the abandoned Verification Protocol could serve as a useful rallying point to work towards compromise solutions that could be presented at the Sixth Review Conference in 2006. It would, hopefully, consolidate the work done in the first four Review Conferences—the Fifth having effectively buried the work done to evolve a Verification Protocol. These are issues that could be taken up for discussion, apart from the limited agenda set out to 'promote common understanding and effective action' by the Fifth Review Conference.
- Third, an important issue for consideration here is how the dangers of BW proliferation emanating from the biodefence work proceeding in several countries within high contain-

ment facilities should be addressed. Not only can such facilities leak as has occurred with the SARS virus from laboratories in Taiwan, Singapore and Beijing, but the empirical evidence from a study published in February 2001 reveals that 'of 21 known germ attacks over the decades, most were conducted not by terrorists, but by professional researchers who had gained access to human pathogens.'[38] Investigations into the anthrax mail attacks in the United States immediately after 9/11 highlight the significance of this issue.[39]

- Fourth, it needs better recognition that the agents that would best serve as biological weapons are not exotic genetically engineered viruses, but agents causing common diseases like plague, smallpox, anthrax and botulism; this list has been further narrowed down to smallpox and anthrax on technical considerations.[40] Although these are common diseases, their lines of treatment have not changed for decades. Even second generation vaccines have not been developed. With the entire human genome having been sequenced much greater attention needs to be focused on improving the detection and treatment of common biowarfare diseases, apart from researching into vectors that could infect livestock and agricultural crops.

It is suggested here that India should show greater activism in rescuing the BTWC from the quagmire into which it has fallen, and work towards establishing an enlightened verification regime. It could rally the NAM group in the BTWC and like-minded countries in the eastern and western regions to press for a multilateral approach to the BTWC and its verification problems. Fortuitously, the 2004 G-8 Summit recognized, 'The BWC is a critical foundation against biological weapons' proliferation, including to terrorists. Its prohibitions should be fully implemented, including enactment of penal legislation. We strongly urge all non-parties to join the BWC promptly.'[41]

NOTES

1. US Arms Control and Disarmament Agency, *Arms Control and Disarmament Agreements: Texts and Histories of the Negotiations*, Washington: US Government Printing Office, 1996, p. 5.
2. Ibid., pp. 95–6.
3. This became apparent over the September 1994-July 2001 period of hard negotiations by an Ad Hoc Group (AHG) established by the Treaty Parties to finalize a Verification Protocol, when the United States expressed its reservations about its adequacy and, in effect, torpedoed the international efforts that had gone into its drafting. But the point needs emphasizing that serious difference persisted between the Treaty Parties of the provisions of the Protocol until the end. Cf. Kalpana Chittranjan, 'History of the BTWC and AHG', in *Working towards a Verification Protocol for Biological Weapons*, P.R. Chari and Arpit Rajain, New Delhi: Institute of Peace and Conflict Studies, July 2001, pp. 9–21.
4. Shared with the author by the Hon. Ron Lehman, US Ambassador to the discussions in Geneva for negotiating the BTWC.
5. P.R. Chari and Giri Deshingkar, 'Putting Teeth into the BWC: An Indian View', in *Current Problems of Biological Warfare and Disarmament*, Susan Wright, special issue of *Politics and Life Sciences*, March 1999, p. 88.
6. http://www.bradford.ac.ik/acad/btwc/convention.btwcres.html accessed on 6 October 2002.
7. Based on interviews with officials in the Ministry of External Affairs. Also, 'Bin Laden's Group has Deadly Weapons', *The Indian Express*, 20 April 1999.
8. K. Santhanam, Director of the Institute of Defence Studies and Analyses, New Delhi, and an architect of India's nuclear weapons programme, expressed these views at the seminar on 'Biological Weapons Convention & Terrorism', held on 12 November 2001. A similar conclusion was reached in a study undertaken by the United Services Institution (a tri Service body largely composed of retired military officials) for the Services Headquarters.
9. Recommendations of the Group of Ministers, *Reforming the National Security System*, February 2001, p. 114.
10. P.R. Chari and Giri Deshingkar, 'India: Straddling East and West', pp. 256-57.
11. Statement made by former Ambassador Arundhati Ghose at the seminar on 'Biological Weapons Convention & Terrorism' held on 12 November 2001.
12. C. Raja Mohan, 'Nuclear Command Authority Comes into Being: No-first Use; Retaliation will be Massive', *The Hindu*, 5 January 2003.

13. This section borrows extensively from P.R. Chari and Giri Deshingkar, 'Putting Teeth into the BWC: An Indian View'.
14. Susan Wright, 'Cuba Case Tests Treaty', *The Bulletin of the Atomic Scientists*, November–December 1997, p. 19.
15. Statement made by Arundhati Ghose to the Fourth Review Conference of the State Parties to the Convention on the Prohibition of the Development, Production and Stockpiling of Bacteriological (Biological) and Toxin Weapons and on their Destruction, 26 November 1996.
16. Malcolm Dando, 'Strengthening the Biological Weapons Convention: Moving towards Endgame', *Disarmament Diplomacy*, no. 21, December 1997.
17. Statement made by Arundhati Ghose to the Fourth Review Conference.
18. John D. Holum, 'Remarks to the Fourth Review Conference of the Biological Weapons Convention', ACDA Home Page, http://www.acda.gov.speeches/holum/bwcover.html, 26 November 1996.
19. Statement by Ambassador Rakesh Sood at the 24th Session of the Ad Hoc Group of State Parties to the Biological Weapons Convention, Geneva, 25 July 2001.
20. Statement by Ambassador Rakesh Sood, Permanent Representative of India to the Conference on Disarmament, at the 57th Session of the First Committee of the United Nations General Assembly on 7 October 2002.
21. Statement by Rakesh Sood to the Fifth Review Conference of the States Parties to the Convention on the Prohibition of the Development, Production and Stockpiling of Bacteriological (Biological) and Toxin Weapons and on Their Destruction, Geneva, 20 November 2001.
22. Ambassador Mahley's Statement at the 24th Session of the Ad Hoc Group on 25 July 2001. Text available at: http://usinfo.state.gov/topical/pol/arms/stories/01072501.htm
23. Government of India, *Ministry of External Affairs, Annual Report 2001-2002*, p. 83.
24. Text available at: http://wwwusinfo.state.gov/topical/pol/arms/stories/01110103.htm
25. Final Report, Fifth Review Conference of the States Parties to the Convention on the Prohibition of the Development, Production and Stockpiling of Bacteriological (Biological) and Toxin Weapons and on Their Destruction, *BWC/CONF.V/17*.
26. John Zarocostas, 'Analysis: Trying to Better Bioweapons Pace', *United Press International Analysis*, 11 November 2002.
27. David Atwood, 'Resumed BW Review Conference: Progress?' *Geneva Reporter*, vol. 21, nos. 3/4, July–December 2002, p. 2.
28. Jez Littlewood, 'Substance Hidden under a Mountain of Paper: The BWC Experts' Meeting in 2003', *Disarmament Diplomacy*, no. 73, October-November 2003, p. 5.

29. Permanent Mission of India to the Conference on Disarmament, Geneva Statement by H.E. Mr. Kanwal Sibal, Foreign Secretary at the Plenary Meeting of the Conference on Disarmament, Geneva, on 23 January 2003, http://meaindia.nic.in/disarmament/dm23jan03.htm
30. Rebecca Johnson, 'BWC Meeting Adopts Minimal Report', *Disarmament Diplomacy*, no. 74, December 2003, pp. 1–2.
31. 'Regulating Biotechnology', Editorial, *The Hindu*, 25 May 2004.
32. Statement by Rakesh Sood, Ambassador, Head of the Indian Delegation, at the First Meeting of the States Parties to the Convention on the Prohibition of the Development, Production and Stockpiling of Bacteriological (Biological) and Toxin Weapons and on Their Destruction on 10 November 2003. http://www.Meaindia.nic.in/disarmament/26da01.htm
33. These views reflect those of the Confederation of Indian Industry and a Task Force established by it to elicit the views of the Indian biotech and pharmaceutical industry. Cf. Sandhya Tewari and Divya Chopra, 'Compulsions of the Biotech Industry/ Reservations Regarding the BTWC Protocol & Suggested Solutions', in *Biological Weapons: Terrorism, Issues and Threats*, ed. P.R. Chari and Arpit Rajain.
34. P.R. Chari and Giri Deshingkar, 'Putting Teeth into the BWC: An Indian View', pp. 61–2.
35. These and other remedial measures are discussed in P.R. Chari, 'Bioterrorism and the Future', in *Biological Weapons: Terrorism, Issues and Threats*, ed. P.R. Chari and Arpit Rajain.
36. United States Department of State, *Patterns of Global Terrorism 2001*, May 2001, p. 66. CRBN is the acronym for Chemical, Radiological, Biological and Nuclear.
37. Nicholas A. Sims, 'Biological Disarmament Diplomacy in the Doldrums: Reflections after the BWC Fifth Review Conference', *Disarmament Diplomacy*, no. 70, April–May 2003, p. 8.
38. William J. Broad, 'In a Lonely Stand, a Scientist takes on National Security Dogma', *The New York Times*, 29 June 2004.
39. These investigations revealed that the weaponized Ames strain of the anthrax bacteria used came from the US Army Medical Research Institute of Infectious Diseases at Fort Detrick, Maryland. Vivek Shankar Mathur and Arpit Rajain, 'The Anthrax Scare', in *Biological Weapons: Issues and Threats*, ed. P.R. Chari and Arpit Rajain, pp. 111–13.
40. P.R. Chari, 'Bioterrorism and the Future', in *Biological Weapons: Issues and Threats*, ed. P.R. Chari and Arpit Rajain, pp. 88–9.
41. G-8 Action Plan on Non-Proliferation, 2004: The Statement, http://fpc.state.gov/fpc/33363.htm

CHAPTER 2

International Efforts to Combat Biological Weapons

KALPANA CHITTARANJAN

The date 26 March 2005 will be an important day in the annals of biological weapons (BW) arms control history. That day will mark three decades since the world's first disarmament agreement (as it banned not just the development but also the production of a whole class of weapons) better known as the Biological Weapons Convention (BWC),[1] entered into force. However, the BWC has an inherent flaw. So far, it lacks verification and enforcement measures, which makes it a 'pact-with-no-punch' and it will remain a paper tiger treaty till it incorporates a mechanism to verify and enforce its provisions. The history of the BWC has largely been about efforts to arrive at a Verification Protocol. This essay examines the efforts made by states parties to the BWC Treaty to arrive at this Protocol.[2] This becomes an imperative necessity in today's world where terrorists' threats to use of weapons of mass destruction could become a reality whenever they acquire the capacity to use such weapons.[3]

BACKGROUND TO MANDATE FOR VERIFICATION PROTOCOL

The BWC signed in April 1972 was negotiated from 1969 to 1971.[4] The operative section of the BWC, which contains fifteen Articles, is to be found in the first Article:[5]

Each State Party to this Convention undertakes never in any circumstances to develop, produce, stockpile or otherwise acquire or retain:

1. Microbial or other biological agents, or toxins whatever their origin or method of production, of types and in quantities that have no justification for prophylactic, protective or other peaceful purposes;
2. Weapons, equipment or means of delivery designed to use such agents or toxins for hostile purposes or in armed conflict.

Though it has an unlimited duration, the BWC called for only one review (Article XII). This led to the First Review Conference which was held from 3 to 21 March 1980. In November 1982, a UN resolution called upon the signatories to establish compliance procedures.

Procedures for consultation in the case of compliance failures were strengthened during the generally positive Second Review Conference, which met in Geneva from 8 to 26 September 1986. A stronger Convention was sought by the participating states with the establishment of several politically-binding confidence-building measures (CBM), including annual declarations of high-containment biological facilities designed for work with dangerous micro-organisms, and reports of unusual outbreaks of disease. A meeting of experts was held (31 March–15 April 1987), to work out details of CBMs in particular, to enable annual exchanges of data about biological research. However, as there was no penalty for failing to file these declarations and no Central Secretariat for urging countries to do so, less than half the states party to the BWC participated in these CBMs.

A decision was taken at the Third Review Conference (9–27 September 1991) to hold future review conferences at least once every five years. This conference recognized the need for stronger measures and mandated the convening of an Ad Hoc Group (AHG) of government experts (also known as Verification Experts or the VEREX group) to identify and examine potential verification measures from a scientific and technical viewpoint.

VEREX eventually identified twenty-one measures that were grouped into two categories. 'Off-site' measures included surveillance over scientific publications, data declarations, notifications of activities, remote sensing, environment sampling and analysis, while possible 'on-site' measures included scientific exchanges, visual inspection, interviews, identification of relevant equipment, sampling and analysis, and continuous monitoring by cameras or other sensors. The VEREX group held four meetings in Geneva—30 March–10 April 1992; 23 November–4 December 1992; 24 May–6 June 1993; and a final session on 13–24 September 1993. At the final session it submitted its consensus report to the BWC member states. In the report, the experts found that, due to the dual-use nature of BW-related equipment and materials, no single measure could fulfil all the mandated criteria for a stand alone verification measure. The group, however, concluded that some measures, used singly or in combination, could strengthen the regime by helping to differentiate prohibited from permitted activities, thus reducing ambiguities about issues of compliance.[6]

FORMATION OF THE AHG AND ITS ATTEMPTS AT ARRIVING AT A VERIFICATION PROTOCOL

A Special Conference of the BWC states parties met in Geneva in September 1994 to consider the VEREX final report and decide on further action. It was agreed that an Ad Hoc Group would be established 'to consider appropriate measures, including possible verification measures, and draft proposals to strengthen the convention, to be included, as appropriate, in a legally binding instrument . . .'.[7] The mandate for the AHG also specifically states that 'the Ad Hoc Group shall, inter alia, consider. . . . Specific measures designed to ensure effective and full implementation of Article X. . . .'

Article X of the BWC states:

1. The States Parties to this Convention undertake to facilitate, and have the right to participate in, the fullest possible exchange of equipment, materials and scientific and technological information for the use of bacteriological (biological) agents and toxins for peaceful purposes. Parties to the Convention in a position to do so shall also cooperate in contributing individually or together with other States or international organizations to the further development and application of scientific discoveries in the field of

bacteriology (biology) for prevention of disease, or for other peaceful purposes.

2. This Convention shall be implemented in a manner designed to avoid hampering the economic or technological development of States Parties to the Convention or international cooperation in the field of peaceful bacteriological (biological) activities, including the international exchange of bacteriological (biological) agents and toxins and equipment for the processing, use or production of bacteriological (biological) agents and toxins for peaceful purposes in accordance with the provisions of the Convention.

Though the AHG held five meetings between 1995 and 1996,[8] it was unable to complete its mandate to finalize draft proposals before the Fourth Review Conference (25 November–6 December 1996). The AHG successfully moved on to negotiation of the rolling text of a Protocol in July 1997. Subsequent meetings had seen the elaboration of language for the various Articles and Annexes to the Protocol.[9]

The key issues at the Fourth Review Conference were the Convention's Article I which defines the basic prohibitions, or the 'scope of the Convention; Article IV, which addresses national implementation measures; Article V, which deals with the consultative process for problems arising from the Treaty; and Article X, which relates to cooperation between states parties for peaceful purposes.[10]

Before the AHG met for the twenty-third time (23 April–11 May 2001), its negotiators had prepared a 250-page draft, containing over 1,000 brackets (indicating points of disagreement) known as the rolling text.[11] To prevent cheating, the text contained complex procedures for conducting on-site inspections. However, a 210-page compromise proposal known as the 'composite text'[12] was tabled by the Chair of the AHG, Ambassador Tibor Toth of Hungary, on 30 March, three weeks before the inauguration of the twenty-third session, to break the impasse in the negotiations, as well as reduce the points of disagreement. It soon became apparent that this session would be devoted to debating the merits of the rolling text over the composite text on the basis of further negotiations on the draft Verification Protocol. Toth devoted the first two weeks of the session to an article-by-article explanation of his composite text.[13] In the third week, Toth compiled a list of issues that was based on feedback from formal and informal sessions with the delegations. By the end of the session, the major outstanding issues were reduced to six areas: definitions; declarations; follow-up after submission of declarations; measures to strengthen the implementation of Article III of the BWC (transfers); investigations; and legal issues.

During the session, it became clear that China was reluctant to allow on-site inspections; Pakistan was concerned that inspectors searching for germ weapons might investigate its nuclear weapons sites. Iran sought a weakening of controls over the export of biological equipment and materials as it believed that this would hurt civilian economies; and the US delegation sat passively, as its officials claimed that it could not act since a policy review on the issue was underway. By the end of the session, however, the composite text had become the de facto basis for the Protocol. How the AHG's final report of the session would address both the composite and rolling texts without turning this issue into a potentially harmful procedural battle became a challenge. The issue was resolved when China's attempt to retain the old formulation, that would have reaffirmed the rolling text as the 'only basis for negotiations', was avoided by referring to this text as 'the underlying basis for negotiations', with a factual description of the AHG's work relating to the composite text. This seemed to satisfy the participants as they concluded the twenty-third session.[14]

In April 2001, indications were available that the US was likely to reject the Protocol. This view was strengthened when a Bush administration policy review team led by Ambassador Donald Mahley, Special Negotiator for Chemical and Biological Arms Control, Department of State, unanimously concluded[15] that Toth's composite text would not be enough to prevent cheating, and that it would burden universities and private industry, as it would leave US companies vulnerable to theft of commercial secrets. Representatives of the State Department, the Pentagon, the CIA and other federal agencies had conducted the review.[16] By the third week of July, it became clear that the Bush administration had 'decided to announce next week that the United States cannot accept a draft agreement for enforcing a 1972 treaty on germ warfare . . .'.[17] Thus, when the AHG met for its twenty-fourth and last scheduled session (23 July–17 August 2001), it did not come as a surprise when Mahley announced on 25 July that the US could not support the draft Protocol as it would 'not improve our ability to verify compliance' with the BWC's global ban on BW and 'would put national security and confidential business information at risk'.[18] The AHG, which then undertook the task of writing its report, failed to reach an agreement on it. Thus, it failed in its mandated task of completing the negotiations on a Verification Protocol before the start of the Fifth BWC Review in Geneva (19 November–7 December 2001).

FIFTH BWC REVIEW CONFERENCE

As Jenni Rissanen put it, 'The Fifth Review Conference of the Biological and Toxin Weapons Convention closed, as it had opened, in eventful and acrimonious fashion.'[19] This was because less than two hours before the conclusion of the Review Conference, the US proposed that the Conference terminate the AHG's mandate,[20] which would have put an end to a little more than a decade-long effort to strengthen the Convention. In order to prevent outright failure, the ninety-one states that were present, adjourned the Conference for a year until 11–12 November 2002. Earlier, during the Conference, the US had tabled a number of new ideas to move forward, which were designed to be politically thought to be not legally binding commitments:[21]

- Make it easier to extradite criminals involved in biological weapons crimes and require BWC member states to enact domestic legislation criminalizing treaty-prohibited activities. About half of the BWC's member states do not have such laws.
- Allow the UN Secretary General to investigate suspected biological weapons use and suspicious disease outbreaks.
- Elaborate vague BWC provisions to clarify and resolve compliance concerns. This would involve voluntary exchanges of information or visits to sites in question.

- Support the World Health Organization's efforts to monitor and respond to global disease and establish an international team to provide assistance 'in the event of a serious outbreak of infectious disease'. States would also be required to 'report internationally' releases of biological agents or other 'adverse events that could impact other countries'.
- Obligate states parties to adopt and implement 'strict regulations for access to particularly dangerous microorganisms'. Related suggestions included calling on states to 'sensitize scientists to the risks of genetic engineering', to 'explore national oversight of high-risk experiments', to adopt a code of conduct for scientists working with pathogenic microorganisms, and to implement 'strict biosafety procedures'.

Other countries were amenable to working with these ideas on the condition that the AHG was left intact. When the US delegation proposed terminating the AHG on the Conference's last day, an action that would have effectively eliminated the Group's mandate to conclude a legally binding protocol to the treaty, it came up with the suggestion that the BWC member states meet annually instead in a new body to assess the implementation of measures agreed to at the Conference and to consider new measures for strengthening the Convention. The uproar that followed led Chairman Toth to suspend the Conference for one year.

In a statement to the Conference, Ambassador Rakesh Sood clarified India's stance,[22]

> We need to adopt a Declaration that will reaffirm the mandate, enable us to resume our stalled negotiations and add to it new measures that will help us deal with new threats to which we have been exposed. This Review Conference cannot end on a note of passivity; it has to issue a call galvanizing the international community into action.

Before the Review Conference resumed in November 2002, the US and the UK proposed alternatives in the interim period.[23] The US demanded that the Review Conference should not make any decisions beyond agreeing to hold another conference in 2006, which angered many of the BWC states parties.

In talking points distributed to the western allies in early September, the United States had suggested that the scheduled 11 November meet in Geneva be 'very short'. In meetings with other delegations, the Assistant Secretary of State for Arms Control, Stephen Rademaker, originally proposed a 10-minute meeting. A State Department official said on 25 September that the United States adopted a slightly more flexible stance after allies and arms control experts indicated that this was impossible. According to the talking points, if the member states attempted to address any issue beyond scheduling another conference in 2006, the United States would publicly list countries it believed to be covertly developing biological weapons.[24]

Ambassador Tibor Tóth tabled his draft proposal in the form of a draft decision when the resumed Review Conference began. As Marie Isabelle Chevrier pointed out:

> Thus the stage was set. The scene, however, was not a document to be discussed, debated, revised and negotiated; rather, it was a new ultimatum. The United States was widely reported to have insisted that no changes whatsoever be made to the draft decision; not a word, not a comma, nothing. And thus it was. After a tense week of meetings—some postponed, others cancelled—a unanimous decision was taken by the conference late on Thursday afternoon of the first week (November 14) to accept the draft decision as tabled by Ambassador Tóth on Monday morning.[25]

THE NEW PROCESS

The states parties issued the following statement during the resumed Review Conference:[26]

THE NEW PROCESS

At the Fifth Review Conference the States Parties in the Final Document agreed that:

At its eighth plenary meeting on 14 November 2002, the Conference decided, by consensus, as follows:

(a) To hold three annual meetings of the States Parties of one week duration each year commencing in 2003 until the

Sixth Review Conference, to be held not later than the end of 2006, to discuss, and promote common understanding and effective action on:

(i) the adoption of necessary national measures to implement the prohibitions set forth in the Convention, including the enactment of penal legislation;
(ii) national mechanisms to establish and maintain the security and oversight of pathogenic microorganisms and toxins;
(iii) enhancing international capabilities for responding to, investigating and mitigating the effects of cases of alleged use of biological or toxin weapons or suspicious outbreaks of disease;
(iv) strengthening and broadening national and international institutional efforts and existing mechanisms for the surveillance, detection, diagnosis and combating of infectious diseases affecting humans, animals, and plants;
(v) the content, promulgation, and adoption of codes of conduct for scientists.

(b) All meetings, both of experts and of States Parties, will reach any conclusions or results by consensus.
(c) Each meeting of the States Parties will be prepared by a two-week meeting of experts. The topics for consideration at each annual meeting of States Parties will be as follows: items (i) and (ii) will be considered in 2003; items (iii) and (iv) in 2004; item (v) in 2005. The first meeting will be chaired by a representative of the Eastern Group, the second by a representative of the Group of Non-Aligned and Other States, and the third by a representative of the Western Group.
(d) The meetings of experts will prepare factual reports describing their work.
(e) The Sixth Review Conference will consider the work of these meetings and decide on any further action.

It was subsequently agreed that Ambassador Tibor Tóth of Hungary would be the representative of the Eastern Group to chair the meetings in 2003 and Ambassador Peter Goosen would be the representative of the Non-Aligned Movement.

CONCLUSION

On 25 July 2001 Ambassador Mahley expressed fears that his country's reluctance to sign the BWC protocol was because implementation would cause problems for the US biological weapons defence programmes, an increased risk of foreign powers stealing commercial US pharmaceutical and biotech secrets through snap inspections, and jeopardize existing American controls over exports of materials which could be used to manufacture bio-weapons. The fate of Verification Protocol efforts by the AHG was doomed. However, some arms control experts concluded that an analysis of US objections to the protocol reveals they were misconceived, as the protocol protects bio-weapons defence programmes from unwarranted prying, has elaborate provisions to protect commercial secrets and would spread US-style export controls more widely around the world.[27] As pointed out, though the decision to hold annual meetings before the Sixth BWC Review Conference is better than nothing, 'it falls far short of developing legally binding ways to help verify the treaty. States-parties did not directly discuss the AHG or the additional protocol in November, and the future of both is uncertain. The AHG appears to be dying a slow, quiet death.'[28]

As a result of the 'New Process', in the first of the three annual 'interim meetings' that is to be convened prior to the 2006 Review Conference, the states parties to the BWC met in Geneva from 10 to 14 November 2003 to discuss issues pertaining to the variety of national legislation that has been passed related to the Convention. However, the meeting yielded little as the states parties avoided offering specific recommendations.[29]

As part of the three-year programme mandated by the Fifth Review Conference, the second *Meeting of Experts from States Parties to the Convention on the Prohibition of the Development, Production and Stockpiling of Bacteriological (Biological) and Toxin Weapons and on their Destruction*, was held in Geneva (19–30 July 2004). A group of 450 experts and officials from 87 BWC member countries, including India, exchanged ideas for strengthening national and international measures against infectious and deliberate diseases. They emphasized the need for strengthening national infectious disease surveillance systems to improve global capabilities for responding to natural or deliberately caused outbreaks.[30]

NOTES

1. The *Convention on the Prohibition of the Development, Production and Stockpiling of Bacteriological (Biological) and Toxin Weapons and on their Destruction (BTWC)* was signed on 10 April 1972 at London, Moscow and Washington with the UK, the US and the Soviet governments being the Depositaries. Forty- three member countries signed at the same time.
2. Up to 20 July 2004.
3. For a comprehensive review of the use and alleged use of biological weapons over the years, and the likely impact of such weapons see Kalpana Chittaranjan, 'Biological Weapons: An Insidious WMD', *Strategic Analysis*, vol. XXII, no. 9, December 1998, pp. 1428–31.
4. For a detailed history of the BWC, see Kalpana Chittaranjan, 'History of the BTWC and AHG', in *Working Towards a Verification Protocol for Biological Weapons*, ed. P.R. Chari and Arpit Rajain, New Delhi: Institute of Peace and Conflict Studies, July 2001, pp. 9–21; Kalpana Chittaranjan, 'The BWC: A Status Report', *Strategic Analysis*, vol. XXV, no. 2, May 2001, pp. 215–25; Kalpana Chittaranjan, 'Verification Protocol: A Must for BWC Effectiveness', *Strategic Analysis*, vol. XXIII, no. 6, September 1999, pp. 947–65.
5. BWC text available at: http://www.opbw.org/convention/conv.html. It currently has 151 states parties and 16 signatory states as of November 2003. List available at: http://www..opbw.org/convention/btwcsps.html
6. Chittaranjan, *Working Towards a Verification Protocol for Biological Weapons*, no. 4, pp. 14–15.
7. Graham S. Pearson, 'Implementation of Article X of the BWC: Present Status and Prospects for the Future', available at http://www.brad.ac.uk/acad/sbtwc/other/articles.htm
8. Ad Hoc Group documents of various sessions available at: http://www.brad.ac.uk/acad/sbtwc/adhocgrp/bw-adhocgrp.htm
9. No. 9.
10. For a comprehensive coverage of the Fourth Review Conference, see Graham S. Pearson, 'The Fourth BWC Review Conference: An Important Step Forward', *Arms Control Today*, vol. 26, no. 10, January–February 1997, pp. 14–18.

11. Parts I, II and III of the Rolling Text revisions available at: http://www.brad.ac.uk/acad/sbtwc/revconf/bw-revconf.htm
12. Text available at: http://www.opbw.org/ahg/docs/CRP8.pdf
13. For a comprehensive coverage of the 23rd AHG Session, see Jenni Rissanen, 'Hurdles Cleared, Obstacles Remaining: The Ad Hoc Group Prepare for the Final Challenge', *Disarmament Diplomacy*, no. 56, April 2001.
14. Chittaranjan, no. 6, pp. 16–17.
15. Michael R. Gordon and Judith Miller, 'US Germ Warfare Review Faults Plan on Enforcement', *The New York Times*, 2 May 2001.
16. Vernon Loeb, 'Bush Panel Faults Germ Warfare Protocol', *The Washington Post*, 27 May 2001, p. AO2.
17. Vernon Loeb, 'US won't Back Plan to Enforce Germ Pact', *The Washington Post*, 21 July 2001, p. AO1.
18. Ambassador Donald Mahley, US Special Negotiator for Chemical and Biological Arms Control Issues Statement by the United States to the Ad Hoc Group of Biological Weapons Convention States Parties Geneva, Switzerland, 25 July 2001 available at: http://www.state.gov/t/ac/rls/rm/2001/5497.htm
19. Jenni Rissanen, 'Left in Limbo: Review Conference Suspended—On Edge of Collapse', *Disarmament Diplomacy*, no. 62, December–January 2002. See ibid., for an extensive coverage and for the BWC Report on the Fifth Review Conference of the BWC.
20. For an immediate reaction to the US action, see Jenni Rissanen, 'Anger after the Ambush: Review Conference Suspended after US Asks for AHG'S TERMINATION', *BWC Review Conference Bulletin*, 9 December 2001 available at: http://www.acronym.org.uk/bwc/revcon8.htm
21. Arms Control Association 'Fact Sheets—Briefing Paper on the Status of Biological Weapons Nonproliferation', May 2003, available at: http://www.armscontrol.org/factsheets/bwissuebrief.asp
22. Full text of the statement 'Permanent Mission of India to the Conference on Disarament Geneva, 20 November 2001 Statement by Ambassador Rakesh Sood Head of Delegation to the Fifth Review Conference of the States Parties to the Convention on the Prohibition of the Development, Production and Stockpiling of Bacteriological (Biological) and Toxin Weapons and on Their Destruction. New Delhi: 20 November 2001' available at: http://meaindia.nic.in/disarmament/dm20nov01.htm
23. For a detailed account of these alternatives, see Kalpana Chittaranjan, 'Endgame in November 2002: US Position—Other Alternative Modalities to Protocol', in *Biological Weapons: Issues and Threats*, ed. P.R. Chari and Arpit Rajain, pp. 46–50.
24. Kerry Boyd, 'US Attempts to Sink BWC Review Conference', *Arms*

Control Today, October 2002, available at:< http://www.armscontrol.org/act/2002_10/bwcoct02.asp?print>

25. Marie Isabelle Chevrier, 'Waiting for Godot or Saving the Show? The BWC Review Conference Reaches Modest Agreement', *Disarmament Diplomacy*, no. 68, December 2002–January 2003, available at: http://www.acronym.org.uk/dd/dd68/68bwc.htm See ibid., for a comprehensive account of the resumed Fifth BWC Review Conference (12–22 November 2002) including the positions taken by various states parties to the BWC.
26. http://www.opbw.org/new_process/new.htm
27. James Meek, 'Killer Germs', *The Guardian*, 24 September 2001.
28. Arms Control Association, no. 21.
29. *Arms Control Today*, 'News Briefs', December 2003, available at: http://www.armscontrol.org/act/2003_12/newsbriefs.asp#BWCStates-Parties
30. UN Press Document, 'Biological Weapons Convention Expert Meeting Concludes', 2 August 2004, available at: http://www.unog.ch/news2/documents/newsen/dc04029e.htm

CHAPTER 3

Biological Warfare Agents: Defining the Threat

GURMEET KANWAL

BACKGROUND

In the prevailing era of strategic uncertainty, ironically, even as the threat of major wars has receded since the end of the Cold War, new threats have emerged that make Armageddon more, not less, likely. Rapidly increasing international terrorism and weapons of mass destruction (WMD) make a potent cocktail. Only a deep survival instinct has stayed the finger on the nuclear trigger and allowed mankind to escape large-scale death and devastation over the last half century since Hiroshima and Nagasaki. However, the finger on the triggering mechanisms of biological and chemical weapons is unlikely to be that of a rational state. In all probability, such weapons would be used by irrational non-state actors. This reality makes their threat more difficult to discern accurately and more complex to counter.

The nature of the threat and its likely ramifications must be understood. Between biological and chemical weapons, bio-weapons are more potent as small quantities can cause large numbers of casualties. Their effects are more persistent and likely to spread quickly over large areas. Unfortunately, due to complacency and inertia and the natural predilection of elected governments to adopt an ostrich-like approach to invisible threats, the international community is ill-prepared to deal with the threat and combat it should it become a reality. While the Biological Weapons Convention (BWC) prohibits the development, production and stockpiling of biological and toxin weapons and has been signed and ratified by 151 countries (16 others have signed but not yet ratified it),[1] it is really only a paper treaty that lacks the wherewithal to detect the development of biological weapons, adopt proactive measures to destroy stockpiles and combat the diseases that may occur if they are used deliberately or inadvertently. The development of bio-weapons is easy to conceal—unlike nuclear weapons, there are no telltale domes hovering in the desert skies. However, the proposed 'Organisation for the Prohibition of Biological Weapons' has remained a non-starter despite several years of painstaking diplomatic efforts.[2] Clearly, the international community has not seriously planned how to fight this threat in a concerted manner.

Organisms and toxins found in nature that can be used to incapacitate, kill, or otherwise impede an adversary are labelled biological weapons. These weapons are characterized by low visibility and high potency. Accessibility to them is not difficult and their means of delivery are relatively easy. Biological weapons are not new in concept and history is replete with examples of their use. Before the twentieth century biological agents were used to deliberately poison food and water. The use of micro-organisms or toxins and of biologically inoculated fabrics have been recorded. Arrows were poisoned by dipping them in blood mixed with manure; decaying carcasses were thrown into wells to contaminate them; corpses of plague victims into cities to spread plague during the siege of Kaffa in the fourteenth century and the Russians who had surrounded Swedish forces at Reval in Estonia in 1710 did the same. The British supplied smallpox-infected blankets to Native Americans.

During the First World War, Germans developed anthrax, glanders, cholera and a wheat fungus for use as biological weapons. They allegedly spread plague in St Petersburg, infected mules with glanders in Mesopotamia, and attempted to do the same with horses of the French Calvary.[3] Research continued and during the Second World War the Japanese conducted bio-weapons experiments on Chinese prisoners and exposed more than 3,000 victims to plague, anthrax, syphilis and other agents. The Americans, British, Germans and Soviets also conducted research in bio-warfare. Since the mid-1980s, terrorist organizations have become the primary users of bio-weapons and several incidents of their use have been recorded. The aim of this paper is to analyse the nature of the threat posed by biological agents and a probable bio-terrorist attack.

BIO-WEAPONS AGENTS

Biological pathogens may be released intentionally or accidentally into the atmosphere. There are some that occur naturally and some that are intentionally developed as tools of warfare to cause disease or death. Human beings can be exposed to these agents through inhalation, skin (cutaneous) exposure, or ingestion of contaminated food or water. The physical symptoms that follow exposure are often delayed and could be confused with other naturally occurring illnesses. Some biological warfare agents persist in the environment and are capable of causing problems over a prolonged period after their release.

A large number of bio-weapon agents have been identified and listed. Bio-warfare agents comprise bacterial agents, viral agents and toxins. The most dangerous ones are as follows:[4]

Anthrax,
Botulinum Toxins,
Brucellosis,
Cholera,
Clostridium Perfringens Toxins,
Congo-Crimean Haemorrhagic Fever,
Ebola Haemorrhagic Fever,
Melioidosis,
Mycotoxins,
Plague,
Q Fever,
Ricin,
Rift Valley Fever,
Saxitoxin,
Smallpox,
Staphylococcal Enterotoxin B,
Trichothecene Mycotoxins,
Tularemia,
Venezuelan Equine Encephalitis.

The nature of illnesses caused by the major agents, their symptoms and locations where they commonly occur are described in detail in the Appendix. Details of the treatment of each disease, the handling of infected patients and the availability of vaccines have not been included as these concern the medical establishment and are easily accessible on the web.

DEFINING THE BIO-TERRORISM THREAT

The bio-terrorism threat covers a wide spectrum. It ranges from hoaxes and the use of relatively low casualty agents by non-state actors or small terrorist groups to the employment of classical biological warfare (BW) agents that can produce mass casualties. In rare cases it may include state-sponsored terrorism. All bio-terrorism scenarios present serious challenges to the international community for the treatment of affected patients and for prophylaxis of exposed persons. Another major hazard is environmental contamination that may pose continuing threats.

The recent history of bio-terrorism is instructive. Among the recorded incidents of bio-terrorism, a large number of cases involved the contamination of food and water. The deliberate contamination of restaurant salad bars in Oregon by followers of Rajneesh in September–October 1984, led to 751 persons being infected with *Salmonella typhimurium*. During Operation Desert Shield and Desert Storm in 1990–1, the coalition forces led by the US, faced a threat from chemical and biological agents. 'Following Gulf War I, Iraq disclosed that it had bombs, Scud missiles, 122-mm rockets, and artillery shells armed with botulinum toxin, anthrax, and aflatoxin. They also had spray tanks fitted to aircraft that could distribute 2,000 litres of agents over a target.'[5]

In 1992, a Virginia man sprayed his roommates with a substance that he claimed was anthrax and 20 people had to be administered chemoprophylaxis. The Japanese sect, Aum Shinrikyo, attempted to release aerosolized anthrax from the tops of buildings in Tokyo in 1994. A year later, two members of a Minnesota militia group, which had produced Ricin for use against local government officials, were convicted for its possession. In 1996, a man in

Ohio had obtained bubonic plague cultures through the mail and was prosecuted.

Over twenty confirmed or suspected cases of anthrax related (ten inhalation, thirteen cutaneous) bio-terrorism acts occurred in the United States between 11/9 terrorist attacks and November 2001. The victims were largely postal workers in New Jersey and Washington DC and media companies in New York and Florida. Letters contaminated with anthrax were handled or opened by these workers. At least five persons died and many more fell sick. At present, seventeen countries are suspected of having offensive BW programmes.

There is a real threat that biological agents may be used against civilian populations as they are readily available, easy to weaponize and use. BW agents are difficult to detect or protect against. They are invisible, odourless and tasteless, and their dispersal can be effected silently. The small quantities required to kill thousands of people in densely populated metropolitan areas make the concealment, transportation and dissemination of biological agents relatively easy. However, the technology is not freely available and trained scientists are required to develop, produce and weaponize these WMD.

BW agents can be spread by aerosol sprays, base ejection artillery shells, missile warheads and bombs whose casing opens up to disperse the agent. They can also be spread through contaminated food or water. 'Variables that can alter the effectiveness of a delivery system include particle size of the agent, stability of the agent under desiccating conditions, UV light, wind speed, wind direction, and atmospheric stability.'[6] As bio-agents are likely to be destroyed or inactivated by a blast, the use of an explosive device to deliver and disseminate such agents is generally ineffective. Another potential threat is the contamination of municipal water supplies, but this requires an unrealistically large amount of agent since drinking water passes through a treatment plant that uses chemicals to purify the supply. Post-filtration contamination is even more difficult to achieve if it is to be widespread.

Aerosolized dispersal of biological agents is the mode most likely to be used by militant groups and terrorists. Airborne pathogens can only be effective biological weapons if they are dispersed in an aerosol cloud as fine microscopic particles that are about five microns in size; only an appreciable dose that can be inhaled and retained in the lungs can cause infection. Advanced weapon systems (such as warheads and missiles) are not required for the aerosolized delivery of biological agents. Low technology aerosolization methods include agricultural crop dusters; aerosol generators on small boats, trucks, or cars; and backpack sprayers. Even purse-size perfume atomizers can suffice for limited targets.

Bio-terrorism using microbes and viruses poses a new threat to national security that is not apparent. The relative ease with which they can be manufactured and dispersed makes biological agents are an ideal weapon for terrorists. It is for this reason that Al Qaeda operatives have tried to acquire them and it is probably a matter of time before they develop and use these weapons of mass terror. As developing, stockpiling and using bio-weapons is relatively inexpensive compared with the cost of defending against them, 'the offence-defence balance in bio-warfare strongly favours the attacker'.[7] The security and public health challenges presented by a single terrorist carrying a vial with a biological agent, whether smallpox, Ebola or something even more lethal engineered in a laboratory are enormous. It is a sad commentary on the management of human affairs by national governments, and their proclivity to procrastinate regarding international cooperation in the face of grave transnational threats, that various nations are seeking to counter the threat virtually single-handedly.

The recent anthrax mailings in the US focused public attention on the current problems in national security planning that expectations of future threats are vastly different from what actually occurs. Like the 11/9 hijacker attacks, the anthrax attacks, too, had not been foreseen. According to Michael J. Powers and Jonathan Ban:

> Rather than planning for a narrow range of least-likely, high-consequence contingencies or focusing only on additional mail-borne anthrax attacks, we must plan for a variety of future incidents—including incidents that cause mass casualties and mass disruption. In fact, planning for a variety of more likely, middle- to low-casualty incidents, while simultaneously being prepared for low-probability, high-consequence incidents is perhaps the most significant challenge facing planners.[8]

The authors contend that the cornerstone of preparedness against future bio-terrorist attacks, regardless of their nature or scope, must be a national public health system capable of detecting, assessing and responding to a broad range of contingencies. While there can be no argument about this recommendation, what is necessary before the process of crisis management starts is an effective, viable and responsive intelligence system to provide timely warning of an impending attack and identify the likely sources of that attack so that a policy and, if necessary, military effort can be mounted to eliminate the threat. As in other maladies, prevention is better than cure.

Powers and Ban further argue that assessments of a bio-terrorist threat are often narrowly focused on single factors.

> The mismatch between threat assessments and preparedness efforts can be explained partly by the failure of threat assessment methodologies to take into account all of the factors comprising the threat. Single-factor threat assessments, for example, focus either on the terrorists' motivations and objectives or on the hypothetical effects of a biological weapon, but they do not indicate which scenarios are plausible or their comparative likelihood.[9]

There is immense merit in this argument.

Powers and Ban recommend consideration of four key elements of the threat: 'The who (the actor), the what (the agent), the where (the target), and the how (the mode of attack).'[10] The interaction of these components determines the direction and impact of a bio-terrorist attack. 'The more casualties bio-terrorists seek to inflict, the more difficult it will be for them to assemble the necessary combination of these components. Thus, the level of risk declines as the level of desired casualties increases because the attack scenario becomes less likely.' It is certainly not easy to launch major bio-terrorist attacks that result in large-scale casualties but it must be accepted that this can be done with extensive preparations. Terrorist organizations have time on their side and, while the intelligence agencies and the police must succeed every time in their surveillance and counter-terrorism efforts, the terrorists need to succeed only once.

Recent advances in the life sciences have brought to the fore fresh concerns about the negative spin-offs of the ongoing biotechnology revolution.[11] The newfound ability of modern science to mutate DNAs combined with sophisticated invitro fertilization techniques could enable rogue elements to develop improved biological weapons. Indications of a possible BW attack include the following:[12]

Disease entity that is unusual or does not occur naturally in a given geographical area.
Multiple disease entities in the same patients, indicating that mixed agents have been used in the attack.
Large numbers of both military and civilian casualties when such populations inhabit the same area.
Data suggesting a massive pointsource outbreak.
Apparent aerosol route of infection.
High morbidity and mortality rates relative to the number of personnel at risk.
Illness limited to fairly localized or circumscribed geographical areas.
Low attack rates in personnel who work in areas with filtered air supplies or closed ventilation systems.
Sentinel dead animals of multiple species.
The absence of a competent natural vector in the area of outbreak (for a biological agent that is vector-borne in nature).

A major weakness in accurately assessing the threat of bio-terrorism is the possibility of an anonymous attack. Such an attack by a third party could even trigger a war between two nations and, therefore, needs to be consciously guarded against by instituting confidence building measures (CBM). 'Biological threat assessments must take into account not only capabilities that are challenging to monitor but also intentions that are even more difficult to discern.'[13] Information on intentions can be gleaned only from apprehended senior members of terrorist networks as they are the ones who may have knowledge of functional details. It is difficult to obtain international and domestic support for a coordinated approach to countering the threat of bio-terrorism unless credible intelligence is available.

INADEQUATE INDIAN RESPONSE

Technical difficulties make the threat of a catastrophic bio-terrorist attack relatively less likely: Only the release of a very contagious or high quality agent by an efficient dissemination route could result in thousands of casualties. In reality, the number of pathways open to terrorists that would result in catastrophic numbers of casualties are few, and those that do exist are technically difficult.[14] However, the low probability of a catastrophic bio-terrorist attack must not lead to complacence since there is ample cause for concern as 'the rapid development of biotechnology and the diffusion of expertise in this field may lower the technical bar over time'.[15]

The strategic discourse in India has a poor track record of scenario building as a tool in threat assessment. This has been a national failing that needs urgent redressal. Unless the process of scenario building is undertaken as a matter of course in conjunction with sophisticated mathematical modelling techniques, threat assessment would continue to remain based on worst case analyses. For example, it needs to be recognized that a bio-terrorist threat is not a one-dimensional threat. The National Security Council Secretariat, now under a new National Security Advisor, should make a concerted effort to take on board and groom young analysts trained in scenario building and analytical modelling techniques.

Given India's strategic culture (or the lack of it!), the government's response to the threat of bio-terrorism has been grossly inadequate. As India's decision makers are mired in the Panipat Syndrome,[16] it is not surprising that there is virtually no recognition of the potential dangers of bio-terrorism, despite the menace of Pakistan-supported Islamist fundamental terrorism in Jammu & Kashmir and elsewhere in the country. The armed services, correctly, do not foresee a large-scale military threat of the use of biological weapons in conventional conflict and are, therefore, not engaged in defending against it. The nuclear threat and, to some extent, the chemical threat are given greater credence by the armed services. There is widespread international acceptance that biological weapons lack military utility. The US unilaterally renounced the use of biological weapons in 1969.[17] However, this realization did not prevent several nations from developing and stockpiling biological weapons as they could be used to soften hardened defences before an assault is launched. If employed in the rear areas of the adversary country, they could disrupt lines of communication and paralyse command centres. Hence, their use cannot be entirely ruled out, particularly as part of an asymmetric strategy by a weaker nation against a stronger adversary.

In India, the threat of bio-terrorism, often referred to as 'a poor man's atomic bomb', is perceived to be primarily directed against the civilian population both because the armed forces are relatively better protected and because the aim of terrorists would invariably be to gain maximum publicity and create a fear psychosis. India's foremost internal security threat is from Jihadi fundamentalism that is mostly sponsored from across India's western border by the ISI agency of Pakistan. Individual Islamist terrorist groups based in Pakistan have often threatened to disrupt peace in India and have succeeded in doing so on several occasions. Bio-terrorism is but a short step to upping the ante by an order of magnitude to dramatically highlight the 'cause' and gain international attention.

Threats against civilian targets are the domain of the Ministry of Home Affairs (MHA). How seriously it takes this threat is a matter of conjecture but its Annual Reports make no mention of bio-terrorism threats. The threat of bio-terrorism requires comprehensive planning and focusing on preparedness and response capacity—integrating the role of the central government with that of state governments, as well as integration of state and national assets. The government should address the challenge of informing the public and educating the people about the reality of bio-terrorism. The support of the people is necessary for early warning, prevention and crisis management. However, such a campaign should be launched with discretion to avoid causing panic.

This essay has sought to focus on the bio-terrorism threat in India. The Parliament and government should focus on the threat of bio-terrorism. The government should draw up and optimize modalities for dealing with the threat of bio-terrorism, both from a budgeting and structural standpoint. Both preventive and pre-emptive strategies are needed to neutralize perceived threats. These should be formulated, debated nationally and resolutely implemented.

NOTES

1. 'Biological Weapons Convention Members to Meet in Geneva from 19 to 30 July 2004', Press Release of the Secretariat of BWC Meeting of Experts, 16 July 2004. (http://www.reachingcriticalwill.org/legal/bw/press16July.html)
2. Oliver Meier, 'Biological Weapons Convention must Prevail', *Defense News*, 27 August–2 September 2001.
3. Daniel J. Dire, 'Historic Aspects Of Biological Warfare Agents', www.emedicine.com/emerg/topic853.
4. Federation of American Scientists website: www.fas.org/nuke/intro/bw/agent.
5. Op. cit., n. 3.
6. Ibid.
7. Gregory Koblentz, 'Pathogens as Weapons: The International Security Implications of Biological Warfare', *International Security*, vol. 28, no. 3 Winter 2003–4, p. 87.
8. Michael J. Powers and Jonathan Ban, 'Bio-Terrorism: Threat and Preparedness', *The Bridge*, vol. 32, no. 1, Spring 2002.
9. Ibid.
10. Ibid.
11. Matthew Meselson, 'Averting the Hostile Exploitation of Biotechnology', *CBW Bulletin*, no. 48, June 2000.
12. Op. cit., n. 3.
13. Op. cit., n. 7.
14. Op. cit., n. 8.
15. Ibid.
16. India's kings never fought invading armies at the Khyber Pass, a natural defensive position, but always waited for the enemy to almost reach Delhi. Three famous battles that decided the course of Indian history were fought at Panipat, a small town 40 miles north of Delhi.
17. Jonathan B. Tucker, 'A Farewell to Germs: The US renunciation of Biological and Toxin Warfare', *International Security*, vol. 27, no. 1, Summer 2002.

APPENDIX
Biological Warfare Agents*

ANTHRAX

Bacillus anthracis is a large, aerobic, gram-positive, spore-forming, non-motile bacillus. The bacterium ordinarily produces a zoonotic disease in domesticated and wild animals such as goats, sheep, cattle, horses and swine. There are normally two types of disease: cutaneous anthrax and inhalation anthrax. About 95 per cent of human anthrax cases in the United States belong to the former category. Cutaneous anthrax develops when a bacterial organism from infected animal tissues is deposited under the skin. When a patient contracts cutaneous anthrax, he develops a small elevated lesion on his skin which becomes a skin ulcer, frequently surrounded by swelling or edema. If the patient is not treated with an effective antibiotic, the mortality rate for cutaneous anthrax is 10–20 per cent.

Inhalation anthrax develops when the bacterial organism is inhaled into the lungs. A progressive infection follows. A biological warfare attack with anthrax spores delivered by aerosol would cause inhalation anthrax, an extraordinarily rare form of the naturally occurring disease. According to an estimate by the US Congress's Office of Technology Assessment, 100 kg of anthrax, released from a low-flying aircraft over a large city on a clear, calm night, could kill between one and three million people. The disease manifests itself after an incubation period varying between one and six days, presumably dependent upon the amount of inhaled organisms. In some cases, there may be a short period of improvement. Shock and death usually follow within 24–36 hours of respiratory distress onset.

An epidemic of inhalation anthrax in its early stage with nonspecific symptoms could be confused with a wide variety of viral, bacterial and fungal infections. Progression over two to three days with the sudden development of severe respiratory distress followed by shock and death in 24–36 hours in essentially all untreated cases eliminates diagnosis other than inhalation anthrax. Other suggestive findings include chest-wall edema, haemorrhagic pleural effusions and haemorrhagic meningitis. Patients suffering from plague or tularemia pneumonia will have pulmonary infiltrates and clinical signs of pneumonia (usually absent in anthrax). Almost all cases of inhalation anthrax in which treatment began after patients became symptomatic have been fatal, regardless of the treatment. Tetracycline and erythromycin have been recommended in penicillin-sensitive patients. Vaccines are available against some forms of anthrax, but their efficacy against abnormally high concentrations of the bacteria is uncertain.

Limited human data suggests that after completion of the first three doses of the recommended six-dose primary series (0, 2, 4 weeks, then 6, 12, 18 months), protection against both cutaneous and inhalation anthrax is available. As with other vaccines, the degree of protection depends upon the magnitude of the challenge dose; vaccine-induced protection is undoubtedly overwhelmed by the extremely high spore challenge.

BOTULINUM TOXINS

The anaerobic, spore forming, gram-positive bacillus *Clostridium Botulinum* produces botulinum toxins. Botulinum toxins are the most lethal toxins known, with an estimated lethal dose of 0.001 mcg/kg in humans to 50 per cent of the exposed population (LD50). Since botulinum toxin is lethal and easy to manufacture and weaponize, it passes a credible threat as a BW agent. When used as a BW or terrorist agent, exposure is likely to occur following inhalation of aerosolized toxin or ingestion of food contaminated with the preformed toxin or microbial spores. Recently, Western sources reported that Iraq had admitted to active research on the offensive use of botulinum toxins and to weaponizing and deploying more than 100 munitions with botulinum toxin in 1995. A biological warfare attack with botulinum toxin delivered by aerosol could cause symptoms largely similar to those observed with food-borne botulism.

In its pure form, the toxin is a white crystalline substance that is readily dissolvable in water, but decays rapidly in the open air. Symptoms of inhalation botulism may begin as early as 24–36 hours following exposure or as late as several days. Initial signs and symptoms include general weakness, lassitude and dizziness. Diminished salivation with extreme dryness of the mouth and throat may cause complaints of a sore throat. Urinary retention may also occur. Motor symptoms are usually present early in the disease; cranial nerves are affected first with blurred vision, diplopia, ptosis and photophobia. Respiratory failure may occur suddenly. Mucous membranes of the mouth may become dry and crusted.

The occurrence of an epidemic with large numbers of afebrile patients showing symptoms of progressive ocular, pharyngeal, respiratory and muscular weakness and paralysis hints strongly at the diagnosis of botulinum. Single cases may be confused with various neuromuscular disorders such as atypical Guillain-Barrè syndrome, myasthenia gravis, or tick paralysis. Respiratory failure secondary to the paralysis of respiratory muscles is the most serious complication and, generally, the cause of death. Reported cases of botulism prior to 1950 had 60 per cent mortality. With tracheotomy and ventilator assistance, fatalities should be less than 5 per cent. Intensive and prolonged nursing may be required for recovery (which may take several weeks or even months).

BRUCELLOSIS

Brucellosis is a zoonotic infection of domesticated and wild animals caused by an organism of the genus *Brucella*. The organism infects mainly cattle, sheep, goats and other ruminants, causing abortion, fetal death and genital infection. Humans, who are usually infected by contact with infected animals, may develop numerous symptoms in addition to the usual ones like fever, malaise and muscular pain. The disease often becomes chronic and may relapse, even with appropriate treatment. The ease of transmission by aerosol suggests that *Brucella* species may be useful as a BW agent.

Brucellosis is caused by one of four species of bacteria: *Brucella melitensis, B. abortus, B. suis and B. canis;* virulence for humans decreases somewhat in the order given. The bacteria reside quiescently in tissue and bone marrow, and are extremely difficult to eradicate even with antibiotic therapy. Their natural reservoir is domestic animals such as goats, sheep and camels (*B. melitensis*); cattle (*B. abortus*); and pigs (*B. suis*). *Brucella canis* is primarily a pathogen of dogs, and only occasionally causes disease in humans, who are infected when they inhale contaminated aerosols, ingest raw (unpasteurized) infected milk or meat, or have abraded skin or conjunctival surfaces that come into contact with the bacteria. Under select environmental conditions (for example, darkness, cool temperatures and high CO_2), persistence for up to two years has been documented. *Brucella* species have long been considered potential candidates for use in biological warfare. The *Brucellae* agent would most likely be delivered by aerosol route.

Brucellosis has an incubation period normally ranging varying from three to four weeks, but it may be as short as one week or as long as several months. The disease is an acute, non-specific febrile illness with chills, sweats, headache, fatigue, myalgias, arthralgias and anorexia. Cough occurs in 15–25 per cent cases, but the chest x-ray is usually normal. Untreated disease can persist for months or even years, often with relapses and remissions. Disability may be pronounced. Lethality may approach 6 per cent following infection with *B. melitensis*, but the disease is rarely fatal (0.5 per cent or less).

Brucellosis may be indistinguishable clinically from the typhoidal form of tularemia or from typhoid fever itself. The disease in humans is characterized by a multitude of somatic complaints, including fever, sweats, anorexia, fatigue, malaise, weight loss and depression. Localized complications may involve the cardiovascular, gastrointestinal, genitourinary, hepatobiliary, osteoarticular, pulmonary and nervous systems. Without adequate and prompt antibiotic treatment, some patients develop a 'chronic' brucellosis syndrome with many features of the 'chronic fatigue' syndrome.

CHOLERA

Cholera is an acute and potentially severe gastrointestinal (diarrhoeal) disease caused by *Vibrio cholerae. V cholerae* is a short, curved, motile, gram-negative, non-sporulating bacillus. Humans acquire the disease by consuming water or food contaminated with the organism. The organism multiplies in the small intestine and secretes an enterotoxin that causes a secretory diarrhoea. When employed as a BW agent, cholera is likely to be used to contaminate water supplies. It is unlikely to be used in aerosol form. Without treatment, death may result from severe dehydration, hypovolemia and shock. Vomiting is often present early in the illness and may complicate oral replacement of fluid losses. There is little or no fever or abdominal pain. Watery diarrhoea can also be caused by enterotoxigenic *E. coli*, rotavirus or other viruses, non-cholera *vibrios*, or food poisoning due to ingestion of preformed toxins such as those of *Clostridium perfringens*, *Bacillus cereus* or *Staphylococcus aureus*.

CLOSTRIDIUM PERFRINGENS TOXINS

Clostridium perfringens is a common anaerobic bacterium associated with three distinct disease syndromes: gas gangrene or clostridial myonecrosis; enteritis necroticans (pig-bel); and clostridium food poisoning. Each of these syndromes has very specific requirements for delivering inocula of *C. perfringens* to specific sites to induce disease, and it is difficult to imagine a general scenario in which the spores or vegetative organisms could be used as a BW agent. There are, however, at least twelve protein toxins elaborated, and one or more of these could be produced, concentrated, and used as a weapon. Water-borne disease is conceivable, but unlikely. The alpha toxin would be lethal by aerosol. Other toxins from the organism may be co-weaponized to enhance effectiveness.

Gas gangrene is a well recognized, life-threatening emergency. Symptoms of the disease may be subtle before fulminant toxemia develops, and the diagnosis is often made at post-mortem examination. The bacteria produce toxins that lead to high mortality from clostridial myonecrosis, and which produce the characteristic intense pain not in proportion to the wound. Within hours signs of systemic toxicity appear, including confusion, tachycardia and sweating. Most *Clostridia* species produce large amounts of CO_2 and hydrogen that cause intense swelling, hence the term 'gas' gangrene, resulting in gas in the soft tissues and the emission of foul-smelling gas from the wound.

EBOLA HAEMORRHAGIC FEVER

Ebola haemorrhagic fever is one of the most virulent viral diseases known to humankind, causing death in 50-90 per cent of all clinically cases. Consequently, it has figured prominently in popular discussions of biological warfare, although its practical applications as a BW agent remain speculative. The disease has been traced to the jungles of Africa and Asia and several different forms of Ebola virus have been identified.

The Ebola virus was first identified in a western equatorial province of Sudan and in the nearby region of Zaire in 1976 after significant epidemics broke out in Yamkubu, northern Zaire, and Nzara, southern Sudan. Between June and November 1976 the Ebola virus infected 284 people in Sudan, with 117 deaths. In Zaire, 318 cases and 280 deaths were reported in September and October. An isolated case occurred in Zaire in 1977, and a second outbreak in Sudan in 1979. In 1989 and 1990, a filovirus, Ebola-Reston, was isolated in monkeys being held in quarantine in a laboratory in Reston (Virginia), Alice (Texas) and Pennsylvania. In the Philippines, Ebola-Reston infections occurred in the quarantine area for monkeys intended for exportation near Manila. There was a epidemic in Kikwit, Zaire in 1995: 315 cases and 244 deaths. One human case of Ebola haemorrhagic fever and several cases of chimpanzees were confirmed in Côte d'Ivoire in 1994–5. In Gabon, Ebola haemorrhagic fever was first documented in 1994 and outbreaks occurred in February 1996 and July 1996. Nearly 1,100 cases and 793 deaths have been documented since the virus was discovered. The natural reservoir of the Ebola virus seems to be the rain forests of Africa and Asia but it has not yet been identified.

The Ebola virus is transmitted by direct contact with the blood, secretions, organs or semen of infected persons. Transmission through semen may occur up to seven weeks after clinical recovery, as with Marburg haemorrhagic fever. Health care workers have frequently been infected while seeing patients. In the 1976 epidemic in Zaire, every Ebola patient infected by contaminated syringes and needles died.

Having an incubation period of two to twenty-one days, Ebola is often characterized by the sudden onset of fever, weakness, muscle pain, headache and sore throat. This is followed by vomiting, diarrhoea, rash, impaired kidney and liver functions, and both internal and external bleeding. Specialized laboratory tests on blood specimens (which are not commercially available) detect specific antigens or antibodies and help to isolate the virus. These tests pose an extreme bio-hazard and are only conducted under maximum containment conditions. Suspected cases should be isolated from other patients and strict barrier nursing techniques practised. All hospital personnel should be briefed on the nature of the disease and its routes of transmission. Hospital personnel who come into close contact with patients or contaminated materials without barrier nursing attire must be considered exposed and put under close supervised surveillance.

MYCOTOXINS

Trichothecene mycotoxins are highly toxic compounds produced by certain species of filamentous fungi (*Fusarium*, *Myrotecium*, *Cephalosporium*, *Trichoderma*, *Verticimonosporium*, *Stachybotrys* species). These mycotoxins (such as T-2, nivalenol) cause multiple organ effects including emesis, diarrhoea, weight loss, nervous disorders, cardiovascular alterations, immunosuppression, haemostatic derangements, skin toxicity and bone marrow damage. Because of their anti-personnel properties, ease of large-scale production and amenability to dispersal by various methods (dusts, droplets, aerosols, smoke, rockets, artillery, mines and portable sprays), mycotoxins have an excellent potential for weaponization. There is strong evidence that trichothecenes ('yellow rain') have been used as a BW agent in Southwest Asia and Afghanistan. Between 1974 and 1981, numerous attacks resulted in at least of 6,310 deaths in Laos, 981 deaths in Cambodia and 3,042 deaths in Afghanistan.

PLAGUE

Plague is a zoonotic infection caused by *Yersinia pestis*, a gram-negative coccobacillus, which has been the cause of three great human pandemics in the sixth, fourteenth, and twentieth centuries. Throughout history, the oriental rat flea (*Xenopsylla cheopis*) has been largely responsible for spreading bubonic plague. Under natural conditions, humans become infected as a result of contact with rodents and their fleas. The mode of transmission of the gram-negative coccobacillus is a bite of the infected flea, *Xenopsylla cheopis*, the oriental rat flea, or *Pulex irritans*, the human flea. Under natural conditions, three syndromes are discernible: bubonic, primary septicemia, or pneumonic. In a biological warfare, the plague bacillus could be delivered via contaminated vectors (fleas) causing the bubonic type or, more likely, via aerosol causing the pneumonic type. Plague may be spread from person to person by droplets. Strict isolation procedures are recommended for all cases.

RICIN

Ricin, a glycoprotein (plant) toxin derived from the beans of the castor plant, is one of the most toxic and easily produced plant toxins. Although the lethal toxicity of ricin is much less than botulinum toxin, the ready worldwide availability of castor beans and the ease with which the toxin can be produced make it significant as a biological weapon. Ricin blocks protein synthesis by altering the RNA, thus killing the cell. Ricin's significance as a potential biological warfare agent relates to its availability worldwide, its ease of production, and extreme pulmonary toxicity when inhaled.

Overall, the clinical picture depends on the route of exposure. All reported serious or fatal cases of castor bean ingestion have followed more or less the same course: rapid onset of nausea, vomiting, abdominal cramps and severe diarrhoea with vascular collapse; death occurs on the third day or later. Following inhalation, nonspecific symptoms such as weakness, fever, cough and hypothermia may be manifested followed by hypotension and cardiovascular collapse. The exact cause of death is unknown and probably varies with the route of infection. Inhalation of high doses produces such severe pulmonary damage as it becomes fatal.

In oral infection, fever, gastrointestinal involvement and vascular collapse are prominent, the latter differentiating it from infection with enteric pathogens. Regarding to inhalation exposure, non-specific findings of weakness, fever, vomiting, cough, hypothermia and hypotension in large numbers of patients suggest several respiratory pathogens.

SMALLPOX

Variola, the causative agent of smallpox, is the most notorious of the poxviruses (family Poxviridae). Smallpox was an important cause of morbidity and mortality in the developing world until recently. In 1980, the World Health Organization (WHO) declared endemic smallpox eradicated, with the last reported case in Somalia in 1977. Variola is highly infectious and is associated with a high mortality rate and secondary spread. Variola poses a significant threat as a BW agent.

The virus is known to exist in only two laboratory repositories in the US and Russia. The emergence of human cases outside the laboratory would signal use of the virus as a biological weapon. Under natural conditions, the virus is transmitted by direct (face-to-face) contact with an infected person and, occasionally, by aerosol. Smallpox virus is highly stable and retains infectivity for long periods outside of the host. A related virus, monkey-pox, clinically resembles smallpox and causes sporadic human disease in West and Central Africa.

The incubation period is typically about twelve days. The illness begins with a prodrome lasting two to three days, with generalized malaise, fever, rigors, headache and backache. This is followed by defervescence and the appearance of a typical skin eruption characterized by progression over seven to ten days of lesions through successive stages, from macules to papules to vesicles to pustules. The latter form crusts and, upon healing, leave depressed depigmented scars. The fatality rate is approximately 35 per cent in unvaccinated individuals. Permanent joint deformities and blindness may follow recovery. Vaccine immunity may prevent or modify illness. A vaccine is fortunately available. Vaccinia virus is a live poxvirus vaccine that induces strong cross-protection against smallpox for at least five years and partial protection for ten or more years.

STAPHYLOCOCCAL ENTEROTOXIN B

Staphylococcal enterotoxin B (SEB) is one of the best studied and, therefore, best understood toxins. SEB is one of the most common causes of food poisoning. Nausea, vomiting and diarrhoea normally occur following ingestion of contaminated foodstuffs. The toxin causes a markedly different clinical syndrome when exposure is through a non-enteric route. In a BW or terrorist attack, the toxin is likely to be acquired through inhalation of a SEB aerosol.

SEB is one of several exotoxins produced by *Staphylococcus aureus*, causing food poisoning when ingested. A BW attack with aerosol delivery of SEB to the respiratory tract produces a distinct syndrome causing significant morbidity and potential mortality. The disease begins one to six hours after exposure with the sudden onset of fever, chills, headache, myalgia and non-productive cough. In more severe cases, dyspnea and retrosternal chest pain may also be present. Fever, which may reach 103–106° F, could last two to five days, but cough may persist for one to four weeks. Many patients may suffer from nausea, vomiting, and diarrhoea. In moderately severe laboratory exposures, lost duty time has been less than two weeks but, based upon animal data, it is anticipated that severe exposures result in fatalities.

In food-borne SEB infection, fever and respiratory involvement are not seen, and gastrointestinal symptoms are prominent. The nonspecific findings of fever, non-productive cough, myalgia and headache seen in large numbers of patients in an epidemic setting would suggest any of several infectious respiratory pathogens, particularly influenza, adenovirus, or mycoplasma. In a BW attack with SEB, the onset may be within a single day, while naturally occurring outbreaks would occur over a more prolonged period.

TULAREMIA

Tularemia is a zoonosis caused by the gram-negative, facultative intracellular bacterium *Francisella tularensis.* The disease is characterized by fever, localized skin or mucous membrane ulceration, regional lymphadenopathy and, occasionally, pneumonia. G.W. McCay discovered the disease in Tulare County, California, in 1911. The first confirmed case of human disease was reported in 1914. Edward Francis, who described transmission by deer flies via infected blood, coined the term tularemia in 1921. *F tularensis* has been considered an important BW agent because of its high infectivity after it is aerosolized.

Under natural conditions, humans beings acquire the disease through inoculation of the skin or mucous membranes with the blood or tissue fluids of infected animals, or the bite of infected deer flies, mosquitoes, or ticks. A BW attack with *F. tularensis* delivered by aerosol would primarily cause typhoidal tularemia, a syndrome expected to have a higher fatality rate than the 5–10 per cent seen when disease is acquired naturally.

There are a variety of clinical forms of tularemia depending on the route of inoculation and virulence of the strain. In humans, as few as 10-50 organisms could cause the disease if inhaled or injected intradermally, whereas 10^8

organisms are required in the case of oral infection. Under natural conditions, ulceroglandular tularemia generally occurs about three days after intradermal inoculation and is manifested as regional lymphadenopathy, fever, chills, headache and malaise, with or without a cutaneous ulcer. Gastrointestinal tularemia occurs after drinking contaminated groundwater, and is characterized by abdominal pain, nausea, vomiting and diarrhoea. Bacteremia is common after primary intradermal, respiratory, or gastrointestinal infection with *F. tularensis* and may result in septicemia or 'typhoidal' tularemia. The typhoidal form may also occur as a primary condition in 5–15 per cent of naturally occurring cases; clinical features include fever, prostration and weight loss, but without adenopathy.

The diagnosis of primary typhoidal tularemia is difficult, as signs and symptoms are non-specific and there is frequently no suggestive exposure history. Pneumonic tularemia is a severe atypical pneumonia that may be fulminant, and may be primary or secondary. Primary pneumonia may be caused by direct inhalation of infectious aerosols, or may result from aspiration of organisms in cases of pharyngeal tularemia. Pneumonic tularemia causes fever, headache, malaise, substernal discomfort and a non-productive cough; radiologic evidence of pneumonia or mediastinal lymphadenopathy may or may not be present. A BW attack with *F. tularensis* would most likely be delivered by aerosol, causing primarily typhoidal tularemia. Many exposed individuals would develop pneumonic tularemia (primary or secondary), but clinical pneumonia may be absent or non-evident. Fatality rates in such cases may be higher than the 5–10 per cent seen when the disease is acquired naturally.

VENEZUELAN EQUINE ENCEPHALITIS

The viral encephalitides, Venezuelan equine encephalitis (VEE) virus, the western equine encephalitis (WEE) virus and the eastern equine encephalitis (EEE) virus belong to the Alphavirus genus and are normally associated with encephalitis. These viruses were first recovered from horses during the 1930s. VEE was isolated in the Guajira peninsula of Venezuela in 1930, WEE in the San Joaquin Valley of California in 1930, and EEE in Virginia and New Jersey in 1933.

Eight serologically distinct viruses belonging to the VEE complex have been associated with human disease; the most important of these pathogens are designated Subtype 1, variants A, B and C. These agents also cause severe disease in horses, mules and donkeys (Equidae). Natural infections are acquired by the bite of a wide variety of mosquitoes. Equidae serve as the viremic hosts and source of mosquito infection. In natural human epidemics, severe and often fatal encephalitis in Equidae always precedes that in humans. A BW attack with virus disseminated as an aerosol would cause human disease as a primary event. If Equidae were present, disease in these animals would occur simultaneously with human disease. Secondary spread by person-to-person contact occurs at a negligible rate. However, a BW attack in a region populated by Equidae and appropriate mosquito vectors could initiate an epizootic epidemic.

Nearly 100 per cent of those infected develop an overt illness. After an incubation period of one to five days, the onset of illness is extremely sudden, with generalized malaise, spiking fever, rigors, severe headache, photophobia, myalgia in the legs and lumbosacral area. Nausea, vomiting, cough, sore throat and diarrhoea may follow. This acute phase lasts 24-72 hours. A prolonged period of aesthenia and lethargy may follow, with full health and activity regained only after one to two weeks. Approximately 4 per cent of patients develop signs of central nervous system infection during a natural epidemic, with meningismus, convulsions, coma and paralysis. These necrologic cases are seen almost exclusively in children. The overall casefatality rate is <1 per cent, but in children with encephalitis, it may reach 20 per cent.

**Note*: Compiled from information given in Federation of American Scientists' website: www.fas.org/nuke/intro/bw/agent and the following sources:

NATO Handbook on the Medical Aspects of NBC Defensive Operations, Part II - Biological.

Guidelines for the Surveillance and Control of Anthrax in Humans and Animals, World Health Organization, WHO/EMC/ZDI/98.6.

WHO Recommended Guidelines for Epidemic Preparedness and Response: Ebola Haemorrhagic Fever (EHF), WHO/EMC/DIS/97.7.

The 'Bad Bug Book' Foodborne Pathogenic Microorganisms and Natural Toxins Handbook, U.S. Food & Drug Administration, Center for Food Safety & Applied Nutrition.

K. Bhushan and G. Katyal, *Nuclear, Biological and Chemical Warfare*, New Delhi: A.P.H. Publishing Corporation, pp. 258-340.

CHAPTER 4

Providing for Bio-Defence: Vaccines for the Future

ASHOK RATTAN

> Biological weapons . . . know no boundaries. They are huge threat to us.
>
> ALBRIGHT

Although often perceived as a recent invention, biological weapons have been used for hundreds of years, even before microbes were discovered. During the siege of Caffa (now Feodossia, Ukraine) in 1346, the Tartars catapulted the dead bodies of plague victims into the city, causing an epidemic among the inhabitants. An outbreak of plague was followed by the retreat of the defending forces and the conquest of Caffa. In the eighteenth century, Sir Jeffrey Amherst deliberately created a smallpox epidemic among hostile Native American tribes by distributing contaminated hospital blankets. The impact on the native Red Indian population was devastating.

The discovery of microbes as the causative agents of many transmissible diseases and the formulation of Koch's postulates leading to the rapid development of modern microbiology during the nineteenth century increased the capability to isolate and produce large stocks of specific pathogens. The discovery of recombinant DNA technology provided the know-how to manipulate genes leading to the real possibility of devising a twenty-first century agent with attributes of an ideal bio-weapon. When the bio-weapon is used against the military, it is bio-warfare; however, when it is directed against the civilian population, it is termed as bio-terrorism.

POOR MAN'S NEUTRON BOMB

A report by the World Health Organization (1970) estimated that if an aeroplane released 50 kg of anthrax spores over a 2 km line, upwind of a population of 500,000 as many as 95,000 people could be killed and 125,000 incapacitated, causing nearly the same devastation as a nuclear explosion while leaving the infrastructure untouched. It is for this reason that anthrax has sometimes been referred to as a poor man's neutron bomb. Even hoaxes alleging the use of biological agents can cause serious disruption.

ATTRIBUTES OF A BIO-WEAPON

The optimum attributes of an effective bio-weapon include identification of a pathogen which consistently produces a given effect—death or disease, is highly contagious, has a low infective dose, has a short and predictable incubation period and is suitable for mass production, storage and delivery. Ideally, it should not deteriorate during dissemination. Weaponization has been achieved in some of the pathogens. While a large number of them can be used as bio-weapons, a recent report by the Center for Disease Control, Atlanta, divided biological agents into three categories according to the level of risk they pose to the public.

CLASSIFICATION OF BIO-WEAPON AGENTS

Category A includes the highest priority agents which are microbes that are easily disseminated or transmitted from person to person with major public health impact, cause high mortality, public panic and social disruption and require special action for public preparedness.

Category B agents include those that are moderately easy to disseminate, cause lower mortality but significant morbidity and require specific enhancements of diagnostic capacity and surveillance.

Category C agents include emerging pathogens that can be engineered for mass dissemination in future due to their availability, ease of production and potential for high morbidity and mortality.

Category A	*Disease caused*
Variola major	Smallpox
Bacillus anthracis	*Anthrax*
Yersinia pestis	*Plague*
Clostridium botulinum toxin	Botulism
Francisella tularensis	*Tularemia*
Ebola virus	Viral haemorrhagic fever

Category B	*Category C*
Q fever	Emerging threat agents
Brucellosis	Nipah virus
Meliodosis	Hanta virus
VEE	SARS
Typhus fever	
Toxic syndrome	
Food safety threats	
Water safety threats	

It must be remembered that the human population can be decimated by lack of food supply as well as human pathogens. Airborne fungal plant pathogens are ideally suited for this role. Similarly, foot and mouth disease can decimate milch cows as can glanders of horses.

WEB OF BIO-DEFENCE

In order to provide an effective bio-defence, a network of preventive and protective efforts needs to be developed, which includes anti-microbials, antitoxin or serum therapy, as also pre- and post-exposure vaccines. In the US, a heavily funded (US$ 6 billion) Bio-shield project has been initiated which will focus on identifying and addressing the unmet bio-defence needs including funding for basic research, target identification, preclinical development as well as clinical evaluation of potential interventions. The regulatory authorities have promised to streamline and shorten the lengthy process for approval of future vaccines.

SUSCEPTIBLE POPULATION

The potential threat of biological warfare is inversely proportional to the number of immune persons in the target population. Thus, biological agents are potential weapons only against a population with a substantial proportion of susceptible persons. Smallpox virus would not have been considered a useful biological weapon in the 1960s when the world population was universally immunized with vaccinia. Similarly, tetanus or diphtheria pose no threat to a population in the industrial world where vaccination against them is available.

NON-SPECIFIC PROTECTION

There is sufficient evidence that there are three principles of immunity maintenance (three lines of defence). Human and vertebrate animals possess all three systems of immunogenesis, which comprise skin and mucous membrane, inflammation and specific immunity, respectively. Constitutional and phagocytic mechanisms are performed by specific inherent mechanisms that are ready to contract infection the moment the infectious agent attacks. They serve as the first and second line of defence which are non-specific mechanism of intracellular determination of microbes. In case they prove to be ineffective, the host has a chance to be rescued by specific immunoglobulin produced by the lymphatic system. Efforts to understand these factors and to specifically enhance non-specific immune response can play an effective role in bio-defence.

PASSIVE IMMUNITY

The only available countermeasure that can provide immediate specific immunity against a biological agent is a passive antibody. Unlike vaccines, which require time to induce protective immunity and depend on the host's ability to mount an immune response, a passive antibody can provide immediate protection regardless of the immune status of the host. Passive antibody therapy has substantial advantages over antimicrobial agents and other measures for post-exposure prophylaxis, including low toxicity and high specific activity. The state of immediate immunity can last for weeks and possibly months. Some IgG isotypes have serum half-lives in excess of 30 days as it has been reported that an average half-life of maternal IgG is 48.4 days, which confer long-lasting protection to passively immunized persons. Although a passive antibody generally has to be given systemically, oral administration can be useful against certain gastrointestinal agents. If vaccines are available, simultaneous administration of vaccines and antibody may be possible to provide both immediate and long-lasting protection.

Stockpiling antibody-based reagents, whether polyclonal or monoclonal, can be rapidly administered to the exposed population and would substantially reduce the threat of many biological agents by providing immediate immunity to susceptible persons. For persistent threats for which vaccines are available, this would provide additional time for immunization as well as for reducing the threat dimensions.

ACTIVE IMMUNITY

Vaccines have the lowest risk and are the most effective method of protecting the public against infectious diseases. Enable force projection by providing continuous long-lasting protection. Army personnel are routinely immunized against a number of possible pathogens before they enter the war zone (e.g. US army personnel in Vietnam, Sudan or Iraq). New and improved vaccines against agents of bio-terrorism must be suitable for the civilian population of varying ages and health status. In addition, vaccines developed to counter civilian bio-terrorist attacks must be safe, easy to administer and capable of immediate protection and/or transmission blocking immune response. Scientists must also develop and characterize adjuvant that can enhance these desirable characteristics. The development of new candidate vaccines for all category A agents is a priority.

A review of the available bio-defence tools against Category A pathogens identifies the unmet needs:

Category A disease	*Vaccine*	*Post-exposure therapy*	*Rapid diagnostic*
Anthrax	Yes	Yes	No
Smallpox	Yes	No	No
Plague	No	Yes	No
Botulism	No	Yes	No
Tularemia	No	Yes	No
Viral Hemorrhagic Fever	No	No	No

PROTECTION AGAINST ANTHRAX

Bacillus anthracis, the agent that causes anthrax, has several characteristics that make it a formidable biological weapon and bioterrorist threat. These characteristics include its stability in spore formation, ease of culture and production, its ability to be aerosolized, the seriousness of the disease it causes and the lack of sufficient vaccine for widespread use. Human anthrax has three major clinical forms: cutaneous, inhalational and gastrointestinal. If left untreated, all three forms can result in septicemia and death.

Major virulence factors include an antiphagocytic outer capsule and at least two well characterized toxins. The two toxins—Edema Factor (EF) and Lethal Factor (LF)—can destroy cells or inhibit their normal functioning. A third component, Protective Antigen (PA), when associated with both EF and LF enables them to bind to a specific receptor on mammalian cells. After this complex is internalized the bacteria's toxic effects are activated.

Although the correlate of immunity has not yet been defined, several animal studies have demonstrated that neutralizing antibodies to PA elicits significant protective immunity against inhalational spore challenge. Vaccination studies have established a direct correlation between antibody fibre to PA and survival after lethal challenge with virulent anthrax spore. The passive administration of polyclonal antibodies raised against recombination PA is protective in mice and guinea pigs. *In vitro* studies have revealed that antibodies to PA recognize spore coat proteins, stimulate the uptake of spores by phagocyte and inhibit spore germination.

Pasteur (1881) demonstrated the protection of sheep by

injection of heat attenuated *B. anthracis* culture. Widespread vaccination of domesticated animals with a live attenuated sterne strains began in 1930 and has led to near eradication of anthrax in domesticated animals. In the US, a human vaccine, Anthrax Vaccine Adsorbed (AVA), an aluminium hydroxide adsorbed has been licensed. This is formulating treated culture supernatant of a toxigenic noncapsulated, nonproteolytic B, anthracis strain, V770-NP1-R, derived from sterne strain. AVA contains a protective antigen; antibodies to this PA confer immunity to anthrax AVA and is safe and efficacious. Six subcutaneous doses need to be administered over a two-year period to obtain immunity. It requires a booster at six months interval. However, the vaccine is not standardized for its PA content and its immune response is not quantitated by measuring neutralizing antibodies to PA.

The development of anthrax vaccines in the future would include, among others, determination of the minimum number of doses required for efficacy. Recombinant vaccines in which the PA gene is cloned into an organism of low pathogenecity such as *B. subtilis*, so that vaccine production would not have to be carried out in a BSL-3 laboratory. Vaccines from a mutant strain which depend upon aromatic amino acids for survival since these compounds are not available in human beings, the vaccine strain would not multiply unchecked. Purified PA preparation combined with various adjuvants may prove to be efficacious after a single dose. An oral anthrax vaccine is also under development.

PROTECTION AGAINST PLAGUE

The bacteria *Yersinia pestis* causes plague. Its potential for use as a biological weapon is based on methods that were developed to produce and aerosolize large amounts of bacteria, and its transmissibility from person to person. Infection by inhalation of even a small number of virulent aerosolized *Y. pestis* bacilli can lead to pneumonic plague, a highly lethal form of plague that can spread from person to person.

A killed whole cell vaccine had been available for individuals considered to be at high risk. Vaccination before exposure has been found to be effective in reducing disease. However, its effectiveness to prevent or reduce pneumonic plague remains untested.

Two *Y. pestis* proteins, F1 and V, are being evaluated as vaccine candidates in animal models. The F1 protein is the principal protective antigen in the plague vaccine. It has been demonstrated that recombinant F1, V or F1+V protein adsorbed by an aluminium hydroxide adjuvant protects animals against both bubonic and pneumonic forms of this disease. The F1+V vaccine provides significant protection as early as fourteen days after immunization. The passive transfer of either V protein specific polyclonal antiserum or a monoclonal anti-V antibody protects animals against a lethal attack by *Y. pestis*.

DRAWBACKS OF ACTIVE IMMUNIZATION

It is true that vaccination can lower the susceptibility of a population against a specific threat but one of the major drawbacks is that inducing a protection response by vaccination may take longer than the time between exposure and onset of disease. Moreover, many vaccines require multiple doses to achieve a protective immune response, which would limit their usefulness in an emergency vaccination programme to provide rapid prophylaxis after an attack.

NON-BIOLOGICAL DEFENSE AGAINST BIO-TERRORISM

Though a number of technological tools for defence against bioweapons are available, it appears that the scientific community is expected to provide answers to problems which political and diplomatic processes have failed to satisfactorily solve. Alternative non-biological solutions to the threat of bio-terrorism like diplomacy and fairness in negotiation to end incentives for the bio-terrorism programme, betterment of human conditions and detection followed by elimination of bio-weapons should all be considered as part of an effective web of prevention. As scientific knowledge increases we should be aware of the dual use of new technologies, for what is powerful for good can be potent for evil.

CHAPTER 5

Bio-Terrorism: Threat Perception

V.M. KALIA

> The threat of biological weapons from a madman with a batch of plague-inducing bacteria that could kill tens of thousands of people in a single act of malevolence is no longer a far-fetched scenario, but a real threat that is here and now.
>
> WILLIAM COHEN
> Former US Secretary of Defence

INTRODUCTION

Humans have been aware of the utility of biological organisms and toxins as weapons of war well before the germ theory of disease was understood. The use of disease as a weapon of war is not new. Warfare with biological weapons dates back to antiquity. In the First World War biological agents were used to attack livestock. There is strong evidence that Germany used *Bacillus anthracis* and *Burkholderia mallei*, the causative agents of anthrax and glanders, to infect Romanian sheep which were being transported to Russia. During the Second World War, Japan conducted extensive biological weapons (BW) research from 1932 to 1945.[1] It attacked at least eleven Chinese cities with biological weapons during the war. The tactics used in these attacks included contamination of food and water supplies as well as tossing cultures directly into homes and spraying agents from aircraft. The United States Biological Warfare Programme was launched in 1942, it included a research and development facility at Camp Detrick (now Fort Detrick), Maryland, test sites in Mississippi and Utah, and a production plant in Terra Haute, Indiana. The United States also collaborated with its allies, including Canada and Great Britain, on biological warfare applications. By the late 1960s the United States had developed a substantial biological arsenal comprising bacterial and toxin agents for anti-personnel use. The Soviet biological warfare programme, which was reportedly launched during the early 1900s, was the largest of all national programmes, and it continued under a clandestine organization called Biopreparat. The Soviet BW programme considered scores of lethal bacteria, toxins and viruses for use in its biological programme, including anthrax, plague, ricin, Ebola, Marburg and smallpox. Hundreds of tonnes of anthrax and dozens of tonnes of plague and smallpox were stockpiled for use against the United States and its allies.

The 9/11 attacks and the subsequent anthrax letters, combined with evidence of terrorist groups' interest in toxic agents, have focused renewed attention on the possibility of biological agents being used by terrorists. The anthrax letters[2] of 2001 were an entirely new phenomenon. They moved the threat of bio-terrorism, which had previously been largely theoretical, closer to reality. Despite hundreds of anthrax hoaxes in the years prior to October 2001, this was the first time that actual, virulent anthrax spores were sent through mail. The attacks were scattered, isolated incidents targeted at prominent media and political figures, but also resulted in a number of people, notably postal workers and congressional staff, suffering from collateral exposure. One of the most significant aspects is that, thus far, the perpetrator remains at large. Rise in bio-terrorism could be attributed to easy accessibility to literature, precursors, ease of production, and the incubation period allowing groups to escape after the attack. Bio-terrorism along with bio-warfare will be a feature of the strategic landscape in the twenty-first century.

According to media reports and intelligence agencies, the possibility of terrorists using chemical or biological materials may increase over the next decade. Interest among non-state actors, including terrorists, in biological and chemical materials is real and growing, and the number of potential perpetrators is increasing. Many terrorist groups have international networks and may not need state sponsors for financial and technical support. Small groups with modest finances and basic training in biology and engineering can develop an effective biological weapons capability. Instructions for manufacturing biological weapons are even available on the Internet.

BIO-WEAPONS AND BIO-TERRORISM

Biological warfare may be defined simply as the use of a biological organism or biologically derived toxin or other substance to cause lethal or incapacitating effects. *Bio-terrorism* refers to the use of biological agents, such as pathogenic organisms or agricultural pests, for the purpose of causing death or disease, to instill a sense of fear and panic in the victims as well as to intimidate governments or societies for political, financial, or ideological gain. Agents may be used to target humans, crops or livestock, or non-living but economically vital material. A bio-terrorist may be any non-state actor who uses or threatens to use biological agents on behalf of a political, religious, ecological, or other ideological cause without reference to its moral or political implications.

Biological warfare agents are characterized by low visibility, high potency, substantial accessibility and relatively easy delivery. One millionth of a gram of anthrax constitutes a lethal inhalation dose. Because of these small quantities, the concealment, transportation and dissemination of biological agents are relatively easy. A number of these agents—bacteria, viruses and toxins—occur naturally in the environment. Moreover, many are used for legitimate medical purposes (such as the development of antibiotics and vaccines), and much of the technology required to produce and 'weaponize' them is available for civilian or military use. Since aerosolization is the prominent method of dissemination, extraordinarily low technology agriculture crop dusters, backpack sprayers, and even purse-sized perfume atomizers are sufficient for bio-agent dissemination.

Biological and toxin weapons are likely to become more attractive to criminals and terrorists in the years ahead. First, as the biotechnology, pharmacology, environmental and health delivery industries grow, the number of persons possessing expertise in microbiology and the biosciences will increase greatly. It is reasonable to expect that a small proportion of this population would be willing for reasons of greed, ideology, or fear to apply techniques in these disciplines for criminal or terrorist purposes. Second, information on the production and dissemination of pathogens and toxins is readily available in open sources. Any one with basic education and training in the microbiological and biotechnological sciences can easily access this information and can probably adapt it for the purpose of weaponizing agents. Third, a small quantity of a pathogen or toxin delivered effectively can lead to widespread illness and death. Fourth, tactical weapons utilizing pathogens or toxins can be so designed that they are easily hidden. Therefore, it would be unlikely that a terrorist or criminal transporting and using a biological weapon would be discovered. Fifth, the delivery and use of pathogens and toxins do not necessarily require sophisticated methods. In particular, it is not technically difficult to contaminate food or beverages, which could lead to hundreds of casualties. Due to significant technical difficulties, it is unlikely that terrorists or criminals would be able to deliver pathogens by aerosol, so a biological attack utilizing this method is unlikely to occur in the next five years. Sixth, there are no defensive technologies available that are, or could be, deployed to detect and identify deliberately disseminated pathogens or toxins in real or near real time. The fact that a biological attack has occurred would, therefore, not become known until sometime later, when the pathogen's incubation period has passed and many individuals fall ill around the same time.[3]

TERRORIST INTEREST IN BIOLOGICAL WEAPONS

Terrorists have evinced an interest in bio-terrorism, and have made efforts to acquire biological agents.[4]

THREAT OF BIO-TERRORISM

Some recent incidents of bio-terrorism are as follows:

Bio-Terrorism Incidents

Date	*Location*	*Incident*
1968	Chicago, USA	The Yippies threatened to 'space-out' the delegates to the Democratic National Convention in Chicago, and everyone else in Chicago as well, by dumping LSD into Lake Michigan.
1972	St. Louis, Chicago, USA	Members of a US right-wing group known as the Order of the Rising Sun, 'dedicated to creating a new master race', had in their possession 30 to 40 kg of typhoid bacteria cultures with the intention of contaminating water supplies in Chicago, St. Louis, and other Midwestern cities.
August 1974	Washington, USA	The 'Alphabet Bomber' claimed that he possessed nerve gas and was going to Washington to kill the President. He also sent toxic material through mail to at least one Supreme Court Judge.
1976	USA	The US Postal Service seized a small package containing a charge, designed to explode a vial of nerve gas when the package was opened. An Arab terrorist group was suspected.
1976	USA	Someone mailed letters to executives that said that the envelope contained a tick infected with a 'dangerous disease'.
1977, 1978, or 1979	Israel and Europe	Palestinian terrorists were reported to have successfully spiked Israeli citrus fruit exports to Europe with liquid mercury.
1980	Paris, France, Germany	The police in Paris discovered a safe house belonging to the German Red Army Faction terrorist organization. It had an improvised laboratory containing flasks of botulism toxin. According to a second report, German police unearthed an RAF safe house that had a stockpile of nerve gas.

1980– May 1983	Galilee, Israel	Israeli government reported that it had uncovered a plot by Israeli Arabs to poison the water in Galilee with 'an unidentified powder'.
1984	Oregon, USA	Members of the Rajneesh religious cult in Antelope, Oregon used salmonella to poison the salad bars of local restaurants in an attempt to affect the outcome of the local elections. Over 700 people were suspected to have become ill. There were no fatalities.
December 1984	England	Four people in England were charged with injecting a weed killer containing mercury into a turkey. An anonymous caller purporting to represent the Animal Liberation Front (ALF) claimed responsibility.
November 1984	United Kingdom	The ALF in the UK claimed that it had contaminated Mars candy bars with rat poison to protest against the manufacturer's funding of research using monkeys. The claim was later found to be a hoax, but millions of chocolate bars were recalled.
1987	Philippines	In the Philippines, 19 police recruits died and nearly 140 were hospitalized after accepting water and sweets from unknown persons.
November 1991	United Kingdom	The ALF (UK) claimed that it had contaminated a popular drink, 'Lucozade'. Five million bottles of the drink were recalled. None of them were found to be contaminated.
January 1992	Edmonton and Calgary	A group calling itself the Animal Rights Militia claimed that it had injected liquid oven cleaner into each of 87 'Cold Buster' bars on store shelves in Edmonton and Calgary. The incident turned out to be a hoax. Two bars sent to the media were injected with a saline solution.
December 1994	Vancouver, Canada	The Animal Rights Militia sent notes to two supermarket chains as well as to the media in the Vancouver area claiming that it had injected Christmas turkeys with rat poison. No evidence of contamination was found.
December 1994	Johannesburg, South Africa	The South African police unearthed a plot designed to spread the HIV virus among

		blacks by sending HIV-positive former guerrillas to patronize prostitutes in Johannesburg.
March 1995	Tokyo, Japan	The Aum Shinrikyo cult placed containers of the deadly sarin nerve agent on five trains on three major lines of the Tokyo subway system. Twelve people died and over 5,500 were injured as the gas spread through the trains. Two of the subway lines were shut down and 26 stations were closed.
May 1995	Ohio, USA	A white supremacist employed at a laboratory in Ohio obtained samples of Yersinia pestis, the organism responsible for plague. He was arrested and the material recovered before he had an opportunity to cultivate the organism.
December 1995	USA and Canada	A man was arrested crossing the US–Canada border and charged with possession of botulism toxin. He also had guns, 20,000 rounds of ammunition, $89,000, and a large quantity of ricin. The man apparently hung himself in jail while awaiting trial.
September 2001	USA	Anthrax letters were sent by mail.

Open source accounts mention at least fifty-four cases in which a terrorist group allegedly expressed an interest in biological agents, but there is little evidence to confirm most of these cases. Only in twenty-seven cases is there more than minimal evidence that a terrorist group possessed, attempted to acquire, threatened to use, or expressed an interest in biological agents. Terrorists have used biological agents, but rarely and with relatively little effect. Of the six groups Rajneesh, Aum Shinrikyo, Dark Harvest, Mau Mau, Polish Resistance and Al Qaeda that used or tried to use biological agents have been identified. Although there may be other cases that have never been publicly identified, only one of these, the Aum Shinrikyo cult, is known to have harmed people.

Rajneesh: There is only one instance of a religious group operating in the United States actually utilizing a chemical or biological agent. Members of the Rajneesh cult used *Salmonella typhimurium*, which causes salmonellosis or food poisoning, to contaminate salad bars of local restaurants.

Aum Shinrikyo: In addition to spreading sarin nerve gas in the Tokyo subway system, Aum Shinrikyo produced biological agents and tried to use them. It expressed an interest in several biological agents, allegedly including *B. anthracis*, botulinum toxin, *C. burnetii* (Q-fever) and even Ebola.

Dark Harvest: This little known group protested the continued anthrax contamination of Gruinard Island, where the British military tested an anthrax bomb during the Second World War. The group carried anthrax-contaminated soil, apparently from the island, and dumped it on the grounds of Porton Down, which houses Britain's biological and chemical weapons research establishment. The anthrax was in a form that was highly unlikely to cause harm.

Mau Mau: According to the British, in late 1952 individuals associated with the Mau Mau African independence movement were responsible for using a plant toxin to poison livestock in what is now Kenya. However, the full extent of these activities is not known.

Polish Resistance: Multiple reports suggest that Polish resistance organizations used biological agents against German forces during the early years of the Second World War. At least one Polish official claimed that 200 Germans were killed in this fashion, but that claim was never confirmed.

Al Qaeda: In January 2003, traces of the toxin ricin were found in an apartment in London used by a group potentially linked to Al Qaeda.

MOTIVES FOR USE OF BIOLOGICAL WEAPONS BY TERRORISTS[5]

Mass Murder: At least two terrorist groups, motivated by apocalyptic, millenarian visions of creating a better society, clearly wanted to kill large numbers of people. In principle, such groups could also be motivated by the desire for revenge against a specific political or ethnic group. Steven Pera and Allan Schwander formed a group, which they called RISE, with the intention of wiping out most of the human race so that the mankind could start over again. The Aum Shinrikyo also wanted to annihilate large numbers of people as part of their efforts to seize control of Japan.

Murder: Several terrorist groups are known to have considered biological agents as weapons to kill specific individuals. In general, the perceived attractiveness of biological agents stems from the belief that the victim would appear to have died a natural death. The perpetrators hope that it would prove impossible either to detect the biological agent (especially if it is a toxin) or to determine that the victim is deliberately infected (especially if it is a pathogen). The Soviet Union also reportedly used biological agents as assassination weapons. For example, ricin toxin weaponized into a small pellet in an umbrella gun was reportedly used by the secret service of the Soviet Union to assassinate Georgi Markov,[6] a Bulgarian defector living in London.

Incapacitation: In at least two instances, the perpetrators wanted to incapacitate large numbers of people without necessarily killing anyone. According to press accounts, the Weathermen attempted to obtain biological agents to contaminate water supplies. They hoped that the repressive reaction of the government to such an incident would radicalize the general population and attract additional supporters for their cause.

Political Statement: In one case, the perpetrators used biological agents to make a political statement. This was the objective of Dark Harvest, a group that was apparently uninterested in causing harm to people or property, but was willing to 'use' biological agents to send a political message.

Anti-agriculture: This can mean either targeting livestock or crops.[7] As mentioned earlier, the Mau Mau used a plant toxin to kill cattle as part of a concerted campaign that involved the known use of other poisons, including arsenic. Apart from this instance, there are no confirmed cases of threats against agriculture.

Criminal Motives: An examination of the criminal use of biological agents reveals additional motives such as extortion. Many of the criminal uses of biological agents involved extortion. For example, extortion was the motive in nearby 9 per cent of the confirmed cases. Generally, the target was a food or grocery company.

TERRORIST GROUPS LIKELY TO RESORT TO BIOLOGICAL WEAPONS

The North Atlantic Assembly conducted a study on the types of terrorist groups potentially attracted to the use of biological agents.[8]

- Groups whose goals include vague notions about world revolution, universalistic goals such as those of the Japanese Red Army and certain European radical leftwing groups.
- Groups unconcerned with the effects of public opinion such as the neo-Nazi groups in Europe and North America.
- Groups with a history of high casualty, indiscriminate attacks, such as pro-Iranian Shiite fundamentalist groups, viz., Hezbollah, and extremists within the Palestinian movement such as the Abu Nidal Organization.
- Groups ideologically opposed to Western society in general.
- Groups noted for their sophistication in weaponry or tactics, such as the Popular Front for the Liberation of Palestine-General Command.
- Groups with state sponsors, especially where the sponsor is known to possess chemical or biological weapons.

TYPES OF BIOLOGICAL ATTACKS BY TERRORISTS

Terrorists are likely to choose four different methods to obtain biological agents: purchase from legitimate suppliers, theft, self-production, and the use of material of natural origin contaminated with biological agents. Terrorists may employ these to attack by first, injecting pathogens or toxins, second, contaminating or poisoning foods, beverages, or fomites such as food supplements and medicines taken orally (if done skilfully, this method could lead to hundreds of casualties); third, suspending pathogens or toxins in a wet or dry formulation and dispersing them over a target area as aerosolized particles. This type of attack could lead to widespread casualties. The dissemination could range from using humans as 'biological bombs' by sending infected, contagious individuals into crowded, confined places, to dropping fleas from aeroplanes. Aerosol dissemination is considered to be the likeliest route for dispersing most of the threatening biological agents.

Terrorists have a target to bring the audience to respond, for them, the best is to produce a mass reaction by spreading this over large areas; however, by killing a leader also an impact can be made. The probability that terrorists or criminals would carry out airborne attacks with pathogens in the next five years is low. The reasons are that it is technically difficult to formulate pathogens and toxins for airborne dispersal, to operate dispersal mechanisms successfully, and to ensure proper meteorological conditions for effective aerosol dispersal. For these reasons, this type of attack is too difficult for most terrorist and criminal groups to attempt. The example of the Aum Shinrikyo is illuminative in this regard. In the biological field, despite having evil intent, a membership that included highly trained bioscientists and chemists, sufficient funding, and ample time to carry out appropriate R&D, the sect failed utterly to produce effective biological and toxin weapons. There are two explanations for this failure. First, the sect used a virulent strain of *Bacillus anthracis* (the causative agent of anthrax) in their weapons, and second, they used a formulation of pathogens and substrate that clogged up the nozzles of their sprayers. The problem of formulation, especially formulations for airborne attacks, is a difficult one to overcome.

The risk of bio-terrorism is escalating because of the geo-political shift to asymmetric warfare, enhanced access to materials and knowledge, covert production facilitated by lack of 'foot print' for easy surveillance, major gaps in medical intelligence, deterrence/defence necessitating special action for medical and health preparedness, advances in biotechnology which increase threat diversity and complexity; bio-terrorism may cause public, social disharmony or economic disruption.

Cost Benefit: When compared to the cost of a nuclear weapons programme, biological weapons are in theory extremely cheap. It is estimated that the cost would be about 0.05 per cent the cost of a conventional weapon to produce a similar amount of mass casualties per square km. According to one analysis, the comparative cost to incur civilian (unprotected) casualties is $2,000 per square kilometer with conventional weapons, $800 with nuclear weapons, $600 with nerve-gas weapons, and $1 with biological weapons'.[9] Advances in microbiology and biotechnology are further reducing the costs of establishing a biological weapons programme.

MILITARY SIGNIFICANCE OF BIO-TERRORISM AND BIO-WEAPONS

Biological weapons may have the greatest military utility at the operational or theatre level of warfare. The goal of attacks on logistical networks, reinforcements and command control facilities 'is to induce operational paralysis, which reduces the enemy's ability to move and coordinate forces in the theatre'.[10] At various times, the United States, the Soviet Union and Iraq developed biological weapons and doctrines for their use at the operational level of warfare.[11] Targets in the enemy's rear area could be selected so that the effects of an attack are at their height when own forces plan on attacking other objectives. The ability of some biological agents to sicken victims for weeks or months could also outweigh the delayed effects of such agents. In addition, the use of incapacitating agents instead of lethal ones may allow an attacker to seize its objectives without provoking regime-threatening retaliation from a nuclear-armed opponent. The deployment of biological weapons against strategic objectives could serve as a potent force multiplier for a conventional military operation.[12]

At the strategic level of warfare the goal is to reduce the willingness or ability of the enemy to continue to prosecute a war. States can achieve this objective either through attacks targeted at civilians with the goal of increasing pressure on the government to yield, or through attacks aimed at damaging the enemy's economy to the point where the state can no longer effectively resist.[13] Biological warfare can target civilians directly with anti-personnel agents or indirectly with anti-livestock or anti-crop agents that could be used against agricultural targets to reduce the enemy's food supply. The ability of biological warfare agents to be disseminated over large areas and for agents such as variola virus and *y. pestis* to cause epidemics makes them well suited for strategic attacks.[14] The delayed effects of biological weapons and the uncertainties associated with the downwind travel of the aerosol cloud are less important for strategic attacks that do not require precision for immediate results. In addition, the disproportionate fear that these 'dreaded' weapons evoke could amplify the psychological impact of even a small-scale biological attack.[15]

The militarily significant quantity of agent depends on the concept of operations envisaged for the use of biological weapons—single overt attack, single covert attack or multiple simultaneous attacks of either type. Biological weapons are seen as strategic in nature because their impact extends beyond the battlefield. They are considered weapons of mass destruction because, under optimal conditions if all the significant problems related to production and delivery are overcome, they could, in theory, cause massive casualties. However, to launch an attack on significant military targets, such as ports, airbases, fixed rear areas and forces, supply points, ammunition dumps, command and control assets and medical facilities using a missile or an aircraft with a dissemination system, at least 100 kg of agent would be needed. Consider a hypothetical scenario in which a single aircraft leaves a trail of 100 kg of anthrax along a line upwind of a metropolitan city, it could claim between 1 and 3 million lives. In comparison, a one megaton hydrogen bomb dropped over a major city would 'only' cause some 0.5 to 1.9 million deaths.

NEW TYPES OF BIOLOGICAL WEAPONS

While any such analysis is speculative, scientists have postulated that the following new types of biological weapons are now deployable or could be manufactured in the coming decade:

1. *Binary biological weapons* may use two safe-to-handle elements which can be assembled before use. This may be a virus and a helper virus like Hepatitis D or a bacterial virulence plasmid like E. coli, plague, anthrax and dysentery.
2. *Designer genes and life forms* may include synthetic genes and gene networks, synthetic viruses and synthetic organisms. These weapons include DNA shuffling, synthetic forms of flu which claimed more lives in 1918 than the number of dead in the First World War and which continues to kill nearly 30,000 Americans every year—and synthetic micro-organisms.
3. *'Gene therapy' weapons* use transforming viruses or similar DNA vectors carrying Trojan horse genes (retrovirus, adenovirus, poxvirus, HSV-1). Such weapons may produce single individual (somatic cell) or inheritable (germ line) changes. They may also attack the body's immunities and wound healing capabilities.
4. *Stealth viruses* may be transforming or conditionally inducible. They exploit the fact that humans normally carry a substantial viral load; examples are the herpes virus, cytomegalovirus, Epstein-Barr and SV40 contamination which are normally dormant or limited in effect but can be transformed into far more lethal diseases. They may be introduced over years and then used to blackmail a population.
5. *Host-swapping diseases* Viral parasites normally have narrow host ranges and establish an evolutionary equilibrium with their hosts. The disruption of this equilibrium normally produces no results, but it can be extremely lethal. Natural examples include AIDS, Hantavirus, Marburg and Ebola. Tailoring the disruption for attack purposes can produce weapons that are extremely lethal and for which there is no treatment. A tailored disease like AIDS could combine serious initial lethality with crippling long-term effects lasting decades.
6. *Designer diseases* use molecular biology to create the disease first and then construct a pathogen to produce it. They may destroy the body's immunity, target normally dormant genes, or instruct cells to commit suicide. Apoptosis is programmed cell death, and specific apoptosis may be used to kill any mix of cells.

Genetically engineered pathogens may be designed to have one or all of the following attributes: [16]

1. *Safer handling and deployment*, including the elimination of risks from accidents or misuse—the 'boomerang effect'.
2. *Easier propagation and/or distribution.* Eliminating the need for a normally hydrated bio-agent or any use of aerosols. Micro-organisms with enhanced aerosol and environmental stability.
3. *Improved ability to target the host*, including the possible targeting of specific races or ethnic groups with given genetic characteristics.
4. *Greater transmissivity and infectivity.* Engineering a disease like Ebola to be as communicable as measles. Micro-organisms resistant to antibiotics, standard vaccines and therapeutics.
5. *New weapons* Benign micro-organisms genetically altered to produce a toxin, venom or bio-regulator.
6. *Increased problems in detection.* Immunologically altered micro-organisms capable of defeating standard identification, detection and diagnostic methods. Problems in diagnosis, false diagnosis, lack of detection by existing detectors, long latency, and binary initiation.
7. *Greater toxicity, more difficult to treat.* Very high morbidity or mortality, resistant to known antibacterial or antiviral agents, immune to existing vaccines, produces symptoms designed to saturate available specialized medical treatment facilities.
8. *Combinations of some or all of the above.*

BIO-TERRORISM THREAT PERCEPTION—INDIA

The state of perception of risk is an important aspect. Developed countries are more conscious of anthrax, botulism, pneumonic plague, tularaemia and smallpox. Websites provide a lot of information on these diseases, their potential risks and the precautions to be taken in the case of an outbreak. However, there is not much focus on diarrhoeal diseases caused by several viruses and bacteria, which can be used as bio-weapons in the Indian context. The website of Medscape and even the official US website of the Centre for Disease Control and Prevention do not contain any information on diarrhoeal diseases, which can cause immense damage in developing countries, more particularly among the poorer sections of the population. Poverty, ignorance, high population density and low levels of hygiene in developing countries, coupled with incompetence and apathy on the part of public and medical authorities, make such diseases as cholera, pneumonic plague, tularaemia, smallpox, haemorrhagic viral infections and other contagious diseases, effective weapons in the arsenal of a bio-terrorist targeting developing countries. Extensive economic damage can be inflicted through the introduction of animal and plant diseases or pests into the livestock and crops.

In mid-December 2001, the Haffkine Institute, one of India's leading research bodies, sent out a message. 'We have just become aware of the threat of bioterrorism. On the question of preparedness, we still have a long way to go,' said Dr. Shreekant Sapatnekar, Director of the Institute. He was addressing a gathering of 600 members of the Association of Medical Consultants of Greater Bombay, an umbrella body covering most disciplines of medical science. The 103-year old Haffkine Institute has had one close brush with bio-terrorism.[17] In the midst of the panic in the US over anthrax, the Institute tested 122 envelopes suspected of containing anthrax, including those received by the offices of the chief minister and deputy chief minister of Maharashtra, as well as celebrities like film stars.

BIOTERRORISM: INDIA'S RESPONSE AND PREPAREDNESS

Plague in Surat: The outbreak of pneumonic plague in Surat in 1995, appeared as a cover story in the Indian national weekly, *The Week*, and was described as a result of biological warfare experiments conducted by the United States.[18] While scientific refutations are unlikely to be entertained by the most extreme of those making such accusations, this incident, along with the previously cited domestic US examples, serves to emphasize the importance of determining that certain outbreaks are *not* the results of terrorism.

India is ill-prepared for bio-terrorism. Eminent Indian medical scientists have warned that India's readiness to face a bio-terrorist attack is hopelessly inadequate. Dr Kamal Dutta, former Director of the National Institute of Communicable Diseases, informed a gathering of scientists in Bombay that India no longer had any stocks of smallpox vaccine or vaccinia seed virus.[19] Global health authorities have identified smallpox as one of the four likeliest ingredients of any biological weapons arsenal. 'All four units where smallpox vaccine was being produced in our country have been closed down. Hence, in the event of a bioterrorist attack, we could be face to face with disaster,' he said.

In no part of the world are the public health and medical authorities adequately prepared to detect and respond to biological hazards, natural or inflicted by bio-terrorists. A majority of the developing countries are virtually unprepared to deal with bio-terrorism. There is a lack of scientific awareness, preparedness and funding. Stocks of antibiotics and vaccines against known pathogens that are essential are woefully inadequate to meet even the periodical natural high incidence, let alone in the event of a bio-terrorist attack. The situation is worse in the developing world and perhaps even in India. The havoc caused by the plague epidemic in Surat in India a few years ago, is a recent example.

Some of the aspects of preparedness against bioterrorism are similar to those needed to face natural disasters like cyclones, floods and earthquakes, as epidemics often follow such disasters. It is important to be proactive and take some urgent measures such as public awareness, stockpiling vaccines and drugs, contingency plan of action, research and development, problems of logistics, and biodefence research and preparedness.

It is generally believed that bio-terrorists have information about the detailed plans and defences built up and would act to circumvent them. At least three considerations favour transparency. First, bio-defence is aimed at facing a bio-terrorist attack, but preventing such an attack is a better choice. Well-advertised preparedness against the best arsenal of bio-terrorists would act as a deterrent. The fight is against bio-terrorism and not the bio-terrorist. Second, if the public is made aware of what measures the national governments and other agencies have taken for their safety, their confidence in public institutions, which is a very important psychological factor, would increase. Third, awareness of governmental efforts may inspire private organizations and individuals to contribute to the national effort. In line with these considerations, it would be unwise to keep bio-defence strategy under warps, on the grounds that military strategy, which is an entirely different issue, is a closely guarded secret.

HOW SHOULD INDIA PREPARE FOR SUCH AN ATTACK?

Three levels of integration are required: a computerized integrated system should instantly be available to a monitoring station where experts can analyse it quickly and take corrective action; all laboratories should be linked. Any occurrence of unusual microorganisms unidentified by laboratories should be investigated by the centre. Like in Surat it was the plague that never was. Surat, Pune, Chandigarh and Delhi's best institution could not identify it correctly. Finally, the laboratory at Gwalior identified that the organism in the specimen was not virulent, it did not cause disease in animals. The Surat experience highlighted the importance of specialized microbiology institutions. The laboratories buy serums, antibodies and antigens from 30 companies and it is difficult to ascertain the quality of their stocks. More high security laboratories like the one in Pune are needed.

CONCLUSION

The threat of bio-terrorism has not receded since the anthrax attacks of 2001, especially since the perpetrators of those attacks remain unidentified. Recent reports of Al Qaeda's efforts to develop biological weapons have only heightened the fears. Despite some empirically based studies and the rich literature on terrorism and WMD issues, the threat of escalation to WMD terrorism remains poorly understood. Continued threat assessments, evaluations and re-evaluations of current policies and heightened vigilance on the part of intelligence agencies are essential to prepare for the future.

Biological warfare has shown its utility in causing disease, hysteria and death, and is not limited to military applications or targeting only humans. The multitude of agents available for use and the variety of dispersion mechanisms that can be utilized increase the complexity in identifying and treating the intentional use of biological agents as weapons of mass destruction. Furthermore, the relative ease of obtaining and producing biological agents increases the chances that they may be used as a terrorist weapon targeting humans, plants or animals.

A review of events related to bio-terrorism reveals that it is a reality and is to be far more feared than either explosives or chemicals, civilian population has scarcely been targeted and the subject of bio-terrorism is generally not discussed publicly, instructions for producing biological weapons are available on the Internet and detection or interdiction of those intending to use biological weapons is extremely difficult.

Bio-terrorism as a full-fledged attack or as a limited tactical strategy by countries or terrorist groups is a possibility. The casualties may not only be army personnel, but civilians as well. The magnitude of casualties and the complex nature of the injuries sustained as a result of a biological attack call for a comprehensive management planning. The dissemination of information and the training of the army, the general public, fire fighters, police and other organizations must be done before disaster strikes. Comprehensive planning is needed for the protection and management of casualties. Networking, including integration in the existing medical and administrative set-up, must be planned and executed. Understanding, planning and implementing a biological casualty medical management set-up are a national challenge.

NOTES

1. G.W. Cristhoph, T.J. Cieslak, J.A. Plavin and E.M. Eitzen, *JAMA*, 278, 412–17 (1997).
2. *Issues & Analysis Assessing the Threat of Mass-Casualty Bioterrorism.* Jason Pate, Senior Research Associate and WMD Terrorism Database Manager and Gary Ackerman, Senior Research Associate, *CNS Chemical and Biological Weapons Nonproliferation Program, October 2001* (updated March 2003).
3. Raymond Zilinskas, *Assessing the Threat of Bioterrorism: Congressional Testimony*, Monterey Institute of International Studies, 20 October 1999.

4. Working Paper: *Bioterrorism and Biocrimes; the Illicit Use of Biological Agents since 1900, August 1998* (February 2001 revision), Washington DC: Center of Counterproliferation Research, National Defence University, p. 7.
5. Working Paper: *Bioterrorism and Biocrimes; the Illicit Use of Biological Agents since 1900, August 1998* (February 2001 revision), Washington, DC: Center of Counterproliferation Research, National Defence University, p. 9.
6. *Chemical and Biological Warfare, an Investigative Guide.* Washington, DC: Office of Enforcement, Strategic Investigative Division, US Customs Service, October 1990.
7. Lester C. Caudle III, 'The Biological Warfare Threat', pp. 459–61, Frederick R. Sidell et al., *Medical Aspects of Chemical and Biological Warfare*, Washington, DC: Office of the Surgeon General, Department of the Army, 1997, provides a summary of the biological warfare threat to animals and crops.
8. Working Paper: *Bioterrorism and Biocrimes; the Illicit Use of Biological Agents since 1900, August 1998* (February 2001 revision), Washington, DC: Center of Counterproliferation Research, National Defence University.
9. North Atlantic Treaty Organization, *NATO Handbook on Medical Aspects of NBC Defence Operations—A-Med-p. 6, part* 2, Biological, June 1992, Final Draft.
10. Robert A. Pape, *Bombing to Win: Air Power and Coercion in War* (Ithaca, NY: Cornell University Press, 1996, p. 72.
11. This potential, however, has been ignored in many analyses of these weapons. Zilinskas, 'Biological Warfare and the Third World'; and Richard Novick and Seth Shulman, 'New Forms of Biological Warfare?' in *Preventing a Biological Arms Race*, pp. 105–6. An exception to this view is W. Seth Carus, *The Poor Man's Atomic Bomb? Biological Weapons in the Middle East*, Policy Paper No. 23, Washington, DC: Washington Institute for Near East Policy, 1991, pp. 36–7. See, respectively, Jonathan B. Tucker, 'Biological Weapons in the Former Soviet Union: An Interview with Dr. Kenneth Alibek', *Nonproliferation Review*, vol. 6, no. 3, Spring–Summer 1999, p. 2 Timothy McCarthy and Jonathan B. Tucker, 'Saddam's Toxic Arsenal: Chemical and Biological Weapons in the Gulf Wars', in *Planning the Unthinkable*, ed. Lavoy, Sagan and Wirtz, p. 62.
12. *Assessment of Impact of Chemical and Biological Weapons on Joint Operations in 2010: A Summary Report*, Mclean, Vaz Booz, Allen, and Hamilton, November 1997.
13. Pape, *Bombing to Win*, pp. 42–7.
14. There are also a number of viral and fungal agents that can cause

epidemics among livestock and crops, respectively. See Simon M. Whity, *Biological Warfare against Crops*, New York: Palagrave, 2002; and Terrance M. Wilson, Linda Logan–Henfrey, Richard Weller and Barry Keliman, 'Agro terrorism, Biological Crimes, and Biological Warfare Targeting Animal Agriculture', in *Emerging Diseases of Animals*, ed. Corrie Brown and Carole Bolin, Washington DC: ASM Press, 2000, pp. 23–57.

15. Jessica Stern, 'Dreaded Risks and the Control of Biological Weapons', *International Security*, vol. 27, no. 3, Winter 2002–3, pp. 102–6.
16. Briefing on the Jason 1997 Summer Study, 'Lear Steven Block, Biological Warfare Threats Enabled by Molecular Biology'; Malcolm R. Dando, 'The Impact of Biotechnology', in Hype or Reality? *The New Terrorism and Mass Casualty Attacks*, ed. Brad Roberts, Alexandria: Chemical and Biological Arms Control Institute, 2000, pp. 193–206.
17. Sumit Ghoshal, 'India Ill-prepared for Bioterrorism', *Medical Post*, vol. 38, no. 5, 5 February 2002.
18. R. Prasannan, 'Military Microbe', *The Week*, 23 July 1995, pp. 30–7.
19. Sumit Ghoshal, op. cit., n. 17.

CHAPTER 6

Biological Weapons and Bio-Terrorism: Meeting the Threat

AJEY LELE

The spectre of biological weapons has haunted humankind for nearly a millennium. Until recently, biological weapons were viewed as strategic weapons. The worth of biological weapons as a strategic military tool is very limited. They are highly dependent on the weather, temperature, wind direction, wind speed and other factors that are beyond human control.[1] However, the changed significance of terrorism post-9/11 attacks, rapid developments in biotechnology and difficulties in policing the proliferation of biological agents heighten the threat from biological terrorism. Biological weapons have the capability to strike psychological terror in the masses. This makes biological weapons an ideal tool for terrorists. Experts on terrorism have identified religious extremist groups, particularly those with an apocalyptic world view, as the most likely groups to use weapons of mass destruction for causing mass casualties.[2]

Following the proliferation of information, the know-how to develop and use biological weapons has become readily available. Information on the manufacture of biological agents is available in open sources. The related principles are published in detail and are available even on the Internet. These sources of information vary in their reliability and details, and may even be erroneous. However, they are based on available information like methods of vaccine manufacture, DNA technology, germ banks and medication for various diseases, besides declassified information on bio-weapons with various nation-states. This information can be used to manufacture bio-weapons.

The technology to develop biological agents (read weapons) does not require large financial investments. Neither does the manufacture of a 'crude' biological weapon require much expertise.[3] Hence, it is essential to analyse whether 'the availability of conventional knowledge puts today's terrorists in any advantageous position and if so, are the states prepared to tackle such threats.'

This paper assesses the possibilities of terrorists indulging in terrorism with conventional biological weapons and ascertains the capabilities of available bio-defence strategies.

In the case of bio-terrorism the task of quantifying risk should not be confused with predicting the next terrorist attack. This important distinction between risk assessment and event prediction has its natural perils. No seismologist is capable of predicting the time, place and magnitude of the next major earthquake,[4] but it is possible for a seismic risk analyst to evaluate the annual probability of loss to a particular area, based on an analysis of plate tectonics. Large earthquakes are impossible to predict because of the random manner in which the rupture of a geological fault propagates and eventually stops. This randomness contributes to the so-called *aleatory*[5] uncertainty in earthquake occurrence, which is readily accounted for within a probabilistic risk assessment, but confounds attempts at deterministic event prediction. This distinction between risk assessment and event prediction could be applied to the threat from bio-terrorism.

It is difficult to appreciate the threat of bio-terrorism if it is analysed through the prism of conventional terrorism. Conventional explosives and firearms continue to be the weapons of choice for terrorists. Terrorists are less likely to use biological weapons than conventional explosives, at least partly because they are difficult to weaponize and their results are unpredictable. However, some groups and individuals of concern have evinced an interest in biological agents. The possibility that terrorists would use biological agents may increase over the next decade.[6] Currently, biological terrorism is still an emerging threat.

During the last few years a small number of terrorist organizations have expressed their intentions of using biological weapons. What remains to be seen is how dangerous these threats are and what could be the nature of damage. Post-9/11 and the subsequent anthrax attacks, bio-terrorism has become one of the key security issues of the twenty-first century. While it is difficult to predict the exact nature of this threat, it is, nonetheless, essential to relate the history of bio-weapons with the future of bio-terrorism to analyse it rationally.

LINKAGES BETWEEN BIO-WEAPONS AND BIO-TERRORISM

The recent history of biological weapons indicates that, along with anthrax and smallpox, many other types of germ weapons using various viruses, bacteria and toxins were produced between the 1970s and 1990s. During these two decades, the involvement of the erstwhile USSR in designing and manufacturing various types of bio-weapons was significantly higher than that of other countries. The Soviets were also involved in the manufacture of anti-agricultural biological weapons, and had made significant advances in genetic engineering, creating new strains of viruses and bacteria for biological weapons.[7]

In the pre-Cold War era, biological weapons were agent specific weapons with variable delivery platforms. Till 1972, the US had weapons that could be fitted with munitions like anthrax, smallpox and plague. The delivery vehicles were rifle shells with dry agent fills or 75 to 100 kg aircraft delivered munitions or liquid agents delivered through dispensers either by aircrafts or by handheld sprays.[8] Details of such weapons are given in Appendix A.

According to Article II of the 1972 Biological Weapon Convention, which entered into force on 26 March 1975, all Parties to the Convention are required to destroy or divert to peaceful purposes all agents, toxins, weapons, equipment and means of delivery relating to existing biological weapons stockpiles within nine months. However, the Soviet Union, which was a signatory to the BWC, enhanced its offensive biological weapons programme just before the Convention came into force and continued this programme for more than a decade and a half.[9]

The Americans were not far behind. Ronald Reagan initiated the germ arms race again in 1984. He approved the sale and transfer of bacteria, viruses and fungi to Iraq.[10] Even after the end of the Cold War, the US did not stop investing in bio-weapons. A week before the 11 September 2001 attacks, American news media reported that the US government had conducted clandestine research on bio-warfare preparedness. The Pentagon had secretly drawn up plans to reproduce a Russian genetically engineered strain of anthrax bacterium to test the US military anthrax vaccine.[11]

The recent history of bio-weapons reveals that the destruction of bio-weapons contemplated in the BWC is far from complete. After the disintegration of the USSR, its bio-weapons programme continues to pose a major threat today. Although bioethics has routinely condemned the use of bio-weapons and bio-warfare, it has not prevented the development of bio-weapons. It has also been observed that the bio-weapons programmes do not end even when the nation abandons them.[12] In these circumstances, it may be inferred that terrorist organizations can 'manage' to obtain bio-weapons from such sources.

The bio-weapons manufactured for fighting a conventional war were essentially in the form of bomb-lets produced from various agents. Terrorists are not likely to use weapons in this manner because of problems in the delivery systems. Terrorist organizations may use modified versions of these weapons, although the agents remain the same. There are three main categories of biological agents which can be used as bio-weapons. The first comprises weapons that disseminate viruses like smallpox, plague and cholera amongst human populations and rabies, foot and mouth disease amongst animals. In plants, they cause mosaic diseases in tobacco, tomato and sugar crop. The second category comprises bacteria, which cause illness by invading tissues and reproducing themselves, or by producing toxins, including botulinum toxin and ricin. Anthrax is an acute infectious disease caused by the spore forming bacterium, *Bacillus anthracis.* This disease could also be used to attack animals. In plants bacteria they can cause rice and corn blight. The third category comprises rickettsia, which lie between viruses and bacteria. They are carried by insects and cause typhus and Q-fever in human populations and heart water disease in animals. In plants, fungi can damage potato and cereals crop.[13]

Theoretically, any non-state actor can procure or manufacture biological weapons to use against human beings or animals or plants. Some non-state actors have both the motivation and skills to selectively cultivate the most dangerous pathogens and use them in acts of terrorism. Today, the connections between biological weapons and threat from bio-terrorism are becoming increasingly evident. For any terrorist group, the hurdles to acquire bio-weapons are minimal. Biological agents are cheap and easily available. No training is required for their use, the production of crude agents is relatively straightforward and terrorist organizations could even use commercially available agents.

It is believed that 30 to 40 countries have the capacity to manufacture biological weapons since many have a pharmaceutical industry adequate for their production. The greatest concentration of existing weapons is believed to be in the Middle East countries like Syria and Sudan. The US bombing of a pharmaceutical factory in Sudan when intelligence information revealed linkages between this laboratory and Osama bin Laden illustrates the concern over the possible use of bio-agents by terrorists.[14] In general, terrorists or criminals can carry out three types of biological attacks. First, the pathogen or toxin may be injected. This method is best used when the terrorist or criminal wishes to elimiante his adversary. Second, a quantity of pathogen or toxin may be used to contaminate or poison foods, beverages, or fomites (such as food supplements and medicines taken by mouth). If done skilfully, this method could lead to casualties on a large scale. Third, pathogens or toxins may be suspended in a wet or dry formulation and dispersed over the target area as aerosolized particles. This type of attack could lead to innumerable casualties, if three conditions are met: (a) the formulation is properly designed for aerosol dispersal; (b) the aerosol particles produced by the dispersal mechanism are of optimal size and can withstand environmental stresses; and (c) meteorological conditions are right for blanketing the target area with aerosol particles.[15]

Although states or terrorists have not successfully employed modern biological weapons based on aerosol dissemination technology, cruder weapons have been used. There are disturbing signs that the normative, operational and political restraints that had limited the use of these weapons earlier are weaker now than they were thirty years ago.[16] The anthrax mail attacks of 2001 represent the first overt use of biological weapons, which has weakened the taboo against the use of biological weapons. The history of terrorism reveals that copycat attacks follow after any successful usage of new methodologies. Hence, it is likely that these attacks could motivate other terrorist organizations to follow suit.

The pathogens market is a new developing one that could sell deadly pathogens to non-state actors willingly or inadvertently. Hundreds of laboratories and companies around the world work with dangerous pathogens, but regulations on access to them vary widely. A World Federation of Culture Collection, a loose association of 472 repositories of living microbial specimens in 61 countries does exist; there are 46 germ banks in countries like Germany, India and Iran that stock anthrax cultures. But, more than 1,000 germ banks worldwide do not belong to this federation, and very few of their culture collections are adequately secured or regulated.[17]

Post-1980, some incidents have come to light of individuals and groups securing and even using bio-weapons. The followers of Bhagwan Shree Rajneesh seeded salad bars at restaurants in Dalles in Oregon in 1984 with Salmonella bacteria, leading to 571 casualties. In the early 1990s, Japan's Aum Shinrikyo cult made unsuccessful attempts to spread anthrax and botulinum toxin in Tokyo. During 1986–8, strains of anthrax were sold to Iraq by an American organization. Attempts were also made by some individuals to procure bubonic plague bacteria, and some were caught in possession of ricin.[18] All these incidents imply that it is possible to easily procure 'germs' from the pathogens market.

MEETING THE THREAT

The conditions that give rise to and motivate bio-terrorism are mired in political, socio-economic, ideological, and cultural perspectives where cause and effect is difficult to quantify. The threat of bio-terrorism cannot be treated in the same manner as that posed by naturally occurring infectious diseases because there is a 'thinking enemy' whose aim is to inflict as many casualties and cause as much damage as possible.[19] A national strategy to address the challenges posed by bio-terrorism should be formulated against this backdrop.

In the case of bio-terrorist attacks, the term risk is used to denote the possibility of an adverse outcome whose probability is between zero and one, which further baffles policy makers. Risk analysts have long observed a tendency among policy makers to respond rapidly to visible crises, even if the baseline danger remains unchanged. This tendency encourages reactive policies crafted in the wake of visible or highly publicized events, resulting in ad hoc policy-making with little regard for competing interests.[20]

Another major problem facing any bio-defence policy is the need for huge investments. In fact, the creation of an offensive biological weapons capability is relatively inexpensive. On the contrary, developing a new bio-defence vaccine costs $300–400 million.[21] It has been argued that the implementation of bio-defence policy forces the diversion of resources from the much-needed public health services, therefore the threat of bio-terrorism has been exaggerated.[22] Nation-states would have to address this criticism while formulating a bio-defence policy and also recognize the fact that most of the projections made about bio-terrorism are based on studies carried out with imaginary scenario build-ups and surrogate laboratory research experiments. Hence, any investment in bio-defence technologies should be done on the basis of realistic threat and risk evaluations.

The basic approach to reduction of bio-terrorism vulnerability should be based on a two-pronged strategy. First, formulation of a policy to prevent a 'germ attack' and, failing that, reducing the effects of disease spread. In combination, the proactive and reactive potentials within these two broad areas form the nucleus of the vital essentials for deterring and combating terrorism. In technical parlance, these proactive and reactive activities could be termed as Active Defence and Passive Defence components of a bio-defence policy.

Active defence comprises measures aimed at preventing a biological attack on reaching the target area. These include various measures for intercepting and destroying enemy missiles armed with biological warheads. Active defence is not merely restricted to counterforce measures to destroy the opponent's biological weapons and associated delivery systems, but also includes arms control, disarmament and sanctions. Passive defence deals with the doctrine and exploiting the entire range of civil defence measures like hazard assessment, detection means and physical protection. It also includes countermeasures to enhance personnel protection by vaccination prior to an attack and by medical treatment after an attack. There are many methods towards allaying civil vulnerabilities that could enhance passive defence.[23]

A method devised by the Americans to disable biological weapons at the production site itself by using the agent defeat weapon or the agent defeat warhead (ADW) is an important element of the active defence policy. This warhead is specifically tailored for use against fixed ground targets associated with the development, production and storage of biological weapons. The effectiveness of the ADW is based on the warhead's ability to destroy biological weapons without dispersing their deadly contents in the atmosphere.[24] However, the efficacy of such weapons to deal with terrorist threats is doubtful, since terrorist organizations are not likely to use conventional biological weapons. Neither are they likely to have large storage facilities for stocking biological weapons. Agent defeat weapons could be of some use if intelligence inputs have identified hideouts where a terrorist/rogue state manufacturing unit is functional or bio-weapons are stored.

Other active defence policies like international mechanisms to restrict the spread of these weapons have their limitations. The BWC has failed to prevent states from proliferating bio-weapons. The question arises whether this failed treaty can restrict further proliferation by terrorists who are not even bound by such constraints? The answer is both no and yes. No, because if the treaty cannot stop states that are bound by international law, how can it be expected to stop terrorists who are free to act on their own. And, yes, because the likelihood of such horrendous acts could catalyse a renewed commitment by the global community to enhance cooperation by strengthening existing multilateral mechanisms and by devising effective ways to address these new security challenges.

However, it is not easy to revive the BWC. Effective biological disarmament faces two major hurdles: (a) the ease of acquiring dual-use materials and technologies required to develop biological weapons, and (b) the difficulty in verifying that these resources are not being used for hostile purposes.[25] The US has not played any constructive role in the fight against the proliferation of bio-weapons, and its current interests are mainly driven by domestic industry compulsions.

The dynamics of existing global geopolitics do not offer much scope for the development of active defence measures to tackle the threat of bio-terrorism effectively. Hence, it is important to concentrate on the design and development of passive defence tools comprising secondary preventive measures, to prevent or minimize the health consequences of an illness or injury by disease after the spread of infection.

A timely reaction against a bio-attack is dependent on the early detection of such an attack. An effective sensor device lies at the heart of any efficient detection technology. Biosensors are electronic devices that identify the existence of a harmful biological agent in the atmosphere. Many new developments in sensor technology have taken place recently, particularly in Western countries. Post-9/11, BW detection has become the focus of attention and an area of rapid development. However, it needs to be appreciated that, in any mode of attack, BW agent organisms are likely to be widely dispersed in the atmosphere. BW attacks may include water contamination or aerosol dispersal. In view of these new threats, the challenges facing BW detection system designers are enormous.[26]

Along with detection equipment, protective clothing and fully equipped hospitals (along with trained manpower), additional investment is required towards accelerating the development of bio-defence vaccine. Vaccination provides adequate protection against known biological agents. Engaging in large-scale vaccination programmes for the civilian population during peacetime is neither practical nor feasible, but the formulation of guidelines to ensure easy availability of vaccine to face any threat is important. Many have predicted that in the wake of rapid developments in biotechnology, terrorist organizations may opt for designer bio-weapons. Hence, more research is necessary to devise technology for need-based vaccine production.

Vaccination is no longer a social and medical issue. At present particularly in the United States, the issue of vaccination involves business interests. Many apocalyptic scenarios are available based on computer simulation exercises, which boost the growth of the private vaccine industry,[27] hence there is a need to critically assess the requirements of emergency vaccination. The global nature of threats and the potential of bio-agents of not limiting themselves to geographical boundaries demands international collaborative efforts to further vaccine development. There is a need to establish global regulatory frameworks to govern biological research and commerce through an international bio-security regime. Globalization strategies for defining international subcontracting and a framework for technological cooperation agreements may provide proper direction to the global vaccine industry.

BIO-DEFENCE IN INDIA

India is at present nowhere near formulating an integrated policy that encompasses a nationwide programme, where a systematic approach to the problem has been put in place that matches a comprehensive set of capabilities to realistically defined threats. The Defence Research and Development Establishment (DRDE) at Gwalior is the primary institution for research in toxicology and biochemical pharmacology and development of antibodies against several bacterial and viral agents. India is capable of responding effectively to threats like anthrax, brucellosis, cholera and plague, viral threats like smallpox and fever and bio-toxic threats like botulism. Also, biological protective gear like masks and suits are available. The National Institute of Communicable Diseases advises the Government of India on issues related to the prevention and control of communicable diseases in the country.[28] Most of the scientific laboratories in India follow a particular line of investigation, which is essentially R&D based. They have succeeded in developing various testing kits, vaccines and protective equipment but an area where the country is lacking today is in integrating these systems so as to be prepared for worst case scenarios.

In 2001, the Central Bureau of Investigation (CBI) set up a cell to tackle bio-terrorism. This core group is expected to work on the basis of a review and assessment of information available on the activities of various terrorist groups. For bio-disaster management, the CBI has also constituted a crack team to meet any eventuality in the country. The team would be assisted by the nodal agencies of the state and the central government and also by the intelligence bureau and other concerned agencies.[29]

The Union Home Ministry has launched a process of

establishing an elite force—comprising four battalions of the central paramilitary forces—to deal with biological, chemical and radioactive attacks.[30] In the overall disaster management plan, the Indian Council for Medical Research (ICMR), New Delhi serves as a disaster nodal organization for biological disasters.[31] India has plans to use its satellites to map and monitor epidemic diseases. It has also been proposed to utilize the Geographical Information Systems (GIS) based mathematical modelling techniques to trace vectors in any part of the country, sometimes even in house clusters.[32] At the local level it has been proposed that disaster management cells would take care off the fallout of NBC attacks. The Indian Armed Forces have their own NBC defence programmes that essentially cater for battlefield requirements.

THE CHALLENGE AHEAD

According to the CIA's top non-proliferation analyst, 'biological weapons pose the most daunting challenge for intelligence collectors and analysts'.[33] The changed nature of terrorism indicates that deterrence may not remain the first line of defence against the use of biological weapons by non-state actors.

Biological threat assessments must take into account not only capabilities, that are challenging to monitor, but also intentions, that are more difficult to discern. Assessing the biological threat posed by terrorist groups is likely to be very difficult given the secretive nature of such organizations. It is possible that terrorist groups with the motivation and capability to use these weapons would emerge with little or no warning. The historical record is replete with flawed biological threat assessments that have resulted in significant overestimates or underestimates of an adversary's biological warfare capabilities and intentions.[34] The attenuation of the threat of bio-terrorism calls for the simultaneous pursuit of policies like counter-terrorism, non-proliferation and formulation of effective defensive techniques.

Advances in molecular biology and genetic engineering have led to the development of new vaccines. At the same time there exists an indirect risk of proliferation because of 'germs creation' by states for the purpose of developing defensive technologies. At present, the US is investing heavily in its bio-defence programme.

For 2004, it has a massive federal bio-defence programme of $6 billion. The major part of its proposed research, however, violates the international norms on bio-weapons. Laboratory studies in the US on genetically engineered germs and methods of dissemination involves the creation of viruses and bacteria to develop new vaccines and other measures to meet a potential biological attack.[35] This gives rise to the possibility of newly engineered pathogens escaping from the laboratory, and there are no guarantees that a scientist may not leak the secrets of weapon manufacture or trade in germs.

For a motivated non-state actor it is not difficult to acquire bio-weapons. A state actor may not be able to identify the exact sources of such weapons. One of the most likely sources is perceived to be the bio-weapons programme of the erstwhile USSR. In spite of massive US efforts, all loose ends have not been tied so far. Information on the full extent of the Soviet biological warfare programme remains incomplete in important details. On 5 May 2004, a Russian scientist died in an Ebola accident,[36] which points to the lack of security measures in bio-weapons laboratories.

The absence of large-scale use of biological weapons since 1945 is a cause for celebration, but not grounds for complacency. The existing pattern of bio-terrorist attacks does not provide a clear basis for predicting the nature of future probable attacks, hence doubts about the seriousness of the threat would always persist till it becomes a reality.

It should be noted that investments in any bio-defence programme caters much beyond the threat of bio-terrorism. During the recent past the world has witnessed outbreaks of a number of serious infectious diseases. In Third World countries India is a classic case of a developing country with a sound medical and biotechnology infrastructure but susceptible to outbreaks of infectious diseases. For example, plague epidemic in Surat/ Himachal Pradesh, dengue fever in Delhi killing 300 people, and Japanese encephalitis in Andhra Pradesh claiming 200 lives (1999).[37] An effective bio-security system could be a boon to the authorities in various nation-states. The advantage is twofold: it caters for disease spread by terrorists as well as its spread by natural outbreak.

NOTES

1. Mark Prelas, Weaponization and Delivery Systems, in *Science and Technology of Terrorism and Counterterrorism*, ed. T.K. Ghosh, New York: Marcel Dekker, Inc., 2002, p. 95.
2. Bruce Hoffman, 'Terrorist and WMD: Some Preliminary Hypotheses', *Nonproliferation Review*, vol. 4, no. 3, Spring-Summer 1997, pp. 45–53. Jessica Stern makes a similar argument in her various writings.
3. http://www.bens.org/pubs_0297.html accessed on 12 March 2004.
4. This argument is based on the writings of Gordon Woo in 'Quantitative Terrorism Risk Assessment', and 'The Evolution of Terrorism Risk Modeling', *Journal of Reinsurance*, 22 April 2003, http://www.rms.com/Publications/EvolutionTerRiskMod_Woo_JournalRe.pdf accessed on 26 February 2004.
5. The meaning of the original word aleatoric according to the *Oxford Dictionary* (1995) is depending on the throw of a die or chance. Aleatory is a technical term used in seismology for describing the uncertainty involved in the prediction of an earthquake.
6. *Testimony Before the Committee on Veterans Affairs and the Subcommittee on Labor, Health and Human Services, Education and Related Agencies, Committee on Appropriations*, US Senate 9:30 a.m., EST Tuesday, 16 March 1999; Combating Terrorism: Observations on Biological Terrorism and Public Health Initiatives.
7. http://www.state.de.us/cjc/terror.html accessed on 8 July 2004.
8. For detailed information see *CB Weapons Today*, vol. II, London: SIPRI, 1975.
9. Malcolm Dando, *Biological Warfare in the 21st Century*, London: Brassey's, 1994, p. 71.
10. http://www.hermes-press.com/bioterrorism.htm accessed on 6 July 2004.
11. Madeline Derexler, 'Understanding International Bio-weapons Controls', http://www.prospect.org/webfeatures/2001/10/drexler-m-10-10.html accessed on 19 June 2004.
12. Ajey Lele, *Bio-Weapons the Genie in the Bottle*, New Delhi: Lancer, 2004, p. 19.
13. Nadine Gurr and Benjamin Cole, *The New Face of Terrorism*, London: I.B. Tauris Publishers, 2002, pp. 51–2.
14. Cindy C. Combs and Marlin Slann, *Encyclopedia of Terrorism*, New York: Facts on File, Inc., p. 32.
15. Raymond Zilinskas, *Congressional Testimony*, Assessing the Threat of Bio-terrorism, Monterey Institute of Intentional Studies, 20 October 1999.
16. Gregory Koblentz, 'Pathogens as Weapons', *International Security*, vol. 28, no. 3 Winter 2003–4, p. 119.
17. Michael Barletta et al., 'Keeping Track of Anthrax: The Case for a Biosecurity Convention', *Bulletin of Atomic Scientists*, May–June 2002, p. 59.

18. G.C. Satpathy, no. 12, p. 43, and *Biological Weapons and Terrorism* (vol. 1), Delhi: Kalpaz Publications, 2004, p. 23.
19. Michael Mair and Julie Samia Mair, 'Complementary Approach to Bioterrorism Prevention', *The Nonproliferation Review*, Fall–Winter 2003, p. 123.
20. Jessica Stern, 'Dreaded Risks and the Control of Biological Weapons', *International Security*, vol. 27, no. 3, Winter 2002–3, p. 90.
21. No. 14, p. 89.
22. Susan Wright, *Biological Warfare and Disarmament*, Maryland: Rowman & Littlefield Publishers, 2002, pp. 80–6.
23. Graham Pearson and Brad Roberts, 'Defending against Biological Attack: Importance of Biotechnology in Preparedness', *Defence Science Journal*, vol. 51, no. 4, October 2001, pp. 382–3.
24. For more details see, 'Destruction of Weapons of Mass Destruction', www.ipcs.org, 12 May 2003.
25. No. 14, p. 94.
26. John Eldridge, 'Patrolling a Biological Frontier', *Jane's International Defence Review*, February 2003, p. 38.
27. For a detailed analysis of the effects of economic globalization on bioterrorist threats see Kendall Hoyt and Stephen G. Brooks, 'A Double-Edged Sword', *International Security*, vol. 28, no. 3, Winter 2003–4, pp. 123–48.
28. Inputs are based on the author's field trip to DRDE, Gwalior and www.nidc.org accessed on 20 January 2003.
29. www.dailyexcelsior.com/01nov14/national.htm accessed on 20 December 2003.
30. *The Times of India*, New Delhi, 3 January 2004.
31. http://w3.whosea.org/gujarat/finalreport10.htm accessed on 12 January 2004.
32. Bhumika Kulkarni, 'Satellites to Monitor Epidemic Diseases', *Times News Network*, 6 January 2004.
33. Statement by Special Assistant to the DCI for Nonproliferation John A. Lauder to the House Permanent Select Committee on Intelligence, 'Worldwide Biological Threat', 3 March 1999, www.cia.gov/cia/public_affairs/speeches/archives/1999/lauder_speech_030399.html accessed on 10 June 2004.
34. No. 14, pp. 114-15.
35. http://www.khilafah.com/home/category.php?DocumentID=9459&TagID=2# accessed on 23 May 2004.
36. Judith Miller, 'Russian Scientist Dies in Ebola Accident at Former Weapons Lab', *New York Times*, 25 May 2004.
37. Reynolds Salemo and Lauren Hickok, 'Warring Germs', *Force*, vol. 1, no. 3, January 2004, p. 40.

REFERENCES

CB Weapons Today (vol. II), Table 1.5, London: SIPRI, 1973.

Tucker, Jonathan, 'The Once and the Future Threat of Smallpox', *Atlantic Monthly Press*, September 2001.

www.vectorsite.net/twgas4.html accessed on 20 November 2002.

Windrem, Robert, 'Soviets Planned Smallpox Attack', www.msnbc.com/news/616710 accessed on 29 October 2002.

APPENDIX A

CONVENTIONAL BIO-WEAPONS

In the pre-Cold War era, biological weapons mainly comprised two categories: agent specific weapons and general type weapons. Agent specific weapons were manufactured to deliver a particular type of germ on the proposed target. In the case of a general type weapon, the nature of munitions and the delivery platforms remain the same irrespective of the germ agent.

A biological weapon includes a payload (agent) of solid or liquid agent capable of dispersing into particles, droplets or vapour. Hence, the nature and characteristics of the different germs impose certain restrictions on the design parameters of that individual germ weapon. The agent specific biological weapons were designed and manufactured on the basis of the technical strengths and weaknesses of individual 'germs' and their survivability post-delivery.

The significant agent disseminating devices that were developed into weapons are discussed in the following paragraphs. These devices were mainly bulk dissemination devices manufactured for fighting a conventional war.

Till 1972 the US had the following anthrax weapons in its stockpile:

1. Anthrax weapons (agent specific weapons)
   (a) *Type and Designation of weapon*: Special munitions E 2.
   Agent: *Bacillus anthracis* (This anthrax bacterium can be cultivated in ordinary nutrient medium under aerobic or anaerobic conditions).
   Mechanism: Bursting.
   Remarks: 7.62-mm rifle shell with dry agent fill.
   (b) *Type and designation of weapon*: Disseminator, dry agent, E 41R 2.
   Agent: *Bacillus anthracis.*
   Mechanism: Dispersion.
   Remarks: Small rectangular can using carbon dioxide propellant.
   (c) *Type and designation of weapon*: Spray tank, dry agent, E 41.
   Agent: Bacillus anthracis.
   Mechanism: Dispersion.
   Remarks: 75 to 140 kg payload for F100, F-4C, A-4D aircraft.
2. General category weapons
   (a) *Type and designation of weapon*: Warhead, guided missile M210:
   Agent: BW agent.
   Mechanism: M143 bomb-lets.
   Remarks: Entered inventory in the mid-60s with 139 km range.
   (b) *Type and designation of weapon*: Spray tank, liquid agent, A/B 45-1.
   Agent: BW agent.
   Mechanism: Spray.
   Remarks: Payload for F-4C aircraft.

(c) *Type and designation of weapon*: Spray tank, liquid agent, A/B Y-1.
Agent: BW agent.
Mechanism: Spray.
Remarks: An expendable munition about 85cm in diameter and 400 cm long, for high speed tactical aircraft.

(d) *Type and designation of weapon*: Spray tank, dry agent, A/B 45 Y-2, A/B 45 y-4, A/B 45 4-4.
Agent: BW agent.
Mechanism: Dispenser.
Remarks: Developed mainly for rice-blast spores and PG toxin agent. Payload designed for F 100, F105 and F4C aircraft.

(e) *Type and designation of weapon*: Bomb cluster, 750-1b, E 108 R2, E61 R4; bomb-let, spherical M143.
Agent: BW agent.
Mechanism: Bursting.
Remarks: These weapons were under development during the 1960s. The M143 bomb-let was developed for Sergeant warhead.

SMALLPOX WEAPONS

- Smallpox weapons were developed by the Soviets for use against the US cities in a war of mutual annihilation, with the aim of killing the survivors in the aftermath of a nuclear exchange.
- Soviet ICBMs: The SS-11, SS-13, SS-17 and SS-18 were equipped with special biological weapon warheads over a 20-year period. Many of the missiles were based in silos near the Arctic Circle on a launch ready status. The cold temperatures in the far north enabled the smallpox agent to remain alive for long periods.
- Soviet engineers had also developed special refrigerated warheads for the SS-18s to enable the biological payload to survive the intense heat of re-entry through the atmosphere.
- American satellite reports during the Cold War era noted that some of the S-11 missiles had oddly shaped warheads that were suspected to be biological weapons.
- According to some reports after 1986, the USSR had included also Chinese cities on its target list. A few officials claimed to have seen Gorbachev's signature on a Soviet Politburo document authorizing the production of smallpox agent for the war against the United States as late as in February 1986.
- According to some analysts, the Soviet Union may have been responsible for distributing samples of the smallpox virus to other countries, including Iraq and North Korea, following the World Health Organization's eradication of the disease in the late 1970s.

OTHER WEAPONS

The modern history of biological weapons indicates that, along with anthrax and smallpox, many other types of germ weapons were produced between the 1970s and 1990s. During these two decades the involvement of the erstwhile USSR in the design and manufacture of various types of bio-weapons was much greater than other countries. The Soviets and others manufactured the following 'germ category weapons'.

Bacteria

Plague
Tularema
Brucellosis
Salmonella

Viruses

Venezuelan Equine Encephalitis (VEE)
Ebola

Toxins

Botulinum
Ricin

CHAPTER 7

Biological Weapons and Bio-Terrorism: Threat to the Environment?

P.K. GAUTAM

INTRODUCTION

In the legitimate conduct of war any act of using biological agents with the intent of injuring, killing or making people sick or harming animals or plants is condemned. Further, it is banned under the provisions of international law. States have institutions and arms control regimes that prohibit the use of biological agents in the conduct of war. The Biological Weapons Convention has imposed a ban on its production. At present there is an impasse over its verification through inspection regimes. Strategies are being developed against non-state actors to nip the problem in the bud. Due to the phenomenon of terrorism and the likely use of weapons of mass destruction (WMD) by non-state actors or clandestine and covert states sponsoring WMD use, defence against biological weapons has assumed paramount importance.

The role of chemical and biological agents till the twentieth century has been well documented. Warfare is harmful to the ecology as it has a direct and long-term impact on it. There is not much evidence linking the use of biological weapons on the environment in the histories of war. However, the case of smallpox infested blankets being supplied to Red Indians in 1793 has been reopened in the aftermath of 11 September 2001.[1] The British who were inoculated and protected against smallpox distributed infected blankets to North American Indians in the eighteenth century.[2] These blankets of bison skin were smeared with body fluid tainted with smallpox and proved to an effective biological warfare agent. Today, the plains around the Great Lakes in North America have been cordoned off and a secret search has been launched to trace those blankets which may not have been destroyed. The worry is that they may fall into the wrong hands.[3]

During the First World War, biological warfare was waged by the Germans using pathogenic micro-organisms to infect the cavalry and draft animal stocks of the opposing forces, especially North America and Romania.[4] Biological agents were last used by the Japanese in mainland China in the 1930s against the Chinese people. The secret work in the former Soviet Union was exposed following an accident in which anthrax leaked into the environment.

The use of biological agents cannot be ruled out by terrorists adopting innovative techniques. This could be as weapons of mass disruption if not destruction. Thus, nations need to be prepared to monitor an attack, contain its spread and cleanse the environment. Although there may be a belief that the threat is hyped by vested interests but in scenario building and worst case contingency planning this cannot be ignored. Many comparisons exist to indicate the potency of weapon grade biological agents. 'Poor man's WMD', something similar to an 'enhanced radiation nuclear bomb or neutron bomb' (killing people but not damaging equipment or buildings) are a few examples.

Paradoxically, a survey of the number of casualties due to the intentional use of bio-weapons by non-state actors reveals that post 9/11, five human beings died and eighteen were injured following an anthrax spore attack via postal service in the USA.[5] Similarly, if it is assumed that the plague in Surat and Himachal Pradesh, the mystery disease in West Bengal, the SARS epidemic of 2003 and the avian flu were acts of biological warfare then the numbers do not add up to any spectacular figures. Their influence and scare effect paralyse and even terrorize governments, financial flows, travel and tourism.

Misuse of Biotechnology

Realists may even link science fiction and biotechnology. The KGB of the erstwhile USSR spread rumours that in the 1980s the AIDS epidemic was the result of US experimentation with biological weapons.[6] There is a fear that AIDS or Ebola[7] may be engineered to be airborne in the near future.[8]

Some are contemplating 'designer ethnic weapons' developed through genome research like an anti-Mongoloid genetic agent to harm the Chinese or an anti-Caucasian time bomb. In a lighter vein, this may not be very effective against India due to the diversity of its people and biological diversity. Informal opinion suggests that herd immunity of Indians is better than what obtains in highly developed countries; thus one finds in India that bottled water is not the preferred choice of many (due to economic and other reasons) and water purification is inadequate. But this should not make us complacent.

GM crops may have a Trojan horse embedded in them to destroy crops by genetic manipulation at the appropriate moment. There may be special cases of adapted organism weapons developed to attack monoculture agriculture. The enormous benefits for medicine and agriculture of genetic manipulation opens up possibilities of malign misuse of biology for the development of new weaponry.[9] In 2001, a gene splicing biologist at the Australian National University in Canberra, while working on a contraceptive vaccine for mice to reduce the pest population, unexpectedly transformed the virus causing the rodent disease mouse pox into a highly lethal pathogen. The effect of this is that instead of the usual side-effect of making the mice mildly ill, lesions break out on the animal's skin with considerable pain. The pulsates grow and bleed and the skin has the appearance of crepe rubber. This could kill 60 per cent of the infected mice, including those that are immune. American researchers have reported a similar vaccine which is almost 100 per cent fatal.[10]

AGRICULTURAL TERRORISM

In 2003, the mad cow disease (bovine spongiform encephalopathy) crippled the Canadian cattle market. In 2002, rumours in the US led to the destruction of poultry coming from southern California, which was suspected to be suffering from an exotic Newcastle disease.[11] This is a highly contagious viral disease of domestic poultry, caged and aviary birds and wild birds. It is characterized by digestive, respiratory and/or nervous symptoms. There are a number of strains of the disease which differ in the severity of their clinical signs ranging from apparent to a rapidly fatal condition. The disease is caused by a virus belonging to the family Paramyxoviridae. ND virus is infective for almost all avian species, both domestic and wild. Most susceptible are domestic chickens, turkeys, pigeons and parrots. A milder form is seen in ducks, geese, pheasants, quails, guinea fowls and canaries. Mild conjunctivitis and influenza-like symptoms have been observed in people working in poultry processing plants and laboratories handling infected birds.

The food supply chain from farm crops to grocery store provides numerous opportunities for infecting them. According to a simulation study carried out in the Pentagon, the virulent foot and mouth disease could spread to twenty-five states in five days and one-third of the nation's cattle herds could get infected.[12] This field is open and bio-attacks on agriculture remain a potent threat. In the US, crop disease research has been undertaken on, for example, production spores of stem rust, rye stem rust, potato blight and rice blast diseases. In counter-insurgency operations in Malaya in the 1950s the UK employed tactics similar to the one used by the Americans under the name of Agent Orange in Vietnam. Initially, a defoliant was sprayed on the edges of jungle roads to reduce the possibility of ambushes but later this was extended to release agents from helicopters as part of the food-denial programme. Iraq was accused of having attempted to develop some anti-crop agents with fungal diseases of wheat.[13] During the Cold War, the US not only used synthetic plant toxins to attack vegetation in Vietnam, but also made detailed plans to destroy the staple crops of its adversaries like wheat in Russia and rice in China.[14]

BIOLOGY, ENVIRONMENT AND SELF-INFLICTED BIO-WARFARE

At the other end of the spectrum lies the threat of 'self-inflicted biological warfare'. If one focuses on human health and security then it is clear that poor infrastructure of public health, mismanagement of the civic environment and waste disposal lead to water-borne diseases, loss of biodiversity, specie intrusion, degradation of the ecology, unsustainable economic growth and the impending doom of global warming plague the developing countries. In India, it is common to suffer from occasional attacks of viral infections and much productivity is lost due to debilitating bouts of viral fevers, stomach or eye disorders.

New and Re-emerging Diseases and Threats due to Environmental Causes

Some of the threats of new and re-emerging diseases due to environmental causes are as follows:

1. Infectious diseases cause nearly 30 per cent of deaths worldwide.
2. In the last two decades more than thirty new and highly infectious diseases have been identified, such as Ebola and AIDS, for which no treatment, cure or vaccine is available so far. In his book, *Hot Zones*, Richard Pearson argues that the resurfacing of viruses like Ebola is due to ecological degradation.[15]
3. Over the last two decades, twenty known strains of diseases like tuberculosis (TB) and malaria have developed resistance to antibiotics due to the widespread use and misuse of these drugs.
4. Old diseases like cholera, plague, dengue fever, meningitis, haemorrhagic fever, diphtheria and yellow fever have re-emerged as public health threats after years of decline.[16]
5. Cholera has spread from Bangladesh to Chile in the ballast tank of a freighter. In India, cholera outbreaks following disasters have been spread by infected travellers.[17]
6. Unknown fevers in many areas have become routine. Since 1986, three major surges of viral fever were observed in Delhi during the changes of season. At any given time between 8 and 12 per cent suffer from viral or unknown fevers.[18]

Devil's Bullets. The indirect link to diseases and man's tinkering with the environment, was reported by *The Hindu*, in 1994.[19]

Impurities found in tap water in places as far removed as Moscow and Washington suppress the human body's immunity against disease, making the person susceptible to infections, AIDS and cancer. The source of these diseases called 'devil's bullet' (DB) is the harmless blue-green algae found in lakes, rivers and oceans. They have been supporting life on earth by acting as carbon dioxide sinks and releasing oxygen. Reacting to spreading pollution, the algae send out alarm signals to one another by generating polymeric molecules or 'alarm molecules' which induce genetic changes in the species, enabling them to adapt to the changing conditions of their habitat. These 'alarm molecules' or DBs help the algae to survive in a hostile environment, but they present a mortal danger to man. Researchers at the NF Gamaleya Institute of Epidemiology and Microbiology in Moscow found that DB molecules can replicate when interacting with the proteins of the human body and attack the human immune system. The threat is believed to be highest in tropical regions such as India where tropical forests are facing extinction. According to the report the Russians have developed a new water filter based on biological filters. It adds a note of caution that the threat can only be eliminated if human beings change their ways and stop poisoning the environment. Dr Alexander Kulberg, the leader of the research team added, 'the tiny blue algae are punishing man for damaging nature.' Whether this was a news item to give publicity to the product or not the story and the underlying scientific rationale appear to be a real possibility.

Genetically Modified Crops. It is not clear what unintentional harm genetically modified crops could cause if they lead to the growth of giant weeds, thus upseting the neighbouring ecology. Some concerns are as follows:[20]

1. GM crops themselves may become weeds and wild population leading to 'super weeds'.
2. They may lead to allergic reactions in human beings.
3. The antibiotic resistance gene in GMO may lead to the development of resistance to antibiotics used to treat human and animal diseases.
4. They may disturb the ecosystem and eliminate the natural

population/biotic communities by altering nutrient cycles due to the introduction of microbes and plants.
5. They may promote genetic uniformity, vulnerability to diseases and narrow down genetic diversity.

Bio(error). In his latest work, *Our Final Hour*, Sir Martin Rees of the University of Cambridge claims that advances in biotechnology, in terms of increased sophistication and decreased costs would mean that weaponized germs pose a huge risk. He foresees that a biological incident which he terms as 'bio(error)' will claim one million lives by 2020.[21] The debate is still on. These new or re-emerging diseases and their threats may lead to instability and disorder.

Health and Environment as Documented by the UN

As a follow-up of Agenda 21 (a blueprint for action for global sustainable development into the twenty-first century worked out at the Earth Summit in 1992) and a prelude to the World Summit on Sustainable Development (WSSD) in 2002, the UN Secretary General had commissioned a study of five areas: Water, Energy, Health, Agriculture and Biodiversity (WEHAB). The study reported that people who are poor are more likely to get sick, and those who are sick are more likely to become poor. Human health depends on a healthy ecosystem. However, environment and poverty can also be a significant source of ill health. Infectious and parasitic diseases account for around 25 per cent of total deaths. Poverty increases vulnerability to HIV infection, and AIDs exacerbates poverty.[22] The study established the various inter-linkages of WEHAB:

1. *Health and Water*: Diseases directly influenced by hygiene, sanitation and water, including infectious diarrhoea, typhoid, cholera, hepatitis, malaria, trachoma, fluorosis and Japanese encephalitis. Improvements in sanitation and hygiene may reduce the incidence, while better water resources management in both agriculture and urban areas may help control malaria and other water-related vector-borne diseases.

2. *Health and Energy.* Long-term changes in the world climate due to the current patterns of energy use could affect the patterns of infectious diseases. The disruption of complex ecological processes has affected the geography of vector-borne and infectious diseases such as malaria, dengue fever and leishmaniasis. Malaria increases markedly during periods of extreme temperature or altered rainfall.
3. *Health and Agriculture.* Millions of people are being poisoned by the use of pesticides and their residues in food. Persistent organic pollutants (POP) accumulate in the food chain, and heavy metals such as mercury, lead and arsenic cause poisoning by contaminating food and drinking water. Chemical contamination of foodstuffs, the outbreak of bovine spongiform encephalopathy and the emergence of a variant of Creutzfeldt-Jakob disease are major concerns.
4. *Health and Biodiversity.* Loss of biodiversity is directly associated with the loss of potential new medicines and medical models that are vital to an understanding of human physiology and disease. Thus, we have lost, before we can discover them, many of nature's chemicals and genes. In addition, the disturbance of the ecosystem and loss of biodiversity may lead to a population explosion in competitive species and the switching of pathogens from primary hosts to humans. This would result in the outbreak of new infectious diseases. Invasive species are spreading worldwide into new environments through intensified human food production, commerce and mobility.

It has been estimated that roughly 60 per cent of the global burden of disease from acute respiratory infections, 90 per cent from diarrhoeal diseases, 50 per cent from chronic respiratory conditions and 90 per cent from malaria could be avoided by simple environmental interventions.[23]

Tropical Region. The Third Assessment Report (TAR) of the Intergovernmental Panel on Climate Change (IPCC) has established with a reasonable degree of confidence that warmer and wetter conditions would increase the potential of infectious diseases in the tropical and temperate regions of Asia. Water-borne diseases would also become more common when higher temperatures and humidity are superimposed on the existing conditions and projected increase in population, urbanization and decline of water quality. Climate sensitive vector-borne diseases like malaria, schistosomiasis and dengue would increase and spread to new regions due to global warming. The fatality rates among newly affected population would be higher. At present, in vulnerable regions, an increase in the epidemic potential of 12 to 27 per cent for malaria and 31 to 47 per cent for dengue is anticipated.[24]

SPECIE INTRUSION AND ITS HARMFUL EFFECTS: NON-LETHAL GUERRILLA WARFARE

An intense debate on the harmful effects of genetically modified crops is raging across the world. One fear is that giant weeds may grow that may decimate the entire crop. Yet, even before GM crops became a debatable issue, alien species have intruded in regions where they are not a part of the ecology as a 'non-lethal weapon'. They have caused great havoc and destruction. Unlike the spectacular anthrax spores attack by postal means, these intruding species and their phenomenon is like a non-lethal weapon, low intensity and guerrilla warfare in nature. They spread slowly, have a low impact and are not a regular media topic. The history of harmful and alien specie intrusion indicates that it is probably inadvertent, though its use as a biological warfare agent cannot be ruled out. This appears to be the missing link between the Convention on Biological Diversity the (CBD) and the BWC.

THE CASE OF LAKE VICTORIA IN AFRICA

It is generally believed that biological war can only be waged by direct means against plants. However, biological agents such as alien plants can cause havoc and destroy the ecology. For example, the choking water hyacinth was introduced into Lake Victoria in Africa as a decorative plant. It has become a breeding ground for the water snail that transmits schistosomiasis and diarrhoeal disease organisms.[25]

In August 1995, the US Defense Intelligence Agency (DIA) studied the water hyacinth plant in Lake Victoria. This lake is the source and lifeline for fish stock of countries like Uganda, Kenya and Tanzania. Given that a single plant can multiply into millions of plants in a single year, this plant could have destroyed the lake and decimated the fish stock. This, in turn, could have led to an outbreak of famine and the attendant political instability.[26] The Global Environmental Facility (GEF) a financial body funded jointly by the United Nations Development Programme, the United Nations Environmental Programme and the World Bank that provides assistance for addressing the environmental problems of developing countries allotted US$ 20 million to save the lake and thus avoid a water and fish war between the 10 million Ugandans, Kenyans and Tanzanians.[27]

Although water hyacinth is a menace in India, it has only been perceived as a threat in choking the waterbodies to death as in the case of the Harike headworks in Punjab where the army had to step in to clear it in 2000–1. As in the case of Lake Victoria, it could have led to unwanted growth of disease organisms and this calls for regular monitoring.

Other Examples

The CBD has noted that after habitat loss, the second most important factor leading to the loss of native species is the introduction of alien species.[28] Some recent examples of assault on the ecology (crops and trees) through the intrusion of alien species (IAS) are:[29]

1. Intrusion of rats via ships to Seychelles and New Zealand.
2. Hedgehogs in Scotland.
3. Rabbits in Australia.
4. Asian longhorn beetle entering the USA and Canada from China (in wood used for making crates) and destroying hardwood forests, including the famous Central Park in New York.

As innovation and unorthodox means are the established strategies and tactics for waging war, some inimical elements may attack the biota by planned species intrusion. In war, causing death is not the only aim. Injuries strain the logistics and administrative system as greater resources are needed for treating casualties, evacuation, treatment and care. In a similar manner, the use of non-spectacular 'bio weapons' makes a lasting economic impact due to the need for treatment of large numbers of people and recurring afflictions. It is in order to examine some practical examples obtaining in India.

THE CASE OF INDIA

In India, a number of intrusive and alien species exist that destroy the ecology. These invasive species have been defined as 'those that produce fertile offspring in large numbers at a considerable distance from the ecosystem they originally belong to.'[30] 'Congress grass' (Parthenium) is one such well-known species which came along with the PL-480 wheat consignments from the USA in the latter half of the twentieth century.

Some other forms of biological invasions reported in India are:[31]

1. *Chromolaena Odorata* (known as *Ranmodi* in Marathi language), or siam weed prevents other species from growing, debilitates agricultural land and commercial plantations.
2. *Mikania Micrantha* or mile-a-minute weed cuts off the light of other plants and consequently destroys them.
3. *Lantana Camara* has spread across the subcontinent. It flowers throughout the year and produces a chemical that inhibits the growth of other plants.
4. The sugar cane wooly aphid is active in many regions of south India.
5. Another alarming specie intrusion is that of an aquatic weed like the water hyacinth (*Eichhornia Crassipes*) which directly affects water bodies and human health.[32]

THE CASE OF 'CONGRESS GRASS' AND THE INDIAN MILITARY

The 'Congress grass' (Parthenium) menace is an environmental problem which India has been tackling silently since the mid-

1960s. This alien specie with tiny white flowers is known to cause Air Borne Contact Dermatitis (ABCD), a common skin allergy. The pollen of the grass can trigger off an asthmatic attack. Medications used to treat the allergy are emollients in mild cases and steroids in severe ones. Steroids are known to have many side effects such as blood toxicity, diabetes and high blood pressure.[33]

This weed came to Pune from America along with a consignment of PL 480 wheat in 1956, which had not been cleaned before being shipped. As it was imported by the Congress government, it was named 'Congress grass'. Years of neglect has allowed this grass to grow wildly and it is as ubiquitous as discarded polythene bags. The weed has adapted well to Indian conditions and it flowers three to four times a year. Being an exotic plant, it does not have any natural enemies such as pests, pathogenic fungi, bacteria and viruses. Nor do herbivores eat it. It out-competes other plants and inhibits their germination and does not allow plant biodiversity. It also makes the soil infertile.[34]

According to Vandana Shiva, this 'wild carrot weed' has spread over five million hectares. It spread to Karnataka in 1961, Jammu & Kashmir in 1963, Madhya Pradesh in 1968, Western Himalayas in 1970 and to Assam and Rajasthan in 1979. It has an adverse impact on crops and biomass productivity. A piece of land yielding 9 to 10 cartloads of grass hardly yields any grass once it has been invaded by the weed.[35]

Although the army is actively involved in weeding out this grass from cantonments, similar effort is almost negligible in non-military stations. Probably, it is part of the general apathy to air and water pollution. Uprooting it completely is next to impossible.[36] Chemical methods of elimination have their side effects such as weedicides entering and lingering in the environment, and damaging other plant life. Biological methods also have harmful side effects. Manual extraction is the best method though some persons may suffer health hazards after being exposed to this grass.

The best and most effective method as suggested by experts and as practised by the military is to uproot the weed every two to three years and burn it. This is a typical example of a silent emergency, like a low intensity unintentional biological conflict.

The environmental lesson in the age of globalization and movement of various pathogens needs to be further studied for remedial measures. At this stage, only societal civic action can counter this threat.

DEFENSIVE MEASURES

SEPARATING THE NOISE FROM THE SIGNALS

The greatest challenge is to create a proactive real-time situational awareness. At each stage the 'root cause' needs to be quickly established. This is possible only if the information is timely, accurate and authentic. The public health care system of a developing country like India suffers from institutional structural problems and inadequate financial resources. These problems need to be addressed immediately. Besides, improved health and human security would more effectively lead to bio-warfare countermeasures.

Second, it would be erroneous to expect a conventional WMD type of attack with technology intensive bio-weapons. Attacks using alien species is a rich area for further research and defensive planning. In the sphere of intrusive species, maximum damage has already been done.

Third, it is of utmost importance to identify the causes of the disease. As is well known, new diseases are surfacing, and old diseases are re-emerging because of ecological degradation. The same may occur in a planned bio-assault. Countering such a bio-assault calls for a high degree of professional competence and coordination. The intelligence community should be better integrated with the ecological and the Infectious Diseases (ID) community. Raising the level of awareness is equally important. The need for an emergency response to bio-terrorism meshes neatly with growing concerns about the rising problems of new and emerging infections like West Nile encephalitis, Hong Kong influenza, HIV/AIDS, bovine spongioform encephalitis, increasing outbreaks of food-borne diseases and large numbers of antibiotic resistant microbes.[37]

Disease Surveillance

During the Ninth Five-Year Plan not much could be achieved in the area of disease surveillance. The important issues that appear in the Tenth Plan Document (2002–7)[38] are:

1. The surveillance of occurrences and the spread of diseases have so far been limited to communicable diseases.
2. Given the inadequate sanitation and problems of the public health system, it would not be possible to completely prevent outbreaks of communicable diseases in the near future.
3. There are inherent delays in the identification and reporting of focal outbreaks/surveillance leading to delayed recognition and response. The Ninth Plan had envisaged the establishment of district based early warning and prompt response measures. However, not much progress was made on this front.
4. Common epidemic prone diseases are not monitored locally.
5. The private sector provides 75 per cent of curative care. However, data from private health providers are not included in any disease surveillance. The Tenth Plan intends to review surveillance, laboratory facilities and reporting.

It should be borne in mind that unlike developed countries such as the USA, in a developing country like India, the military would be better prepared than the civil administration. Thus, the military needs to be involved and integrated in all counter measures. Central police organizations such as the Central Reserve Police Force (CRPF) have been specially earmarked for disaster management in line with Disaster Management plans that are the responsibility of the Ministry of Home Affairs. Four battalions are being trained to counter WMD terrorism in metropolitan cities.[39] How they deal with their counterparts in the military is not clear. It has been recommended that this should be an integrated effort. Unlike radiological bombs or gas/chemical disasters, biological agents are more difficult to locate, contain and eliminate.

Reporting of Infectious Diseases

Under the International Health Regulations (IHR), it is mandatory for countries to report the occurrences of several infectious diseases: cholera, plague and yellow fever. Emerging diseases like Ebola haemorrhagic fever, severe acute respiratory syndrome (SARS) and avian influenza are not included in this list.[40] This calls for urgent modification when it is presented to the World Health Assembly in 2005.[41] Although the World Health Organization swings into action to survey and institute remedial measures in the event of an outbreak of strange and new diseases, much time may be lost before reporting and setting up of teams. The reasons for not including suspicious diseases may be due to geopolitical rivalries when countries may want to conceal such details for fear of confirming that a clandestine bio-weapon had been effectively used against them by an enemy. This old-fashioned thinking in reporting only mainstream diseases may have served the purpose of checking appropriate vaccination or immunization of travellers, but it is not likely to solve the problem of elimination of the scourge of biological warfare in its totality. Shedding secrecy and overcoming barriers in reporting diseases is one aspect that should be tackled universally.

Need for an Integrated and Multi-disciplinary Approach

According to R. Uma Shankar in the Department of Crop Physiology, University of Agricultural Sciences, Bangalore, there is no comprehensive study of the impact of invasive species in India.[42] There is a growing threat that this simple biological assault may be used against an adversary to inflict a slow-acting, non-lethal, ecological war or bio-war.

The Cartagena Protocol, as a supplementary agreement to the Convention on Biodiversity, has provisions to protect biodiversity from the risk of genetically modified technologies.[43] The World Trade Organization (WTO) includes the Agreement on Sanitary and Phytosanitary Measures (SPS Agreement) for human, plant and animal health protection. But debate on the negative effects of GM crops on the natural habitat or human health remains undecided. In the UK, the planting of GM crops has been deferred by a year to fix the separation distances between crops and the liability regime for contamination of conventional or GM crops.[44] Investigations in the Philippines on illnesses among people living near GM maize fields noted that GM crops may have triggered fevers, respiratory illnesses, and skin reactions. Blood tests revealed that villagers had developed antibodies to resist the maize's in-built pesticide.[45]

Ballast of Ships. Biological war can be waged by the movement of alien species as also pathogens in the ballast of ships and may never be detected or the originator identified. This is because it may be very difficult to establish whether the disease or sickness in humans, plants or livestock is unintentional or intentional. As alluded to earlier, cholera spread from Bangladesh to Chile in this manner. Measures should be adopted to get rid of these intrusive species. A global treaty, 'The International Convention for Control and Management of Ships Ballast Waters and Sediments', was approved in February 2004, under the aegis of the International Maritime Organization (IMO).[46] About 10 billion tonnes of ballast water is transferred each year across the world. In India, 5,000 ships release two million tonnes of ballast water in Mumbai alone. About 400 alien organisms are reported to be travelling by these means. The Ballast Water and Sedimentation Management Plan under the Treaty would require new vessels to be fitted with equipment for treating ballast water after 2009 and a complete switch-over by the year 2016.[47] The intentional use of specie intrusion as a bio-weapon also needs to be considered as a potential threat. The Indian Coast Guards and other central and state authorities should draw up contingency plans to meet this threat.

Preserving Our Ecology and Biodiversity

Perhaps, the best defence against biological warfare is to preserve our ecology, biological diversity and mitigate the adverse effects of climate change. This would provide an in-built mechanism for defence against biological assaults. Throughout recorded history about 10,000 species were used by humans for food and agriculture. Today, only 150 plant specimens constitute our diet.[48] Along with the unintended damage that GM crops may have done to agriculture due to loss of plant diversity, the resistance and coping capability has been reduced.

The livestock resources of India have great genetic variability and environmental adaptation. In the animal husbandry sector the endangered breed of indigenous livestock should be conserved. It has around 30 breeds of cattle, 12 breeds of buffalos, 20 breeds of goats and 40 breeds of sheep.[49] This diversity needs to be preserved.

Preserving diversity, though not a direct and visible defence against biological warfare, is a long-term protection. Unlike the industrial and mechanized monoculture obtaining in the USA, agriculture in India is different due to the large number of small-size holdings and varying micro-climates in various regions. This may give us inherent defence against any assault on agriculture even if the assault is via the unintentional ill effects of GM crops or an intentional one by a non-state actor or a state sponsoring such terrorism.

NOTES

1. Pranay G. Lal, 'Pox Americana: Is the West a Victim of its Own Past?', *Down to Earth*, 29 February 2004, pp. 44–5.
2. Malcolm Dando, 'The Impact of the Development of Modern Biology and Medicine on the Evolution of Offensive Biological Warfare Programs in the Twentieth Century', *Defense Analysis*, vol.15, no. 1, p. 47.
3. Pranay G. Lal, op. cit., explains that knowledge of inoculation was denied to indigenous people in the colonies. The West remains in mortal fear of strange new diseases that originate in Asia (like severe acute respiratory syndrome [SARS], and avian influenza) and Africa (like acquired immune deficiency syndrome [AIDS], Ebola and monkey-pox). But almost all vaccination measures are designed to protect citizens of the developed world and the focus is not on the source regions.
4. Malcolm Dando, op. cit., p. 47.
5. Matin Zuberi, 'WMD in Hands of Non-State Actors: An Emerging Threat Assessment of the Possibility and Its Impact on National Security', *The Journal of the United Service Institute of India*, vol. CXXXII, no. 549, July–September 2002, pp. 354–65.
6. George H. Quester, *Before and After the Cold War, Using Past Forecasts to Predict the Future*, London: Frank Cass, 2002, p. 166.
7. The exact origin, location and natural habitat of the Ebola virus remains unknown. Evidence indicates that the virus is zoonotic (animal borne) and is normally present in an animal host native to Africa. Confirmed

cases of Ebola haemorrhagic fever (HF) have been reported from Congo, Gabon, Sudan, Uganda and the Ivory Coast. People can be exposed to this virus by direct contact with blood and/or secretions of an infected person or needles contaminated with the infection. See K. Bhushan and G. Katyal, *Nuclear Biological and Chemical Warfare* (New Delhi: A.P.H. Publishing Corporation, 2002, pp. 282–3. There is no known cure or treatment for Ebola, with 90 per cent of infected persons dying in the particularly horrifying circumstances of the progressive destruction of their bodies' connective tissues. See C.J. Williams, 'A Pocketful of Posies?: A Review of National Plans for the Protection of Civilians against Chemical, Biological or Radiological Weapon', *Seaford House Papers*, selected papers written by members of the course at the Royal College of Defence Studies, UK, 1999, p. 143, n. 5.

8. Jerome C. Glenn and Theodore J. Gordon, *The Millennium Project: 2002 State of the Future* (Washington: American Council for The United Nations University, 2002), p. 24.
9. Ibid., p. 39.
10. 'SA Perspective', *Scientific American*, January 2004, p. 6; Jamie Wilson, 'In the Shadow of Bio-terrorism', *Frontline*, 21 May 2004, pp. 88–90.
11. Daniel G. Dupont, 'Food Fears', *Scientific American*, October 2003, pp. 20-1.
12. Ibid.
13. Willie Russell, Book Review of Simon M. Whitby's, *Biological Warfare against Crops (Global Issues)*, UK: Palgrave, accessed from the Internet on 16 March 2004.
14. Malcolm Dando, *The New Biological Weapons*, Boulder: Lynne Rienner Publishers, 2001, p.123.
15. Quoted in *Down to Earth*, 15 November 2001, p. 31.
16. Op. cit., n. 8, p. 24.
17. *State of the World Population* 2001, Chap. 5, UN (Internet Version) quoting World Health Organization (WHO), *Health and Environment in Sustainable Development: Five Years after Earth Summit*, Geneva: WHO, 1997.
18. Pranay G. Lal, 'Virus Attack', *Down to Earth*, 15 November 2001, p. 29.
19. Vladimir Radyuhin, 'Algae Seek Balance by Punishing Man', *The Hindu* (Hyderabad), 3 May 1994.
20. Syamal Krishna Ghosh, 'GM Crops: Rationality Irresistible', *Current Science*, vol. 81, no. 6, 25 September 2001, p. 656.
21. Quoted by Julie Wakefield, 'Doom and Gloom by 2100', *Scientific American*, July 2004, p. 48.
22. WEHAB Working Group, *A Framework Action on Health and the Environment*, Johannesburg: WSSD, August 2002, pp. 5–11 (Internet version).
23. Op. cit., n. 17.

24. James J. McCarthy et al., eds, *Impacts, Adaptation, and Vulnerability*, New York: Cambridge University Press, 2001, paragraph 5.2.6 (Internet version) and Internet Version of *Regional Impact of Climate Change*, Chap. 11, Tropical Asia, Executive Summary.
25. WEHAB Working Group, *A Framework for Action on Health and the Environment* (Johannesburg: World Summit on Sustainable Development, 2002).
26. Colin H. Kahl, 'Population Growth, Environmental Degradation, and State Sponsored Violence', *International Security*, vol. 23, no. 2, Fall 1998, p. 81.
27. Roger A. Payne, 'The Limits and Promises of Environmental Conflict Prevention: The Case of GEF', *Journal of Peace Studies*, vol. 23, no. 2, Fall 1998, p. 81.
28. *The World Resources: A Guide to Global Environment 1998-99, Environmental Change and Human Health*, Joint publication of World Resources Institute, UNEP, UNDP and World Bank, New York: Oxford University Press, p. 197.
29. BBC TV Earth Report of 2 March 2004.
30. Nitin Seth, 'It's a Pogrom out There', *Down to Earth*, 29 February 2004, pp. 27–34.
31. Ibid.
32. This water hyacinth should not be confused with the common *singhara* or water chestnut which is relished as a food and is found in most water bodies in India. It is sold like any other fruit in the post monsoon period and its flour or *atta* is consumed by Hindus instead of cereals during the fasting period when the consumption of grains is taboo. It is also used in the preparation of Ayurvedic medicines.
33. Veenu Singh, 'Deadly Grass', the *Hindustan Times*, 19 November 2000.
34. Dipankar Ghosh, 'A Menace for Sure', *Down to Earth*, 31 January 2004.
35. Vandana Shiva, 'Specie Invasion', *Geography and You*, vol. 2, no. 10, 2002, p. 7.
36. Op. cit., n. 34.
37. D.A. Henderson, 'US Response to Possible Bioterrorism', National Academy of Sciences, reproduced in *Strategic Digest*, May 2001, p. 603.
38. *5 Year Plan, 2002–2007*, vol. II, Planning Commission, Government of India, pp. 117–18. Also see Lieutenant General D. Raghunath, 'Health Hazards and National Security', in *India's National Security: Annual Review 2003*, ed. Satish Kumar, New Delhi: India Research Press, 2004), pp. 184–95.
39. Colonel M.S. Patial, talk delivered at the United Service Institute (USI) of India, New Delhi on 23 June 2004 on 'Strategy for Consequence Management of WMD Terrorism', forthcoming as a book.
40. 'Wider Ambit', *Down to Earth*, 31 May 2004, pp. 18–19.

41. Ibid.
42. Interview in *Down to Earth*, 29 February 2004, p. 31.
43. The Cartagena Protocol, which entered into force in September 2003, is designed to ensure the safe transfer, handling and use of GMOs that may adversely affect the conservation and sustainable use of biological diversity, taking also into account risks to human health. On 27 February 2004, it adopted labelling and documentation to promote safety of international trade in GM organism. All bulk shipments of living or genetically modified organisms (known as LMOs and GMOs) intended for food, feed or processing (such as soyabeans and maize) are to be identified as 'may contain LMOs'. See *UN News*, vol. 59, no. 10, 6–12 March 2004.
44. Paul Brown, 'GM Crops Delayed by at least a Year after Cabinet Leak', *Guardian Weekly*, 4–10 March 2004.
45. Ibid.
46. Clifford Polycarp, 'Decks Cleared, Partly', *Down to Earth*, 31 March 2004, p. 46.
47. Ibid.
48. 'Agricultural Biodiversity', *UN News*, vol. 57, no. 24, 15–21 June 2002.
49. 'Animal Husbandry and Dairying', *10th Plan Document*, vol. II, Planning Commission, Government of India, Chap. 5.2, p. 569.

CHAPTER 8

Non-State Actors in South Asia: Who will Use Bio-Weapons and Against Whom?

SUBA CHANDRAN

For the last decade, especially after the use of chemical and biological agents by Aum Shinrikyo in 1995, the threat of terrorists using biological weapons has increased manifold. Numerous studies have been commissioned and published in recent years by various research institutes, universities and think tanks especially in the US.[1] Though the attack did not result in a high number of casualties[2] like that in a conventional bombing, 'the use of an invisible, lethal poison created a pervasive sense of fear and insecurity'.[3] While focusing on 'bio-terrorism' some crucial questions need to be raised to assess the feasibility and possibility of a non-state actor using biological weapons and materials.

IS THE BIOLOGICAL WEAPON A WMD?

It is essential to analyse the nature of threat posed by biological weapons to determine whether they would become part of militant warfare. History is replete with instances when biological weapons have been used by states and non-state actors; however, they have never been used by a non-state actor as a weapon of mass destruction. For example, the Mongols used plague (*Yersinia pestis*) in the battle of Kaffa in 1346; the British employed smallpox (*Variola*) against the Delaware Indians and against General George Washington's forces during the Revolutionary War; the Germans chose anthrax (*Bacillus anthracis*) and glanders (*Pseudomonas mallei*) to attack the horses and mules of the US army and its allies in the First World War; and the Japanese used typhoid (*Salmonella typhi*) in the Second World War.[4]

Available records reveal that the biological agents and weapons used by non-state actors have not resulted in mass deaths, when compared to the casualties caused by other weapons. For example, major attacks involving biological weapons by non-state actors include those by Aum Shinrikyo, in which 12 people were killed;[5] Rajneesh followers in Oregon in 1984 in which 751 people fell ill but no one was killed;[6] and the anthrax mail attacks in the US in 2001 in which 5 people were killed and 22 fell ill.[7] Besides these high profile attacks, there were numerous incidents in which biological agents were used by both state and non-state actors to eliminate individuals for political and criminal reasons.[8] Considering that militant groups could potentially use biological weapons along with nuclear weapons as a WMD 'blurs the threat and consequence assessment."[9]

IS EVERY INCIDENT OUTSIDE THE STATE INVOLVING BIOLOGICAL WEAPONS A TERRORIST ACT?

A distinction needs to be drawn between various attacks involving biological weapons, especially between bio-terrorist and bio-criminal acts. A further distinction should be made, if one is to define terrorism as use of violence for political purposes and criminal activities for economic purposes. The use of biological weapons by cult groups like the Aum Shinrikyo and Rajneesh cannot be defined as use by terrorist groups. Their efforts have not succeeded; for example, according an analysis, most of the Aum Shinrikyo's efforts at using biological weapons have been exaggerated and 'despite semi-professional capabilities, substantial time and effort, all of (Aum's) efforts failed'.[10]

A survey of incidents involving biological weapons reveals that most of them were perpetuated for criminal rather than political purposes. According to one study of the 54 confirmed and possible uses of biological agents and weapons in the last century, 32 were criminal in nature and only 9 were terrorist.[11]

AN ANALYSIS OF 54 EVENTS INVOLVING BIOLOGICAL WEAPONS IN THE TWENTIETH CENTURY

Motivation/Type	*Number*	*Percentage*
Criminal	32	59.26
Terrorist	9	16.67
State	12	22.22
Unknown	1	01.85

According to another analysis, 'many of the listed cases could arguably classify as attempts at homicide, suicide, or criminal extortion motivated by financial rather than political gain'.[12] One study identified 244 incidents of chemical and biological weapons terrorism since the First World War and concludes that of these '60 per cent involved the actual use of chemical or biological agents, 30 per cent involved threatened use, and 10 per cent acquisition only. Only 25 per cent of the surveyed incidents were linked to political motives; the rest were perpetrated by criminals, psychotics, disgruntled employees and others.'[13]

Exaggerating the threat perceptions may compel the state to adopt massive countermeasures. In this process, the state may undermine or ignore the threat from those actors who are likely to use biological materials for purposes other than terrorism.

IS A DIFFERENCE BETWEEN BIOLOGICAL WEAPONS AND BIOLOGICAL MATERIALS ESSENTIAL FOR DEFINING BIOLOGICAL TERRORISM?

Jean Pascal Zanders draws a distinction between biological terrorism with biological materials and biological weapons. According to him:

> Terrorism with CB (Chemical and Biological) materials deals with the use of any toxic substance or pathogen in pursuit of certain goals. Terrorism with CB weapons refers to the use of warfare agents that is a toxic chemical designed, developed and selected by the military to support certain missions laid out in the military doctrine of a state. This distinction highlights the deeper significance of the 1995 sarin attack in the Tokyo

subway; for the first time, a terrorist organization turned to a warfare agent.[14]

The distinction between these two is essential to forecast the future strategies of a militant group. If a militant group uses biological materials for biological terrorism, it could be an either a one-time threat or a series of threats that the state should counteract. The use of biological materials for terrorism is then defined by the presence and availability of such materials with the militant group. In such cases, there is no long-term threat, as these biological materials do not become a part of militant strategy.

On the other hand, if a militant group uses or seeks biological weapons then the threat of use from that particular group needs to be taken seriously. Seeking biological weapons would indicate the level of importance attached to bio-terrorism as a strategy against the state. This approach would focus counter actions against bio-terrorism. Instead of perceiving the threat of bio-terrorism from every single militant group, it would enable the state to focus on specific groups.

Second, this distinction is crucial as biological weapons are difficult to procure or assemble, unlike biological materials. Irrespective of its organized efforts to produce biological weapons, Aum Shinrikyo's efforts failed, mainly due to 'the challenge of acquiring sufficiently lethal strains of botulinum toxin and anthrax bacilli (and) the difficulty in preparing those agents for dissemination and dispersing them'.[15] However, this view is not accepted by those who perceive terrorists as likely to use biological weapons. According to an analysis, Aum failed to produce biological weapons in the early 1990s because biological warfare then was too difficult; however, the '1990s brought a proliferation of information and biotechnological advances' to overcome these initial difficulties.[16]

HOW TO DEFINE THE COVERT USE OF BIOLOGICAL WEAPONS BY STATE ACTORS?

While the focus has been on bio-terrorism by non-state actors in recent years, what has gone unnoticed or under noticed is its state sponsorship. It has been reported that 22 per cent of attacks with biological weapons in the twentieth century have been carried out covertly by different states.[17] Some of the most prominent state sponsored attacks include the following use and alleged use:[18]

1. The murder of Georgi Markov in 1978 by the Bulgarian secret police using a pellet containing ricin.
2. The use of poison and biological agent by the apartheid regime in South Africa against the blacks.
3. Biological agents utilized by the US against North Korea and China in 1952 and later against Cuba in the 1960s.
4. The use of anthrax in Rhodesia during 1979–80.
5. Mycotoxins employed by the Soviets in Afghanistan.
6. The attempted assassination of the head of Hamas in 1997 by Mossad with the opiate fentonyl.

NON-STATE ACTORS IN SOUTH ASIA WHO WILL USE BIOLOGICAL WEAPONS AGAINST WHOM?

Non-state actors in South Asia include terrorists; communal/ sectarian organizations, naxalite groups, criminal groups and private militias. All these groups have different objectives and strategies though each group uses violence either against the state or against the people or both. Within this group, who would use biological weapons? Do biological weapons fit into their warfare and objectives for which they are resorting to violence?

MILITANT GROUPS IN SOUTH ASIA

In the context of bio-terrorism, militant groups are seen as the most likely non-state actors to resort to biological weapons or bio-materials. South Asia as a region has the highest number of terrorist groups compared to any other region in the world. (For a list of militant groups in South Asia see Appendix 1.) Before analysing who are likely to use biological weapons, it is essential to focus on three questions: Has there been any instance of use or threat of use of biological weapons by terrorist groups in South Asia? Do any of the terrorist groups in South Asia have linkages with other groups who have used or threatened to use biological weapons? Do biological weapons fit into their warfare strategy?

Has there been a threat?

The only instance of a threat to use biological materials by a terrorist group in South Asia has been in Sri Lanka, where it has been alleged that the Tamil militants had warned the Government of Sri Lanka through a communiqué of biological warfare.

According to this communiqué:[19]

> The Ceylon Government had announced that it will get the help of the devil to fight the terrorists—that is to subjugate the Tamil race. It is now quite apparent to the whole world that the Government is doing exactly that by its diabolical acts against innocent Tamils. Hence it is quite fit and proper for the Tamils to counter the Government in a similar manner, and with this object in view, we have formed an operation squad to wage total war against the Government in all parts of Ceylon. One strategy is to wage a biological war, which we believe will cripple Ceylon in a few years. Doctors and scientists have got over their scruples and are now working on methods to implement the following:
>
> 1. Sending qualified volunteers to bring infected material, cultures and infected water snails to spread Bilbariasis (River Blindness) in the canals and reservoirs of the Mahaweli at several points. It may take sometime before infected people come to the hospitals, but by that time the damage would have been achieved.
> 2. Similarly, bring infected material and mosquitoes to spread Yellow Fever in the South, where the carrier mosquito is already found.
> 3. A Tamil in South America has already volunteered to supply infected material for rubber trees (Leaf Curl) not presently found in Ceylon. It is hoped to wipe out the rubber plantations by spreading the infection at widely separated points.
> 4. Arrangements are being made to send competent volunteers to collect infected tea to propagate diseases not presently found in Ceylon tea plantations. Diseases not found in Ceylon tea bushes are prevalent in Assam.
> 5. Other activities such as poisoning water supplies of the army in the North and East, continuing the overseas propaganda to halt tourism and investment in Ceylon, will continue on an intensified scale. We have little doubt that unborn Sinhalese generation will curse the folly and wickedness of the government, which will make Ceylon a cursed land shunned by the world. History will record the just demands of the Tamils and diabolical actions and policy of the Ceylon Government. Actions speak louder than words.

The communiqué issued before 1987 has not been ascribed to

any particular militant group in Sri Lanka. Nor has this communiqué been published elsewhere.

Has there been a linkage?

Are there linkages between terrorist groups in South Asia with groups that have used or threatened to use biological weapons? One major terrorist organization which has close links with terrorist outfits in South Asia is Al Qaeda. According to a CIA report:

> Al Qaeda and associated extremist groups have a wide variety of potential agents and delivery means to choose from for chemical, biological, radiological, or nuclear (CBRN) attacks. Al Qaeda's end goal is the use of CBRN to cause mass casualties; however, most attacks by the group—and especially by associated extremists—probably will be small scale, incorporating relatively crude delivery means and easily produced or obtained chemicals, toxins, or radiological substances.[20]

The report also highlights the efforts of members of the Al Qaeda to procure biological agents. It emphasizes that 'Spray devices disseminating biological warfare (BW) agents have the highest potential impact. Both 11 September attack leader Mohammad Atta and Zacharias Moussaoui expressed interest in crop dusters, raising our concern that Al Qaeda has considered using aircraft to disseminate BW agents.'[21]

A report prepared by the Pentagon for the US Congress noted: 'Osama bin Laden's terrorist network has been pursuing a sophisticated biological weapons research programme and is seeking chemical weapons.'[22] In 2002, the Pentagon reported finding traces of anthrax at a suspected Al Qaeda biological weapons site in Kandahar, along with some equipment for converting the bacteria into a weapon. Other samples found at the site tested positive for the poison ricin.[23] George J. Tenet, then director of the CIA, was quoted, 'Documents recovered from Al Qaeda facilities in Afghanistan show that bin Laden was pursuing a sophisticated biological weapons research programme. . . . We also believe that bin Laden was seeking to acquire or develop a nuclear device. Al Qaeda may be pursuing a radioactive dispersal device, which some call a "dirty bomb".'[24]

According to a report prepared by a UN panel of experts, 'The risk of Al Qaeda acquiring and using weapons of mass destruction also continues to grow,' and 'undoubtedly, Al Qaeda is still considering the use of chemical or bio-weapons to perpetrate its terrorist actions.'[25]

Al Qaeda's linkages with militant groups in South Asia have been proved beyond doubt. In particular, five militant organizations—Lashkar-e-Toiba, Jaish-e-Mohammad, Harkat-ul-Jihad-ul-Islami, Harkat-ul-Mujahideen and Lashkar-e-Jhangvi—have close linkages with Al Qaeda.[26] While the first four are terrorist organizations whose presence in India has been documented, the last one is a sectarian organization whose activities are limited to Pakistan, especially Punjab.

The influence of Al Qaeda over these militant groups has been explained by Rohan Gunaratna. According to him:

> [T]hese militant groups' ideologies are influenced by Osama's organisation in three ways. They conduct suicide bombings, which are the hallmark of Al Qaeda. And they all attack the heart of the government, that is New Delhi. Finally, they have all attacked and killed foreigners. The Harkat did it in Kashmir, the Jaish recently killed Daniel Pearl in Pakistan. Their influence comes through infiltration. Al Qaeda is under pressure from the international coalition, so it is now operating through other groups by funding their operations. Evidence of this can be found in the recent attacks in Pakistan on diplomatic targets and churches. This is the Al Qaeda operating through front and sympathetic organizations like Jaish and others.[27]

In short, there exists a linkage between some South Asian terrorist groups and the Al Qaeda which, it is suspected, possesses or is developing biological agents. Therefore, the possibility of use of biological agents or weapons would be restricted to these few groups, provided this use forms an integral part of their warfare strategy.

Will a biological attack suit their purpose?

An analysis of terrorist attacks reveals that they are increasingly focused and less indiscriminate. For example, in Jammu & Kashmir, the favoured targets of militant attacks are the security forces, counter-insurgents and factions. Attack on civilians follows a pattern: most of the civilians targeted are political activists, village defence committee members, informants, shepherds, surrendered militants (other than Ikhwans), and the minority community.

CIVILIANS KILLED IN JAMMU & KASHMIR: 1990–2003

Phase I	*Phase II*
1990: 862	1998: 877
1991: 594	1999: 799
1993: 1,023	2000: 842
1994: 1,012	2001: 919
1995: 1,161	2002: 922
1996: 1,333	2003: 608 (up to October)
1997: 840	

SOURCE: Based on Institute of Conflict Management Data.

Militant groups are wary of becoming alienated from the people, whose cause they allegedly espouse. One of the reasons why they decided to use improvised explosive devices was to make their attacks target specific instead of idulging in random indiscriminate killings. However, both these arguments are limited only to those militant groups that have been waging an indigenous struggle against the state with or without external support. Since their strategy is premised on target specificity, it is unlikely that they would resort to the use of any weapon that would result in indiscriminate deaths. For this reason, it is unlikely that they would use biological weapons or agents.

There are other terrorist groups like the Lashkar-e-Toiba and the Jaish-e-Mohammed that are fighting for a totally different cause. Comprised mostly of Pakistanis and Afghans, these two groups have been waging a battle to establish Islamic rule in India and have very different objectives from those of the Hizbul Mujahideen, which is engaged in a struggle for an independent Kashmir and comprises largely of Kashmiris. There have been numerous incidents where these foreign groups have targeted the minority community in Jammu & Kashmir.

Is there any likelihood of these foreign militant groups using biological materials against the minority community in Jammu & Kashmir? If at all biological weapons are employed in Kashmir, the Lashkar and Jaish groups would use them, especially against the minority community, as part of their ethnic cleansing strategy. The fact is that there are select villages and areas even in Jammu & Kashmir where the population is entirely non-Muslim. These groups, especially the Lashkar, could also launch such an attack elsewhere in India.

Criminal Mafia

The question arises: will the criminal mafia led by Dawood Ibrahim decide to use biological weapons? Till 1990, the focus of the mafia groups was solely on economic targets. Initially, Dawood Ibrahim was opposed to being a part of any political or terrorist network. Prior to their involvement in the Mumbai serial bomb blasts of December 1992–January 1993, the organized criminal gangs of Dawood Ibrahim and Tiger Memon did not want to engage in any political or terrorist activity as it 'understood that backing terror would damage its core business interests'.[28]

The ISI-terrorist (especially the Lashkar-Dawood link) has been strengthened in recent years. This nexus has been responsible for at least eight bomb blasts since 2002 in Mumbai alone, killing more than 60 persons.[29] The Dawood gang provided manpower, the Lashkar organized the training and the ISI provided the funds.[30] The attack on the American Centre in Kolkata in January 2002 was the handiwork of militants belonging to the Jaish and Lashkar with Aftab Ansari, a member of the Dawood-led mafia, providing the necessary assistance.[31]

The criminal syndicate led by Dawood Ibrahim along with the Lashkar-e-Toiba is antagonistic to India and its people, and does not represent any constituency. Hence, there are no constraints or inhibitions that would prevent these groups from using weapons of mass destruction. The fact that they were involved in serial blasts amply reflects their motives and modus operandi, as also their indifference to killing their own co-religionists in the process. Outside Jammu & Kashmir, if a non-state actor decides to use

ATTACK ON MINORITY COMMUNITY:
SOME TRENDS IN ATTACKS SINCE 1998

District	*Number of Attacks*	*Numbers Killed in each Attack*	*Total*
Udhampur	6	9, 4, 5, 7, 8, 3	36
Doda	17	26, 15, 20, 29, 13, 4, 5, 6, 5, 5, 15	143
Rajori	10	11, 9, 3, 12, 10, 5, 4	54
Poonch	4	9, 5, 2, 6	22
Anantnag	4	15, 7, 13, 2	37
Pahalgam	3	23, 5, 8	36
Jammu	4	13, 30, 28, 13	84
Pulawama	1	24	24

SOURCE: Compiled from various sources.

biological weapons in India, then it would be these criminal groups targeting areas of economic interest and high population.

PRIVATE MILITIAS OF BIHAR: WILL THEIR CONFLICT BASED ON CASTE TURN BIOLOGICAL?

A number of caste militias operate in Bihar and parts of Uttar Pradesh. One of the main reasons for their emergence is the social hierarchy and economic exploitation by the upper class, who also belong to the upper castes. When the lower classes and lower castes decided to unite under the influence of naxalites, the middle and upper classes formed private militias to protect their self-interests.

Ever since these caste militias have been involved in indiscriminate killings on a regular basis. Amongst them, the Ranvir Sena is the most powerful private militia of the upper caste landlords. Since its formation, the Ranvir Sena has been implicated in at least five major massacres, apart from a number of killings of the lower castes, especially dalits. In certain areas of Bihar and Uttar Pradesh the lower castes live in isolated clusters and villages. The possibility of the private militia using biological materials cannot be completely ruled out. Poisoning has always been used in certain areas.

NOTES

1. Some of the recent studies include W. Seth Carus, *Bioterrrorism and Biocrimes: The Illicit Use of Biological Agents since 1900*, Washington DC: Center for Counter Proliferation Research, National Defense University, 1998; D.W. Brackett, *Holy Terror: Armageddon in Tokyo*, New York: Weatherhill, 1996; Brad Roberts, ed., *Terrorism with Chemical and Biological Weapons*, Alexandria, Virginia: Chemical and Biological Arms Control Institute, 1997; Jonathan B. Tucker, *Biosecurity: Limiting Terrorist Access to Deadly Pathogens*, Washington DC: USIP, November 2003; Michael Barletta, *Biosecurity Measures for Preventing Bioterrrorism*, Report by the Center for Non-proliferation Studies, November 2002; *Chronology of Incidents Involving Ricin*, Report by the Center for Non-proliferation Studies, February 2004; Jonathan B. Tucker, ed., *Toxic Terror: Assessing Terrorist Use of Chemical and Biological Weapons*, Mass.: MIT Press, 2000; *Bio Terrorism Threat Assessment and Risk Management Workshop*, Special Report, Center for Non-proliferation Studies, 2003.
2. The attack took place on 20 March 1995, when five members of the cult released the deadly nerve agent sarin, killing 12 people and injuring over 1,000. Aum Shinrikyo was implicated in seventeen such attacks, ten involving chemical agents and seven involving biological agents.
3. Jonathan Tucker, 'Introduction', in *Toxic Terror: Assessing Terrorist Use of Chemical and Biological Weapons*, ed. Jonathan B. Tucker, Mass: MIT Press, 2000, p. 1.
4. See Jim A. Davis, 'The Looming Biological Warfare Storm: Misconceptions and Probable Scenarios', *Air & Space Power Journal*, Spring 2003. http://www.airpower.maxwell.af.mil/airchronicles/apj/apj03/spr03/davis.html
5. For a complete account of Aum Shinrikyo's operations see David E. Kaplan and Andrew Marshall, *The Cult at the End of the World* (New York: Crown Publishers, 1996) 'Chronology of Aum Shinrikyo's CBW Activities', Center for Non-proliferation Studies. http://cns.miis.edu/pubs/reports/pdfs/aum_chrn.pdf
6. W. Seth Carus, *Bioterrorism and Biocrimes: The Illicit Use of Biological Agents since 1900*, p. 50.
7. See 'Small-scale Terrorist Attacks Using Chemical and Biological Agents: An Assessment Framework and Preliminary Comparisons', http://www.fas.org/irp/crs/RL32391.pdf
8. See W. Seth Carus, *Bioterrorism and Biocrimes: The Illicit Use of Biologcal Agents since 1900*, pp. 8–10.
9. Jean Pascal Zanders, 'Assessing the Risk of Chemical and Biological Weapons Proliferation to Terrorists', *The Nonproliferation Review*, Fall 1999, p. 21.

10. See Milton Leitenberg, 'Aum Shinrikyo's Efforts to Produce Biological Weapons: A Case Study in the Serial Propagation of Misinformation', *Terrorism and Political Violence*, vol. 11, no. 4, Winter 1999, pp. 149–58.
11. Numbers are compiled from Appendix A: List of Cases in *Bioterrorism and Biocrimes: The Illicit Use of Biologcal Agents Since 1900*, W. Seth Carus, pp. 181–5.
12. Jean Pascal Zanders, 'Assessing the Risk of Chemical and Biological Weapons Proliferation to Terrorists', *The Nonproliferation Review*, Fall 1999, p. 19.
13. Harvey J. McGeorge, 'Chemical and Biological Terrorism: Analysing the Problem', *The ASA Newsletter*, no. 42, 16 June 1994, pp. 12–13 quoted in Jonathan Tucker, 'Introduction', in *Toxic Terror: Assessing Terrorist Use of Chemical and Biological Weapons*, ed. Jonathan B. Tucker, pp. 1–2.
14. Jean Pascal Zanders, 'Assessing the Risk of Chemical and Biological Weapons Proliferation to Terrorists', *The Nonproliferation Review*, Fall 1999, pp. 18-19.
15. See William Rosenau, 'Aum Shinrikyo's Biological Weapons Program: Why did it Fail?', *Studies in Conflict and Terrorism*, vol. 24, no. 4, July 2001, pp. 289–310.
16. Jim A. Davis, 'The Looming Biological Warfare Storm: Misconceptions and Probable Scenarios', *Air & Space Power Journal*, Spring 2003. http:/ /www.airpower.maxwell.af.mil/airchronicles/apj/apj03/spr03/davis.html
17. W. Seth Carus, *Bioterrorism and Biocrimes: The Illicit Use of Biologcal Agents Since 1900*, Appendix A: List of Cases, pp. 181–5.
18. See Mark Wheelis, 'A Short History of Biological Warfare and Weapons'. http://microbiology.ucdavis.edu/faculty/mwheelis/BW_history.pdf; Jean Pascal Zanders, 'Assessing the Risk of Chemical and Biological Weapons Proliferation to Terrorists', *The Nonproliferation Review*, Fall 1999.
19. Rohan Gunaratna, *War & Peace in Sri Lanka with a Post Accord Report from Jaffna*, Sri Lanka: Institute of Fundamental Studies, 1987, pp. 51–2. The author fails to mention the year in which the threat was issued and by whom and why it has not yet been carried out. Better counsel may have prevailed with the realization that Tamils would suffer as much as the Sinhala population.
20. 'Terrorist CBRN: Materials and Effects Terrorist CBRN', CIA Report, June 2003. http://www.cia.gov/cia/reports/terrorist_cbrn/CBRN_threat_wo.pdf Also see Bill Gerta, 'CIA Says Al Qaeda Ready to Use Nukes', *The Washington Times*, 3 June 2003.
21. 'Terrorist CBRN: Materials and Effects Terrorist CBRN', CIA Report, June 2003. http://www.cia.gov/cia/reports/terrorist_cbrn/CBRN_threat_wo.pdf Also see Barton Gellman, 'Al Qaeda Near Biological, Chemical Arms Production', *Washington Post*, 23 March 2003.

22. 'Pentagon: Al Qaeda Pursuing Bio Weapons', *USA Today*, 23 May 2003. http://www.usatoday.com/news/washington/2003-05-23-us-wmd_x.htm. Also see 'U.S.: Bio Weapons A Qaeda Focus'. http://www.cbsnews.com/stories/2003/05/23/attack/main555367.shtml
23. 'Al Qaeda Program to Make WMD Halted by Afghan War', *USA Today*, 21 January 2004. http://www.usatoday.com/news/world/2004-01-26-al-qaeda-wmd_x.htm Also see Michael R. Gordon, 'US Says It Found Qaeda Lab Being Built to Produce Anthrax', *New York Times*, 23 March 2002.
24. Michael R. Gordon, 'US Says It Found Qaeda Lab Being Built to Produce Anthrax', *New York Times*, 23 March 2002.
25. 'Qaeda Might Use Biological Weapons', *The Indian Express*, 16 November 2003. Also see 'UN Details Al Qaeda Threat: Biological, Chemical Attack "A matter of Time"', http://www.cnn.com/2003/US/11/20/un.alqaeda/
26. See B. Raman, 'Al Qaeda in India'. http://www.rediff.com/news/2003/apr/04spec.htm; B. Raman, 'Al Qaeda and Lashkar-e-Toiba', http://www.saag.org/papers7/paper678.html . According to Rohan Gunaratna, 'the Al Qaeda has infiltrated three Pakistani and Kashmiri groups: Harkat, Jaish-e-Mohammed and Lashkar-e-Toiba. They shared operational training and infrastructure with the Al Qaeda in Afghanistan before 9/11'. See 'Al Qaeda has Infiltrated Harkat, Lashkar & Jaish, They Want to Increase Heat in Valley', interview with Rohan Gunaratna, *The Indian Express*, 30 August 2002.
27. Ibid., interview with Rohan Gunaratna, *The Indian Express*, 30 August 2002.
28. Praveen Swami, 'Extending Terror', *Frontline*, vol. 16, no. 6, 13–26 March 1999. http://www.flonnet.com/fl/606/16060160.htm
29. See 'The Mirror Cracked', *The Outlook*, 8 September 2003, p. 34.
30. Anupama Katakam, 'The New Pawns', *Frontline*, vol. 20, no. 19, 13–26 September 2003.
31. Tapash Ganguly, 'Kolkata's Killer Crew', *The Week*, 17 February 2002, p. 10.

APPENDIX 1

Militant Groups in South Asia*

INDIA

Assam

United Liberation Front of Asom (ULFA)
National Democratic Front of Bodoland (NDFB)
United People's Democratic Solidarity (UPDS)
Kamtapur Liberation Organisation (KLO)
Bodo Liberation Tiger Force (BLTF)
Dima Halim Daogah (DHD)
Karbi National Volunteers (KNV)
Rabha National Security Force (RNSF)
Koch-Rajbongshi Liberation Organisation (KRLO)
Hmar People's Convention-Democracy (HPC-D)
Karbi People's Front (KPF)
Tiwa National Revolutionary Force (TNRF)
Bircha Commando Force (BCF)
Bengali Tiger Force (BTF)
Adivasi Security Force (ASF)
All Assam Adivasi Suraksha Samiti (AAASS)
Gorkha Tiger Force (GTF)
Barak Valley Youth Liberation Front (BVYLF)
Muslim United Liberation Tigers of Assam (MULTA)
United Liberation Front of Barak Valley
Muslim United Liberation Front of Assam (MULFA)
Muslim Security Council of Assam (MSCA)
United Liberation Militia of Assam (ULMA)
Islamic Liberation Army of Assam (ILAA)
Muslim Volunteer Force (MVF)
Muslim Liberation Army (MLA)
Muslim Security Force (MSF)
Islamic Sevak Sangh (ISS)
Islamic United Reformation Protest of India (IURPI)
United Muslim Liberation Front of Assam (UMLFA)
Revolutionary Muslim Commandos (RMC)

* Institute for Conflict Management, New Delhi in its website has published in detail all the militant groups operating/that have operated in South Asia. http://www.satp.org/

Muslim Tiger Force (MTF)
People's United Liberation Front (PULF)
Adam Sena (AS)
Harkat-ul-Mujahideen Harkat-ul-Jehad

JAMMU & KASHMIR

Lashkar-e-Omar (LeO)
Hizb-ul-Mujahideen (HM)
Harkat-ul-Ansar (HuA, now known as Harkat-ul Mujahideen)
Lashkar-e-Toiba (LeT)
Jaish-e-Mohammad Mujahideen-e-Tanzeem (JeM)
Harkat-ul Mujahideen (HuM, previously known as Harkat-ul-Ansar)
Al Badr Jamait-ul-Mujahideen (JuM)
Lashkar-e-Jabbar (LeJ)
Harkat-ul-Jehad-i-Islami
Al Barq
Tehrik-ul-Mujahideen
Al Jehad
Jammu & Kashmir National Liberation Army
People's League
Muslim Janbaz Force
Kashmir Jehad Force
Al Jehad Force (comprising Muslim Janbaz Force and Kashmir Jehad Force)
Al Umar Mujahideen
Mahaz-e-Azadi
Islami Jamaat-e-Tulba
Jammu & Kashmir Students Liberation Front
Ikhwan-ul-Mujahideen
Islamic Students League
Tehrik-e-Hurriat-e-Kashmir
Tehrik-e-Nifaz-e-Fiqar Jafaria
Al Mustafa Liberation Fighters
Tehrik-e-Jehad-e-Islami
Muslim Mujahideen
Al Mujahid Force
Tehrik-e-Jehad
Islami Inquilabi Mahaz

MANIPUR

United National Liberation Front (UNLF)
People's Liberation Army (PLA)
People's Revolutionary Party of Kangleipak (PREPAK)

Kangleipak Communist Party (KCP)
Kanglei Yawol Kanna Lup (KYKL)
Manipur Liberation Tiger Army (MLTA)
Iripak Kanba Lup (IKL)
People's Republican Army (PRA)
Kangleipak Kanba Kanglup (KKK)
Kangleipak Liberation Organisation (KLO)
Revolutionary Joint Committee (RJC)
National Socialist Council of Nagaland—Isak-Muivah (NSCN-IM)
People's United Liberation Front (PULF)
North East Minority Front (NEMF)
Islamic National Front (INF)
Islamic Revolutionary Front (IRF)
United Islamic Liberation Army (UILA)
United Islamic Revolutionary Army (UIRA)
Kuki National Front (KNF)
Kuki National Army (KNA)
Kuki Revolutionary Army (KRA)
Kuki National Organisation (KNO)
Kuki Independent Army (KIA)
Kuki Defence Force (KDF)
Kuki International Force (KIF)
Kuki National Volunteers (KNV)
Kuki Liberation Front (KLF)
Kuki Security Force (KSF)
Kuki Liberation Army (KLA)
Kuki Revolutionary Front (KRF)
United Kuki Liberation Front (UKLF)
Hmar People's Convention (HPC)
Hmar People's Convention-Democracy (HPC-D)
Hmar Revolutionary Front (HRF)
Zomi Revolutionary Army (ZRA)
Zomi Revolutionary Volunteers (ZRV)
Indigenous People's Revolutionary Alliance (IRPA)
Kom Rem People's Convention (KRPC)
Chin Kuki Revolutionary Front (CKRF)

MEGHALAYA

Hynniewtrep National Liberation Council (HNLC)
Achik National Volunteer Council (ANVC)
People's Liberation Front of Meghalaya (PLF-M)
Hajong United Liberation Army (HULA)

Nagaland

National Socialist Council of Nagaland (Isak-Muivah) (NSCN [IM])
National Socialist Council of Nagaland (Khaplang) (NSCN [K])
Naga National Council (Adino) (NNC [Adino])

Tripura

National Liberation Front of Tripura (NLFT)
All Tripura Tiger Force (ATTF)
Tripura Liberation Organisation Front (TLOF)
United Bengali Liberation Front (UBLF)
Tripura Tribal Volunteer Force (TTVF)
Tripura Armed Tribal Commando Force (TATCF)
Tripura Tribal Democratic Force (TTDF)
Tripura Tribal Youth Force (TTYF)
Tripura Liberation Force (TLF)
Tripura Defence Force (TDF)
All Tripura Volunteer Force (ATVF)
Tribal Commando Force (TCF)
Tripura Tribal Youth Force (TTYF)
All Tripura Bharat Suraksha Force (ATBSF)
Tripura Tribal Action Committee Force (TTACF)
Socialist Democratic Front of Tripura (SDFT)
All Tripura National Force (ATNF)
Tripura Tribal Sengkrak Force (TTSF)
Tiger Commando Force (TCF)
Tripura Mukti Police (TMP)
Tripura Rajya Raksha Bahini (TRRB)
Tripura State Volunteers (TSV)
Tripura National Democratic Tribal Force (TNDTF)
National Militia of Tripura (NMT)
All Tripura Bengali Regiment (ATBR)
Bangla Mukti Sena (BMS)
All Tripura Liberation Organisation (ATLO)
Tripura National Army (TNA)
Borok National Council of Tripura (BNCT)

Mizoram

Bru National Liberation Front
Hmar People's Convention-Democracy (HPC-D)

Arunachal Pradesh

Arunachal Dragon Force (ADF)

LEFT WING EXTREMIST GROUPS

People's Guerrilla Army
People's War Group
Maoist Communist Centre

OTHER NON-STATE ACTORS

Tamil National Retrieval Troops (TNRT)
Akhil Bharat Nepali Ekta Samaj (ABNES)
Tamil Nadu Liberation Army (TNLA)
Deendar Anjuman
Students Islamic Movement of India (SIMI)
Asif Reza Commando Force
Ranvir Sena

BANGLADESH

Harkat-ul-Jehad-al-Islami (HuJI)

PAKISTAN

Lashkar-e-Omar (LeO)
Sipah-e-Sahaba Pakistan (SSP)
Tehreek-e-Jaferia Pakistan (TJP)
Tehreek-e-Nafaz-e-Shariat-e-Mohammadi
Lashkar-e-Jhangvi (LeJ)
Sipah-e-Muhammad Pakistan (SMP)
Muttahidda Quami Movement—Altaf Hussain (MQM)
Haqiqi Muhajir Quami Movement (MQM-H)
Baluch People's Libration Front (BPLF)
Baluch Students' Organistaion (BSO)
Jamaat-ul-Fuqra
Nadeem Commando
Popular Front for Armed Resistance
Muslim United Army
Harkat-ul-Mujahideen Al-Alami
Baluch Students' Organistaion–Awami (BSO–A)
Hizb-ul-Mujahideen (HM)
Harkat-ul-Ansar (HuA, now known as Harkat-ul Mujahideen)
Lashkar-e-Toiba (LeT)
Jaish-e-Mohammad Mujahideen-e-Tanzeem (JeM)
Harkat-ul-Mujahideen (HuM, previously known as Harkat-ul-Ansar)
Al Badr
Jamait-ul-Mujahideen (JuM)

Lashkar-e-Jabbar (LeJ)
Harkat-ul-Jehad-i-Islami
Muttahida Jehad Council (MJC)
Al Barq
Tehrik-ul-Mujahideen
Al Jehad
Muslim Janbaz Force
Kashmir Jehad Force
Al Jehad Force (comprising Muslim Janbaz Force and Kashmir Jehad Force)
Al Umar Mujahideen
Mahaz-e-Azadi
Islami Jamaat-e-Tulba
Islamic Students League
Tehrik-e-Hurriat-e-Kashmir
Tehrik-e-Nifaz-e-Fiqar Jafaria
Al Mustafa Liberation Fighters
Tehrik-e-Jehad-e-Islami
Muslim Mujahideen
Al Mujahid Force
Tehrik-e-Jehad
Islami Inquilabi Mahaz

INVESTIGATION 1

SARS: First Pandemic of the Twenty-first Century

ANIMESH ROUL

> Beware the threat of the spores, Bad news parcels bide their time.
> They lurk to enter the unsuspecting, and unleash dormant evil that multiplies.
>
> SETU K. VORA, 'Threat of the Spores', *Emerging Infectious Diseases*, vol. 10, no. 4, April 2004 www.cdc.gov/eid

INTRODUCTION

Infectious disease and related health concerns have rarely found a place in national security discourse in the past. Of late, the issue has assumed prominence and has been included in the national security debate. Disease spread poses a threat to human and national security. The entire gamut of human and public health concerns rests on the proposition that 'it could seriously threaten both the individual and quality of life that a person is able to attain within a given society, polity or state'.[1] The argument that the transnational spread of disease poses a threat to (human) security is validated by recent developments, such as the HIV/AIDS epidemic, the spread and virulence of emerging and re-emerging infectious diseases (ERID),[2] the threat of bio-terrorism and epidemics that weaken fragile state structures.[3]

The emergence of infectious diseases on the global agenda highlights the discovery of new disease agents, increasing antibiotic resistance and the devastating impact of epidemics—cholera in Latin America, plague in India, the Ebola virus in Africa,[4] and more recently, severe acute respiratory syndrome (SARS) which transcended national boundaries and assumed the form of a global pandemic in 2003. This paper focuses on the outbreak of SARS as the first pandemic of the twenty-first century, reviews the causes and course of the disease and explores key lessons learnt from the outbreak that could shape the future of infectious disease control.

THE OUTBREAK

The severe acute respiratory syndrome hit the world in a virulent form within three months of its outbreak in Foshan and Guangzhou of Guangdong province in South China as atypical pneumonia in mid-November 2002. Soon it spread to Vietnam and Hong Kong and from there it made its way to other parts of the world including most of the Southeast Asian countries. According to the World Health Organization's (WHO) latest estimation, it had afflicted 8,096 persons and had caused 774 deaths affecting at least 29 countries spread over five continents.[5] These 'vectors without borders' clearly demonstrated the potential hazards of unrestricted air travel and human mobility that transcends national boundaries and regions during the disease outbreak.

Although the initial cases of the disease affected more than 300 people and caused five deaths in Guangdong, the official report of the outbreak was received by the WHO after almost three months on 11 February 2003.[6] Subsequently, the new disease was named SARS and a new coronavirus[7] was identified as the causal agent after preliminary case definition was established. An analysis of the complete genome sequence of the SARS virus suggested that it is not closely related to any of the three previously identified coronavirus subfamilies, nor does it seem to have arisen through a chance genetic recombination between known coronaviruses. According to Malik Peiris, a virologist at the University of Hong Kong, its unique sequence suggests that it evolved independently from other members of the family, in some animal host, over a long time.

Before the WHO surveillance team could establish that the cases matched the definition of SARS, an infected doctor in Guangdong province triggered the spread of the virus in the ninth floor of the Metropole hotel in Hong Kong, where he had stayed, and days later guests and visitors to that hotel had seeded a cluster of cases in the hospital systems of Hong Kong, Vietnam, Singapore, and even Canada, that became 'hot zones' within no time. The initial 'hot zones' were characterized by a rapid increase in the number of cases, primarily among health care workers and their close contacts. In Hong Kong, Canada and Vietnam, SARS first took root in hospital settings, where the staff exposed themselves to the infectious agent without taking adequate precautions. They were unaware that a new disease had surfaced. All these initial outbreaks were subsequently characterized by chains of secondary transmission outside the health care environment. Most of the infected doctors and health care workers who had treated the early cases, and foreign nationals, mainly tourists flew home or elsewhere, and acted as a vector of the deadly virus. Soon the whole world came under the grip of SARS which created panic among people and nations alike.

EPIDEMIOLOGY OF SARS

The earlier suspicions about the epidemiology of SARS are now better understood. The genesis of the SARS-CoV has been traced to wild civets and raccoon dogs that are considered culinary delicacies in southeastern China. At this stage domestic pigs and poultry do not appear to have been the hosts. Serologic data indicates that there had been previous infections of humans and animals in this region. In humans, who are infected with the virus, the incubation period varies from 5 to 15 days. This lag time allows these people to travel by air almost anywhere in the world after they have been exposed. Once it becomes symptomatic, the disease spreads by person-to-person contact. Most, but not all, cases arise from close contact with an infected person. However, details regarding transmission have yet to be analysed.

SARS, CHINA AND BEYOND

When SARS crossed the political boundaries of mainland China, it spread almost everywhere in the Asia Pacific. Its spread within the host country and its virulence varied, probably due to adequate protective measures and climatic conditions. Among the 30 affected countries worldwide, China, Hong Kong, Taiwan, Canada and Vietnam bore the brunt of the SARS pandemic.

China. The origin of the disease was traced back to the Chinese mainland where sporadic cases of SARS have been reported till recently. Lately, three cases of SARS infection came to light after the containment of the disease since its outbreak in 2003. The first instance was reported on 5 January 2004 when Chinese health officials confirmed that a 32-year-old man had contracted SARS in southern Guangdong province. Immediately, China announced a plan to slaughter thousands of civet cats, believed to be the natural host of the SARS-CoV. Again, on 17 January, the health officials confirmed two new cases of infection in the same province. On 22 April 2004, the Chinese Ministry of Health informed the WHO that a nurse working in a Beijing hospital had contracted the virus fifteen days earlier and was in intensive care. Out of the 171 close contacts under medical observation, five suspected patients were isolated following fever. [8] China's Ministry of Health confirmed that a woman who had died in Anhui province had SARS—the first death from the illness in 2004. This confirmation brought the total number of confirmed SARS cases in China to five—two in Anhui, three in Beijing—with four more suspected cases in the capital.[9]

Hong Kong. The Special Administrative Region, Hong Kong (China) was the second most affected region, fatality-wise, and the city had more cases in proportion to its population than any other affected region. There were 1,755 reported cases and 299 deaths.[10] In Hong Kong, the first officially recognized outbreak of SARS occurred in the first week of March 2003 in the Prince of Wales Hospital.[11] Soon after more than 300 cases were reported from the Amoy Gardens apartment block in Kowloon Bay and as per investigation reports the virus had spread through a sewage pipe. This was the only instance of an environmental transmission of SARS.[12]

Educational institutions were closed down in mid-March, and the economy was hit hard by a sharp decline in the inflow of foreign tourists resulting in a substantial loss of foreign exchange earnings. In late May the infection rate dropped and the WHO lifted its warning against travel to Hong Kong. Although the Hong Kong authorities were criticized for their slow response and failure to quarantine the early cases, they swung into action thereafter to contain its horizontal spread.

Taiwan. The first case of SARS in Taiwan was reported on 18 March, but the outbreak really occurred in late April and early May 2003. When the total worldwide death toll was 229, Taiwan had only 29 probable cases without any fatality. At that time it was believed to be a minor outbreak as most of the cases were imported and local transmission was negligible. On 22 April, a new cluster of seven infections was reported in Hoping Hospital in Taipei, leading to a number of local transmissions that culminated in 116 probable cases and 10 deaths within a fortnight.[13] The death toll reached 180 out of 665 reported cases by the time SARS completely subsided in Taiwan. According to the WHO, 90 per cent of the cases in Taiwan occurred in a hospital setting. The rapid spread of SARS in Taiwan was attributed to lack of experience in containing outbreaks, delayed expert assistance from the WHO along with poor health infrastructure, hospital mismanagement, and lack of seriousness on the part of the health authorities. The situation was exacerbated when more than 150 medics and para-medics including Taipei's top health official Chiu Shu-ti, resigned from their jobs as a protest against inadequate safeguards. On 5 July, Taiwan was the last country to be removed by the WHO from its list of SARS infected areas.

Canada. This is the only country outside Asia which witnessed severe outbreaks in two phases. The virus entered Canada via an infected woman who returned home from Hong Kong. Within a short span of time she transmitted the infection to five members of her family. On 5 March 2003, the woman died of SARS in Toronto followed by one of her sons. However, the failure to immediately identify the causative agent led to nosocomial transmission[14] in the Toronto area, extending to health workers at Scarborough Grace Hospital. The suspected and most of the probable SARS cases identified in Toronto occurred within health care facilities. In small number of cases, the infection was due to household and community transmission, mostly after hospital visits.

However, quarantine measures instituted in late April seemed to have brought SARS under control. To the utter astonishment of the health authorities, the disease resurfaced a month later with a new cluster of cases in a hospital on the northern side of Toronto. On 23 May, the medical community realized that nosocomial transmission of SARS to patients and visitors had been occurring in a single ward of the North York General Hospital (NYGH) throughout April and early May.[15] A second phase of the outbreak (SARS II) was declared at the NYGH, and was designated as a level-3 institution, which implied that SARS had been transmitted through unprotected exposure.[16] Toronto became the first area to be taken off and then put back on the WHO's list of affected areas. On 2 July, the city was declared SARS-free by the WHO authorities; by that time SARS had infected 251 people and killed 41 of them.

Singapore: Like Canada, SARS spread to Singapore by an infected woman, Esther Mok, who returned home after staying on the ninth floor of the Metropole hotel in Hong Kong. Singapore reported 238 cases and 33 deaths. Unlike other affected regions, Singapore had adopted 'exemplary' and stringent measures to contain SARS, primarily by thermal imaging of air passengers to detect those who had high temperatures.[17] The health authorities even distributed digital thermometers to school students to enable them to check their temperature daily. Most importantly, the battle against SARS led to a drastic new legislation to punish those who might break the home quarantine orders or expose the community to the infection by other means of wilful action or sheer neglect. The law, an expansion of the scope of the Infectious Diseases Act, provides for severe fines and/or jail terms.[18] Despite all these measures, the disease resurfaced in Singapore in September when a researcher working in the Environmental Health Institute (EHI) Laboratory contracted SARS.[19] It was the first case of infection in Singapore since the WHO declared the country SARS-free on

31 May 2003. However, effective measures and readiness prevented the virus from creating havoc.

Vietnam: Vietnam has been praised as a model case in the fight against SARS; it was the first country to contain an outbreak of the deadly virus. The disease killed 5 people out of a total of 63 infected cases.

Other SARS affected regions. Although SARS reached the borders of the US, the UK, Spain, Sweden and even India, it proved fatal in at least four other countries. Malaysia, the Philippines, Thailand and South Africa reported SARS-related deaths, though not on the same scale as in Asia or North America. Malyasia reported five cases of SARS, including two deaths. The country was the first to impose travel restrictions after the first death occurred in early April 2003. The Philippines was declared SARS-free on 21 May but it reported fourteen cases and two deaths. Thailand's first celebrated SARS patient was Dr Carlo Urbani, who died of SARS after identifying the causative agent and warned the world of the impending anarchy. Out of a total of nine cases, only two died of the disease. South Africa, the only country affected in Africa, reported one death in April. The victim was infected in Hong Kong in March.

SARS SCARE IN INDIA

Although SARS was not fatal in India, it created panic and confusion within the health establishments, as well as among the people. The first case of SARS was reported from Goa, where a 32-year-old marine engineer tested positive. The patient, who sailed from Hong Kong to Mumbai, reached Goa on 1 April and was admitted to the Goa Medical College Hospital from where he was discharged on 14 April. The Director-General of the Indian Council of Medical Research (ICMR) had confirmed the case. At least nineteen more persons have tested positive for the SARS virus in laboratory tests but none of them fall within the WHO definition of SARS. The WHO had categorically stated that a mere laboratory diagnosis is not enough to declare a person as suffering from SARS but the person should have clinical symptoms too. The WHO had described India as SARS-free on 1 May 2003. After a week, the WHO put India back on the list of countries reporting probable cases. According to the WHO's representative in India, N. Kumara Rai, the world body had taken into account one new case in Kolkata.[20] These declarations by the WHO and the Health Ministry caused considerable confusion in the general populace.[21]

Regarding its impact on trade and commerce, the Federation of Indian Chambers of Commerce and Industry (FICCI) had described SARS as the 'most serious single factor' which could adversely affect growth in Asia. A survey conducted by the FICCI following its initial reaction had revealed that there was no catastrophic effect on Indian trade and commerce, and the SARS scare had a moderate effect on trade and investment flows between India and ASEAN countries.[22] The Confederation of Indian Industry (CII) had stressed that SARS could lead to uncertainty in the global as well as Indian economy and it may prove to be a major hindrance to economic growth.[23] Citing Chinese customs statistics, a study observed that bilateral trade between India and China during January and March 2003 had witnessed an impressive growth of 77.8 per cent, with total trade touching US$ 1.66 billion. India's exports to China during the first quarter of 2003 crossed all previous records in bilateral trade by shipping $ 947 million worth of goods, registering a growth of 119.2 per cent.[24] Though an exhaustive study of the real impact of SARS on Indian economy is not available, it is more or less clear that the panic did not affect India's economy as the Plague outbreak did in 1994.

CONTROVERSY OVER ORIGIN

The controversy surrounding the origin of SARS became the most debated issue in 2003. On 16 January 2004, the WHO declared that it had found evidence suggesting that civet cats do carry SARS. Before that several questions had been raised on the source and natural host of the disease. Since the initial cases were reported from China, which is known for its secrecy and subsequent efforts to suppress the early outbreaks, this raised many eyebrows. Two major controversies gained ground in the wake of the outbreak: SARS as a creation of communist China for bio-warfare purposes, and it is an alien virus from space.

SARS as a bio-weapon. Regarding the origin of SARS, the alarmists had their say. According to them, the outbreak may not have been caused by a naturally found virus. They alleged that the Chinese military had a hand in it and its massive cover-up. According to Richard Fisher, senior fellow at the Jamestown Foundation, a Washington-based think tank, a bio-weapon link should not be ruled out. There were speculations about a possible leak from a secret military bio-weapon programme.[25] Russian medical expert Professor Sergei Kolesnikov, a renowned member of the Russian Medical Sciences Academy, claimed that the SARS virus is a hybrid of two viruses—measles and mumps—and could only be produced in laboratory conditions. This indicates that the SARS virus could be a biological weapon developed by China.[26]

Wei Jingsheng, a Chinese dissident in exile, without dismissing reports that SARS emanated from China's biological weapons research facilities, noted that the Chinese President, Hu Jintao, had conducted an inspection tour, including a visit to the Chinese Military Medical Academy, a bio-military research facility, to dismiss rumors of a bio-weapon leak.[27] This suspicion gained strength when WHO officials were denied access to Chinese military hospitals during a field inspection. A media story claimed that Beijing's hospital administrators had ordered large numbers of SARS infected patients to be transferred from No. 309, one of the city's military-run hospitals, to No. 3 Armed Police Hospital in Fengtai before a WHO inspection team visited the former (No. 309) in the last week of April 2003. Most of the cases, including severe ones, were transferred out, leaving just a small number of cases to be inspected by WHO officials. This cover-up, it was alleged, followed the army's experimentation with this deadly bio-war weapon.[28]

On the other hand, many believed that the bio-weapon theory was far-fetched. Stephanie Lieggi, an expert in the East Asia Nonproliferation Program at the Center for Nonproliferation

Studies, Monterrey, described the speculations as baseless, owing to the lack of plausible evidence to support these claims.

Space theory. Scientists claimed that the SARS virus could have reached the earth from outer space, piggyback on a comet or on a extra-terrestrial object. Chandra Wickramasinghe at the Center for Astrobiology, University of Cardiff, forcefully advocated this theory called 'panspermia'. According to him, several aspects of the SARS outbreak like the strange nature of Coronavirus, supported the unorthodox point of view about panspermia.[29] The other advocates of this theory include the Indian scientist Jayant Narlikar at the Inter-University Center for Astronomy and Astrophysics, Pune. The virus, according to this theory, may have entered the atmosphere east of the Himalayas, where the stratosphere is thinnest, and was subsequently deposited in southern China. An earlier collaborative study between these two scientists recovered bacteria from stratospheric samples collected from a height of 20 miles.[30] Refuting the claim, Edison Liu of the Genome Institute of Singapore debunked the theory as scientific imagination bordering on fantasy.[31] However, there is no concrete evidence to confirm the panspermic theory as responsible for SARS.

LESSONS LEARNED

What have we learned from the SARS outbreak to prevent future situations involving these infectious pathogens? The emergence of a disease follows two steps: introduction into the human population and perpetuated transmission. Although preventing the introduction of a new disease is ideal, containing a zoonosis[32] is a necessity. First, the most important requirement is the need to report, promptly and accurately, cases of any disease with the potential for spreading worldwide in this interconnected and mobile world. Second, timely global alerts prevent imported cases from triggering widespread outbreaks in new areas. Third, travel recommendations, including screening measures at airports, help to contain the international spread of an emerging infection.

There are other loopholes and related lessons that can be

derived from the existing health establishments of many countries. An outbreak can be contained even without curative drugs or vaccines if existing interventions are tailored to circumstances and backed by political commitment. Although risk analysis about new and emerging infections is a major challenge, it is vital to ensure that accurate information is successfully and unambiguously communicated to the public. [33]

ASSESSMENT

Following the outbreak of SARS, government authorities had adopted various strategies to cope with the killer virus. The most effective mechanism was to promptly set in place modalities to prevent the further spread of the disease. These included quarantine of infected patients, issuing travel advisories to SARS-affected countries, immigration checks and border controls, public information programmes, and even closure of schools and institutions. While Singapore and other affected countries acted promptly, China was severely criticized for complacency, lack of seriousness and its slowness in responding to the request of WHO for a medical team inspection in Guangdong. According to the WHO Director-General, Gro Harlem Brundtland, the spread of the disease could have been contained had the Chinese authorities treated the matter seriously at an early stage and with greater alacrity. China's belated response was due to the authorities' concern with the economic fallout. The slow process of 'silence-denial' to acknowledge and cooperate is not really surprising given the prevailing attitude towards infectious diseases in the country.[34]

The SARS outbreak was eventually brought under control by a coordinated response. Measures like improved screening and reporting of cases, immediate isolation of SARS patients, enhanced hospital infection control practices, and quarantine of close contacts were the most effective ways to prevent further proliferation of the virus through person-to-person transmission.[35] Many health practitioners opined that containment, quarantine and Internet (information dissemination) helped conquer SARS, which otherwise would have spelt disaster on an unprecedented scale. The current belief is that SARS had species-jumped from an animal to humans. The virus is capable of infecting several species including monkeys and common cats. Mice and rats have been shown to be relatively resistant to SARS.

However, much about SARS remains a mystery, including its origins. How it actually started and from which animal source it came remains unclear. There is serious concern that SARS could re-emerge. As some cases have recently resurfaced in China, the outbreak is a wake-up call for the world.

NOTES

1. For a complete analysis of the changing nature of security concerns and disease see, Jennifer Brower and Peter Chalk, *The Global Threat of New and Re-emerging Infectious Disease*, New York: RAND Corporation, 2003, pp. 1-12.
2. 'Emerging infectious diseases are those whose incidence in humans has increased during the last two decades or which threaten to increase in the near future. The term also applies to newly appearing infectious diseases or diseases that are spreading to new geographical areas. Re-emerging diseases are those that were easily controlled in the past, but which have developed anti-microbial resistance.' This definition of ERIDs is quoted from Andrew T. Price-Smith, *The Health of Nations*, Cambridge: MIT Press, 2002, p. 2.
3. Commission on Human Security, *Human Security Now*, New York, 2003, pp. 97–8.
4. Ibid.
5. See WHO Summary of Probable SARS Cases with Onset of Illness from 1 November 2002 to 31 July 2003 (based on data as of 31 December 2003). http://www.who.int/csr/sars/country/table2004_04_21/en. Accessed on 25 April 2004.
6. Joseph Fewsmith, 'China and Politics of SARS', *Current History*, vol. 122, no. 665, September 2003, p. 250.
7. Human coronaviruses cause up to 30 per cent of colds but they rarely cause lower respiratory tract disease. In contrast, coronaviruses cause devastating epizootics of respiratory or enteric disease in livestock and poultry. The SARS-associated Coronavirus (SARS-CoV) could have arisen as a mutant of a human coronavirus that acquired new virulence factors. For a detailed description, see, Kathryn V. Holmes, 'SARS-Associated Coronavirus', *New England Journal of Medicine*, vol. 348, no. 20, 15 May 2003, pp. 1948-51.
8. 'SARS: One Suspected Case Reported in China', www.who.int/csr/don/2004_04_22/en

9. The deceased 53-year-old woman, with the surname Wei, contracted the illness from her daughter—the second confirmed in case Anhui. The daughter, was a laboratory worker in Beijing, is in a stable condition. The mother, previously diagonsed as a suspected SARS case, died on 19 April. 'First 2004 SARS Death', 30 April 2004 [http://edition.cnn.com/2004/WORLD/asiapcf/04/30/china.sars/]
10. See WHO Summary of Probable SARS Cases with Onset of Illness from 1 November 2002 to 31 July 2003. http://www.who.int/csr/sars/country/table2004_04_21/en. Accessed on 25 April 2004.
11. B. Tomlinson and C. Cockram, 'SARS: Experience at Prince of Wales Hospital', *Lancet*, vol. 361, 2003, pp. 1486–7.
12. 'SARS: Lessons From a New Disease', *The World Health Report*, 2003, p. 74.
13. Ying-Hen Hsieh, C.W.S. Chen and S.B. Hsu, 'SARS Outbreak, Taiwan, 2003', *Emerging Infectious Disease*, vol. 10, no. 2, February 2004, p. 201.
14. Nosocomial infections are those that originate or occur in a hospital or hospital-like setting.
15. Center for Disease Control and Prevention, 'Update: Severe Acute Respiratory Syndrome—Toronto, Canada, 2003', *Morbidity Mortality Weekly Report* (*MMWR*), 13 June 2003, vol. 52, no. 23, 13 June 2003, pp. 547–50. URL<http://www.cdc.gov/mmwr/preview/mmwrhtml/mm5223a4.htm>
16. Mona R. Loutfy, et al., 'Hospital Preparedness and SARS', *Emerging Infectious Diseases*, vol. 10, no. 5, May 2004, p. 771. www.cdc.gov/eid
17. 'Singapore Deploys New Weaponry in SARS Battle ', *Reuters*, 16 April 2003.
18. 'SARS Spread: Singapore to Punish Violators', *The Hindu* (Chennai), 26 April 2003.
19. 'SARS in Singapore', 10 September 2003. http://www.who.int/csr/don/2003_09_10/en
20. 'SARS: India Back on List', *The Hindu*, 9 May 2003.
21. About the confusion and chaos, see R. Ramachandran, 'The SARS Confusion', *Frontline*, vol. 20, no. 10, 10–23 May 2003.
22. 'SARS Effect on Indo-ASEAN Trade Moderate', 2 May 2003. www.rediff.com/money/2003/may/02sars.htm
23. 'SARS a Threat to Indian Economy, says CII', http://www.rediff.com/money/2003/apr/12sars.htm
24. See Mehmood-ul-Hassan Khan, 'Global Comparative Study and Socio-economic Implications of SARS', 24 January 2004. http://usa.mediamonitors.net/content/view/full/4252
25. 'SARS Leaked from Bio-weapon Program', *The Age*, 1 May 2003. www.theage.com.au
26. 'SARS Virus could be China's Bio-weapon: Russian Expert', *Indian Express*, 12 April 2003.

27. Wei Jingsheng, 'SARS Tests Communist Rule in China', *International Herald Tribune*, 29 April 2003.
28. John LeBoutillier, 'SARS: Chinese Biowar Accident', Friday, 2 May 2003. http://www.newsmax.com
29. According to the theory of Panspermia, comets seeded life on the earth four billion years ago and living organisms like microboes continue to arrive on this planet. Towards the end of the nineteenth century this hypothesis on the origins of life gained currency, particularly after the suggestion by a Swedish chemist, S.A. Arrhenius, that life on earth arose from panspermia, micro-organisms or spores floated through space by radiation pressure from planet to planet or solar system to solar system.
30. 'SARS from the Stars?', *The Hindustan Times*, 9 May 2003. Also see for a detailed analysis, Ajay Lele, *Bio-Weapons: The Genie in the Bottle*, New Delhi: Lancer, 2004.
31. 'Scientist Sinks SARS Space Theory', http://www.news.com.au/
32. Zoonoses are responsible for most of the emerging infectious diseases, including Ebola virus, West Nile virus, monkey-pox and HIV. In the case of SARS Coronavirus (SARS-CoV), according to Malik Peiris of the University of Hong Kong, serological evidence indicates that the virus was spread through interspecies transmission from wild game markets in Guangdong, China.
33. 'SARS: Lessons from a New Disease', *The World Health Report*, 2003, p. 73.
34. Mely Caballero-Anthony, 'SARS: A Security Priority', http://www.ntu.edu.sg
35. For a detailed study, see, United States General Accounting Office (GAO), *Asian SARS Outbreak Challenged International and National Responses*, April 2004, pp. 28–9.

INVESTIGATION 2

Bird Flu

RESHMI KAZI

The recent bird flu pandemic is the worst in the medical history of the world. Within four months, avian influenza, commonly known as bird flu erupted twice in Asia. The killer disease left behind several people dead and a poultry population massacred by millions. It also gripped Asians in a panic that left them feeling vulnerable. This affects national security interests raising the threat of a biological conflict. The outbreak of bird flu in Asia necessitates the need to reassess our public health system.

The term 'influenza' was coined by the Italians during an epidemic in 1743. Avian influenza was first identified during an outbreak in Italy over a century ago. A highly pathogenic form of avian influenza known as fowl plague emerged in Italy around 1878. In 1889–90, Pfeiffer isolated Homophiles influenza and identified it as the causative agent of the pandemic.[1] In 1918–19 a severe influenza epidemic swept across the world and claimed an estimated 20 million lives. Investigations revealed that Pfeiffer's bacillus was the primary cause of the outbreak, though it could have been a secondary causative agent.[2] Medical virology made a breakthrough in 1933 when Smith, Andrews and Laidlauw isolated the influenza virus.[3] They reproduced the disease in ferrets by intranasal innoculation with bacteria free filtrates of nasopharyngeal secretions obtained from patients.

A notable advance was made in 1940 by Francis and Magill who independently isolated a serotype of the influenza virus, which was antigenitically unrelated to the strains known until then.[4] This was designated as type B influenza virus to distinguish it from the original serotype, identified as type A. In 1949, Taylor isolated a third serotype of the influenza virus, type C. The classification of the influenza virus into these three serotypes—A, B and C—is determined by the antigenic nature of the 'internal' or ribonucleoprotein antigen (RNA). In simplified terms, the influenza virus subtypes are divided into groups based on their differences in protein.

AETIOLOGY

Avian influenza is a highly contagious viral infection, which can affect all bird species. However, the poultry population is particularly susceptible. Influenza viruses are segmented, negative strand RNA viruses that belong to the *Orthomyxoviridae* family and are divided into three types as mentioned earlier.[5] Only influenza A viruses are reported to cause infections in birds. Type A influenza viruses are further divided into subtypes based on their antigenic relationships in the virus glycoproteins—haemagglutinin (HA) and neuraminidase (NA).[6] Today, fifteen HA subtypes (H1-H15) and nine neuraminidase subtypes (N1-N9) have been identified.[7] Each virus has one H and one N antigen in any combination.[8] The range of subtypes and combinations naturally occurring in mammals are restricted, but all subtypes and the majority of the possible combinations have been isolated from Asian species.

Influenza A viruses infecting poultry are divided into two distinct groups on the basis of their ability to cause disease: Highly Pathogenic Avian Influenza (HPAI) and Low Pathogenic Avian Influenza (LPAI). HPAI, the more virulent form of avian influenza is also known as 'fowl plague', and is one of the most dreaded diseases in poultry and other birds with flock mortality almost 100 per cent.[9] Besides, there may be economic devastation due to trade sanctions and embargoes placed on the infected regions. Worldwide, there have only been twenty-one reported primary isolates of such viruses from domestic poultry between 1999 and 2002.[10] An acute epidemic occurred in Italy in 1999–2000 causing 413 outbreaks with 16 million birds affected. So severe is the effect of bird flu that the World Organization for Animal Health (OIE) recognizes it as a list A disease.[11]

LPAI viruses cause a mild form of disease. Their pathogenecity is lower than the virulent HPAI. Clinical signs are far less evident or even absent and mortality rate is lower. Sometimes secondary infections or environmental conditions may cause exacerbation of LPAI infections leading to a more serious disease.[12] Evidence indicates that certain avian influenza virus subtypes of low pathogenicity may mutate into highly pathogenic virus strains after circulation for some time in a poultry population.

CLINICAL SYMPTOMS

The clinical symptoms of HPAI infection may vary from sudden death with little or no overt symptoms to a more characteristic disease with excessive lacumination sinusitis (uncomfortable swelling of sinus tissues), oedema of the head (swelling due to excess of watery fluid in the cavities and body tissues) and cyanosis of the unfettered skin (skin becoming loose and showing bluish symptom).[13] Respiration may be laboured in some cases. Other notable symptoms of HPAI in poultry include depression, loss of appetite, sudden cessation in egg laying, nervous signs, swelling and blue discoloration of combs and wattles due to disturbance in blood circulation, coughing, sneezing and profuse diarrhoea. At times, birds show signs of weakness and a staggering gait. Sick birds may sit or stand in a semi-comatose state with their heads touching the ground. The mortality rate may be 100 per cent depending on the species, the age, the virus type involved, and environmental factors like concurrent bacterial infections. Clinical signs of LPAI include primarily mild respiratory disease, depression and decrease of egg production in laying birds. The incubation period of these viruses range from as short as a few hours to three days in individual birds, and up to fourteen days to spread throughout the flock.[14]

Post-mortem findings of affected poultry populations vary considerably, but congestion and haemorrhage affecting the organs usually predominate. Necrotic foci may be found in the liver, lungs, spleen and kidneys.[15] There may also be exudates in the air sacs and peritoneum and occasionally a fibrinous pericardites.[16] When the disease afflicts adult laying birds, egg peritonitis may be a constant abnormality.

TRANSMISSION

The spread of avian influenza viruses is chiefly related to the excretion of high concentrations of virus in the faeces, salvia and nasal secretions of infected birds. The indications are that viruses of H5 or H7 subtype are initially introduced by feral birds as viruses of low virulence, which subsequently mutate and become virulent. Bird flu viruses are passed on to the poultry population through primary and secondary transmission.

PRIMARY TRANSMISSION

Available evidence reveals that the primary introduction of bird flu viruses into an area is effected by wild birds, usually waterfowl, but gulls and shorebirds also act as potential carriers. There is evidence of a higher prevalence of infection of poultry on migratory routes, e.g. Minnesota in the USA and Norfolk in England.[17] Chances of infection are higher in poultry living in exposed conditions such as turkeys on range and ducks on fattening fields. Such transmissions may not involve direct contact as the affected waterfowl may carry the viruses into an area and transmit to poultry by various mechanisms, e.g. mechanically through infective faeces and respiratory secretions. Surface water, used as potable water, may also be contaminated with influenza viruses and act as a source of infection. Although migratory waterfowl and other wild birds appear as a reservoir of bird flu, other possibilities should not be ruled out. There is, for example, a high probability that bird flu viruses may pass between pigs, turkeys and humans. Reports on the introduction of avian influenza virus of HINI subtype in turkey flocks by infected pigs are well documented.

SECONDARY TRANSMISSION

Secondary transmission of bird flu viruses occurs mainly by mechanical transfer of infected faeces, in which the virus may be present in high concentrations and may survive for considerable periods.[18] Birds or other animals that are not vulnerable to infection may become contaminated and spread the virus. Shared water or food may also become contaminated. However, man is the main source of secondary spread for domestic poultry. Several instances of HPAI infections confirm that the movement of caretakers, farm owners and staff, trucks and drivers moving birds or delivering food, visiting farms and artificial inseminators play a major role in the spread of avian influenza virus from farm to farm. The virus may be carried by contaminated equipment, vehicles, feed, cages or clothing—especially shoes—from farm to farm. The virus can be transmitted by the feet and bodies of animals, such as rodents, which act as a mechanical vector for spreading the disease. Flies can also act as mechanical vectors.

ZOONOTIC POTENTIAL

Avian influenza poses a serious risk to human health. It is a zoonotic illness—native to animal populations, but capable of being passed to humans by direct contact with infected birds. A number of conditions make transmission to humans likely such as poor sanitation of the chicken stalls in retail outlets, the presence of markets in proximity to living areas, the lack of central slaughtering facilities and the practice of slaughtering chickens at retail outlets. Direct human susceptibility to avian influenza occurs from the faeces of infected birds. People working in the poultry farms are in close proximity to infected birds increases. The risk of exposure to bird flu increases following the use of contaminated clothing, shoes and farming equipment by the staff.

Influenza viruses are highly unstable and tend to mutate rapidly. Studies have shown that mildly pathogenic viruses, if allowed to circulate for sometime in a poultry population, mutate into highly pathogenic viruses. There is deep concern in the medical fraternity and the World Health Organization (WHO) that the pathogen could adapt itself into new virus types associated with human-to-human transmission. The association of HPAI viruses with human viruses could facilitate the swapping of genetic material. The infection may then spread rapidly among humans resulting in an epidemic. The most severe flu pandemic in recent times was the 'Spanish Flu' outbreak. In 1918–19, the aquatic bird flu made its way to Kansas, where it spread rapidly among the US cavalry horses and soldiers. These troops were sent to Europe to fight in the First World War, but many arrived in the throes of a lethal disease. In just 18 months, the flu had claimed an estimated 40 to 50 million lives.

All type A influenza viruses, including those that regularly cause seasonal epidemics in humans, are genetically well adapted to elude host defences. This is due to the genetic instability of these viruses that enables them to undergo change in two different ways, viz., antigenic drift and antigenic shift. The former refers to small changes in the virus that occur over time because of the lack of efficient 'proof-reading' and error repairing mechanisms even as it replicates itself in human beings and animals.[19] As a result, the genetic composition of the virus changes, and the existing strain is replaced with a new antigenic variant which necessitates constant monitoring of the global situation and the development of influenza vaccines.

A second characteristic of influenza viruses is also a human health concern: influenza A viruses, including subtypes from different species, can swap or 'reassort' genetic materials and merge, which results in a new subtype different from the parent viruses. As populations have no immunity to the new subtype, and existing vaccines do not confer protection, this has caused highly lethal pandemics. Conditions favourable to human infection include humans living in close proximity to domestic poultry and pigs. Since pigs are susceptible to infection with both avian and mammalian viruses, including human strains, they may act as a 'mixing vessel' for the scrambling of genetic material from human and avian viruses, resulting in the creation of a new subtype.[20] The new virus may infect humans and cause person-to-person transmission. Recent evidence of direct transmission to humans in some fifteen avian subtypes indicates that humans may serve as a 'mixing vessel' as well.

During the last six years, avian influenza virus infections among humans have been detected on four occasions, with three different subtypes. In 1996, H7N7 virus was detected in England in the eye of a woman suffering from conjunctivitis who kept ducks. This virus was demonstrated to be genetically closest in all eight genes to viruses of avian origin. In May 1997, a virus of H5N1 subtype was isolated from a young child who died in Hong Kong, and by December of the same year, the virus was confirmed by isolation to have infected eighteen people, six of whom died. Evidence indicated limited human-to-human spread of this virus; hence the efficiency of transmission would have been extremely low.[21] What aroused attention, however, was that the viruses isolated from human cases appeared to be identical to those isolated from chickens in Hong Kong following an outbreak of a highly pathogenic disease in March 1997.

In recent years, outbreaks in poultry due to viruses of H9 subtype, usually H9N2, have been widespread. During the second half of the 1990s, outbreaks due to H9N2 subtype were reported in Germany, Italy, Ireland, South Africa, the US, Korea, China, the Middle East, Iran and Pakistan. In March 1999, H9N2 subtype was isolated independently from two girls aged 1 and 4 years who suffered from flu-like illnesses in Hong Kong. Subsequently, five isolations of H9N2 virus from humans were reported on mainland China in August 1999. The inference drawn was that the extremely high mortality, 6 out of 18, among people infected with H5N1 virus in Hong Kong was because the virus was capable of systemic inflection. These 18 patients manifested severe respiratory symptoms, and several of the dead were suffering from complicated medical conditions prior to infection; pneumonia appeared to be the main cause of death occurring as a result of infections with influenza viruses. The outbreak of the HPAI virus strain H7N7 in the Netherlands in February 2003 claimed the lives of 1 veterinarian, 83 poultry workers and 6 members of their families. In both the outbreaks in Hong Kong and the Netherlands in 1997, mild person-to-person transmission probably occurred, indicating the emergence of a new strain, but with limited human-to-human transmission potential.

The isolation of the H7N7 virus from the woman suffering from conjunctivitis in England was fortuitous; so was the first isolation of H5N7 in Hong Kong after the death of the patient, besides other isolates of avian viruses from humans that were due to enhanced awareness and surveillance exercises. In all these cases there was no evidence of human-to-human transmission, with the exception of infections with H5N1, which showed evidence of a very limited spread. This substantiated the finding that these viruses possessed all eight genes of avian origin.[22] It may well be that infection with avian influenza viruses among humans occurs more frequently than was originally assumed, but due to their limited effect go unrecognized. The main danger for the human population, is if persons infected with an 'avian' virus are simultaneously infected with a 'human' influenza virus. In such a situation a reassortment may occur resulting in the emergence of a virus fully capable of spreading within the human population, but with a surface protein (HA and/or NA), for which the human population is immunologically vulnerable. Although this is an extremely rare coincidence it could lead to the outbreak of a true influenza pandemic. Because of this possibility experts like Robert B. Webster have warned 'An influenza pandemic may be inevitable and probably imminent'.

OUTBREAK IN ASIA

Avian viruses have opportunities to mutate and become lethal for human beings, which is almost entirely based in the Chinese ecology, and has probably been true for more than 4,000 years. The reason can be found in the Chinese style of agriculture. It is estimated that the poultry population of eastern and southeastern parts of Asia runs into millions. Farms in China tend to be small scale family operations, packed densely, one adjoining another across vast spans of the nation. Farm animals are usually housed together and are allowed to roam during the day inside a small, shared canal or pen area, and are thus exposed to viruses carried by wild birds. Seasonal seeding of influenza viruses into backyard poultry systems by waterfowl migrating through the east and central Asian flyways (recognized migration routes from northern China/Siberia to South-East Asia and South and West Asia) allows a regular addition of new viruses to the diverse domestic poultry virus pool. Once high density commercial poultry flocks are affected, infection may spread rapidly within these units and the high quantities of virus produced may be easily carried to other units, humans and the environment. This transmission cycle may be described as virus shifting from 'the flyways to the highway and byways'.

INVESTIGATION AND CONTROL MEASURES

Avian influenza emerged in November 2003 when Thailand reported an outbreak of what it described as 'chicken cholera'. A month later, South Korea confirmed reports of avian flu. This was the onset of a deadly virus epidemic that eventually swept across Southeast Asia and created panic worldwide. Fifteen days later, Taiwan reported its first case on 31 December 2003 that later destroyed thousands of chickens suffering from a milder form of avian flu. With Vietnam reporting cases of bird flu in many of its poultry farms, panic spread. However, matters came to a head when, on 13 January 2003, the WHO confirmed that the deaths of three persons in Vietnam were linked to avian flu. The killer disease spread across Cambodia, Indonesia, Japan, Taiwan, Hong Kong, China and Laos devastating the poultry population. On 26 January 2004, Pakistan reported that 2 million chickens had died due to H7 and H9 subtypes. On the same day, Thailand confirmed the death of a 6-year-old boy, the first human victim. As he slipped into unconsciousness, Kaptan Boonmanuj, told his mother, 'Mum, my chest feels like it's going to explode.'[23] On 26 January, after being in coma for two weeks, Kaptan died in Bangkok's Siriraj Hospital. Incidentally, Kaptan, spent long hours everyday at his uncle's fighting-cock farm. He had contracted H5Ni, the most fatal subtype of avian flu. On 1 February, the WHO reported the death of two sisters in Vietnam following exposure to bird flu virus. Though preliminary investigations revealed that the virus could have been transmitted by their brother (who had earlier contracted the disease and had died) these speculations were ruled out. In the same month, the WHO confirmed that new genetic tests showed no evidence that the deadly bird flu was spreading through human-to-human transmission. By March 2004, there were confirmed outbreaks of bird flu in 10 Asian countries, killing 23 people in Vietnam and Thailand.

What is alarming is that there was an outbreak of avian flu in Asia after an interval of just four months. An important question is what led to this massive outbreak of bird flu virus in Asia? Geographical contiguity is a critical factor that led to the epidemic. Many scientists identified migratory wildfowl, which can carry numerous viruses without being affected, as responsible for the initial spread of the disease. Besides geography, other factors include transport of infected chickens across borders, both legally and illegally, and government inactivity despite mounting evidence of an avian flu outbreak. Factors such as ignorance about bird flu and its transmission, official reluctance to admit mistakes, insufficient money and manpower to implement measures and sheer incompetence further exacerbated the situation.[24] Together, these factors make the task of eradicating H5N1 virus difficult and expensive.

CONTROL AND ERADICATION STRATEGIES

The FAO and the WHO stated that avian flu could not be eradicated in the near future. The avian influenza virus spreads in domestic birds with a rapidity that makes it difficult to control, especially in the affected regions of Asia where there is a high concentration of poultry. According to them, the only way to contain the disease is mass culling or killing of the infected poultry. The agencies propose a method called ring isolation whereby infected poultry are identified and destroyed. Mass 'culling' quarantining and disinfecting infected farms are the only means for the effective control and eradication of the virus. During the 1997 outbreak, the entire poultry population of Hong Kong (about 1.5 million chickens and other birds) was culled in three days. Similarly, the outbreak in the Netherlands in 2003 led to the culling of 30 million birds within a week out of a total population of 100 million. In the recent campaign against the epidemic, more than 100 million poultry birds have been slaughtered.

The FAO has established an avian flu Technical Task Force, led by its Animal Health Service, to closely monitor the current situation in Asia, provide technical support to FAO's country representative offices for handling the crisis and facilitate communication between relevant international organizations, such as the OIE and the WHO. In addition, the FAO, the OIE and the WHO recommended several measures for controlling the avian flu virus.[25]

Awareness of the disease, early detection and notification of the disease.

Stamping out is the preferred control option for an outbreak of HPAI and should be applied to all flocks manifesting the clinical disease. The culled poultry should be safely disposed off.

Feed equipment and litter should be destroyed or treated to inactivate the virus.

Movement restrictions on affected farms and farms within a 10 km radius.

Recognizing that it may not always be desirable to proceed with massive culling in some situations, vaccination is considered a suitable option. The rationale underlying this is that vaccination reduces susceptibility to infection.

The 'Differentiation of Infected from Vaccinated Animals' (DIVA) strategy using a vaccine containing a heterologous neuraminidase is an effective tool for the control of infections in poultry.

The UN agencies advocate bio-security as an essential part of the control of avian influenza and recommend that it should be given adequate importance in devising control measures.

SARS *VS* AVIAN FLU

Is avian flu more deadly than the severe acute respiratory syndrome (SARS)? The WHO has declared that bird flu is potentially more dangerous than SARS. With a small genetic change, it could easily spread among humans around the world. In it worst form, it could mutate into a killer of the kind that claimed tens of millions of lives after the First World War. Although the symptoms of avian influenza are similar to SARS, completely different viruses cause bird flu. Avian influenza is more contagious and cannot be contained like SARS by isolating injected individuals. The mortality rate of H5N1 is higher than SARS—the pneumonia-like disease killed 1 in 10 of the 8,000 persons infected in the outbreak of 2002–3. What makes H5N1 so lethal, according to a study published in December 2002 by the Peireis team, is its ability to excite an almost suicidal response from the body's immune system.[26] The more the virus replicates, the more the body releases cytokines—small proteins that are triggers for increasing immune response and play a major role in inflammation.[27] As the virus proliferates, cytokines flood the bloodstream, causing massive self-injury to body tissues.[28] What is worrying experts is that if H5N1 crossbreeds with human influenza it would be transmissible from humans to humans by airborne droplets, driven by coughs and sneezes, which could eventually result in a human pandemic.

POSITION IN INDIA

It is curious that India escaped the spread of HPAI infection or infection by H5N1 or H9 and H7 subtypes, while Pakistan was affected. The possible reasons are that first, India does not fall in the migratory routes of waterfowl from the north. Second, Indian culinary practices do not include the consumption of wild and exotic birds. The livestock markets do not keep or sell such birds alongside domestic poultry. The Indian government was quick to respond to the prevailing epidemic. On 29 January, the centre issued a blanket ban on the import of all poultry and related processed foods from the affected countries.[29] According to Dr Hare Krishna Pradhan, Director of the High Security Animal Disease Laboratory (HSADL) in Bhopal, surveillance measures were put in place, particularly in states along the north-eastern and western borders. Even zoo officials exercised precautions. Following an order from the Zoo Authority of India, tigers were fed beef and pythons were given guinea pigs. In addition, a small functional laboratory was set up in Ghazipur mandi to test and isolate sick birds.[30] A strict vigilance was maintained on any illegal meatshop. The authorities paid visits to such establishments to monitor the health of the birds and workers.

The poultry population in India is very large (about 150 million) and, should avian flu strike, the results would be disastrous. The avian industry, which provides livelihood to thousands, would be devastated, leaving them on the brink of an economic disaster and crippling the economy seriously. According to T.S. Johri of the Central Avian Research Institute, Izatnagar, while the virus may be present in a dormant form in wild bird populations, no surveillance of migratory birds has been systematically conducted for avian influenza virus.[31] However, Dr Pradhan revealed that around 13,000–14,000 birds of all kinds were tested in 2003 and no bird flu virus was detected.[32] There have been occasional alarms as the one in 2003 where a suspected outbreak in Chandigarh was actually a bacterial infection. A mild strain, H9N7, was found in some poultry in a farm in north Gurgaon.

The chances of avian influenza virus spreading to India, argued A.R. Subba Rao, Chairman, Compound Live Stock Feed, Manufacturers Association, are remote as the country is self-sufficient in poultry products and does not import chicken, eggs or feed.[33] Moreover, in terms of technology, management and efficiency, the Indian poultry industry is well equipped to handle any eventuality. Adequate bio-security measures have been initiated at all levels. In addition, effective surveillance and vaccination measures are very much in place to contain any infection. This argument is strengthened by the fact that the 1997 bird flu epidemic in Hong Kong did not affect birds in India. The Asian outbreak of the highly pathogenic avian flu has emphasized the importance of promoting and strengthening veterinary research and animal husbandry in India.

CONCLUSION

Poultry is a vital source of food and income security in Asia, a fact borne out by the fact that the region has 200 million small farmers, who have between 10 to 100 birds in their farms. Avian influenza has wrecked the poultry industry. For WHO, the most worrisome aspect is the very high per cent (70) of fatalities.

Apart from spelling economic disaster, the crisis poses a grave threat to national security. At present, no vaccines have been developed to combat the highly pathogenic avian influenza. Vaccines can be made only from chicken eggs, though there is ongoing research on other possibilities. In 1995, the US National Institutes of Health and the WHO convened a meeting in Washington to find a solution to a 1918-type pandemic. The meeting concluded that, even if it was possible to identify a new virus and make seed stock for vaccine production promptly, it would take six months to produce millions of doses.[34] If production is done on a campaign basis in pharmaceutical plants all over the world, it would still be impossible to produce sufficient doses to protect more than a small percentage of the world's population. This is because there are so many live chicken eggs sitting in incubators under sterile conditions worldwide.[35] Even in non-pandemic years, the US did not possess sufficient vaccine doses. If avian flu becomes lethal for human beings and spreads globally, the moot question of who would have access to vaccines could well become a national security issue with affected nations helplessly looking for immunization while other populations survive. With the US already facing a shortage of vaccines, it would deny them even to its neighbours, Canada and Mexico—neither of whom has the capacity to produce bird flu vaccine. This could destabilize relations between these countries, proliferate illegal vaccine smuggling and increase long-standing animosities between the nations. The outbreak of a human pandemic in Canada and Mexico would also increase the risk potential of avian influenza viruses spreading back to the United States. Bird flu is an airborne disease and its virus type A mutate rapidly. With a slight reassortment in its genetic character, avian influenza could lead to an endemic disease through human-to-human transmission. If this were to be the future scenario in developed nations like the US, the condition of developing nations in Asia could be worse. In the South Asian region, if adequate steps are not undertaken promptly to prevent avian influenza from contaminating its troposphere, the result would be catastrophic. The lethal infection has already wreaked havoc in the poultry population in Vietnam, Thailand, Bangkok, South Korea and Pakistan. In the absence of an effective vaccine to combat avian flu, there is an extremely high possibility of outbreaks in South Asia.

Can the pandemic be averted? If Asia is to limit the epidemic and avoid another avian flu crisis, it has to change the current ways in which its poultry industry has developed and put into place new surveillance systems to detect animal diseases. The WHO and FAO officials have warned that the bird flu outbreak may not be contained and the possibility of a pandemic is on the cards. Constant surveillance and hard work could play a vital role in combating the avian influenza virus. This is one battle that Asia cannot afford to lose.

NOTES

1. Sudhir Gupta, 'Bird Flu Strikes', *Science Reporter*, vol. 41, no. 3, March 2004, p. 16.
2. Ibid.
3. Ibid.
4. Ibid.
5. 'Prelimimary Final Report/OIE Terrestrial Animal Health Standards Commission/December 2003', http://www.oie.int/eng/AVIAN_INFLUENZA/AHG_AI_Nov2003.pdf.
6. 'Classification of Influenza Viruses', http://www.avian-influenza.com/Disease/intro/classification.asp.
7. Dr Predeep Seth, 'Bird Flu', paper presented at the Dimensions of Science lecture series held on 25 February 2004, New Delhi.
8. Op. cit., n. 5.
9. R. Ramachandran, 'Avian Epidemic', *Frontline*, vol. 21, no. 4, 27 February 2004, p. 48.
10. N. Gopal Raj, 'Bird Flu Fears', *The Hindu*, 13 July 2004.
11. Avian Influenza', http://www.avian-influenza.com?Disease/AI_in_poultry?HPAI.asp
12. Op. cit., n. 5.
13. 'Highly Pathognenic Avian Influenza', http://www.oie.int/eng/normes/mmanual/A_00037.htm
14. 'Avian Influenza: A Few Facts', http://www.avian_influenza.com.binaries/95_60642.pdf
15. 'Avian Influenza', http://www.defra.gov.uk/diseases/notifiable/disease/avianinfluenza.htm
16. Ibid.
17. Op. cit., n. 5.
18. Ibid.
19. Op. cit., n. 9.
20. Ibid.
21. Op. cit., n. 5.
22. Ibid.
23. 'Is a Human Pandemic Next?', *Time*, vol. 163, no. 5, 9 February 2004, p. 15.
24. Ibid.
25. 'Animal Health Special Report: Technical Consultations', http://www.fao.org/ag/againto/subjects/en/health/diseases-cards/avian_recomm.html
26. 'Why 'Bird Flu' is more lethal than SARS', http://sify.com/printer-friendly,php?id=13372297&ctid=2&lid=1
27. Ibid.

28. Ibid.
29. Smita Mitra, 'Cock-a-doodle-flu', *Outlook*, vol. 44 no. 5, 9 February 2004, p. 51.
30. 'Delhi Measures to Prevent Bird Flu', *The Hindu*, 30 January 2004.
31. Op. cit., n. 9.
32. Ibid.
33. Amarnath K. Menon, 'Fowl Fear', *India Today*, vol. 29, no. 6, 16 February 2004, p. 70.
34. 'Can Bird Flu be Halted Before it Becomes a Global Epidemic?' http://www.khaleejtimes.com/Displayarticle.asp?xfile=data/editorial/2004/February/edtori. . . .
35. Ibid.

Biological Weapons: A Chronology

PRAFULLA KETKAR

Despite the proven effectiveness of the inadvertent spread of disease and the potential effectiveness of its deliberate use, many people believe that the use of biological weapons (BW) would be limited. On the other hand, some argue that biological agents may have been used more frequently than documented, though they may not have been employed in direct warfare. This controversy suggests that the secret use of biological agents for 'deliberate spreading of disease in humans, animals and plants by introducing living micro-organism into the victims', and the general ignorance about the utilization of such weapons makes the documentation on biological weapons use a Herculean task. Perhaps, this is the reason very few attempts have been made to record these events, but there is a general agreement among scholars that biological warfare is not new. This essay describes the episodes of biological warfare in a chronological manner and highlights the changes that have occurred in the use of bio-weapons in modern times.

ANCIENT PERIOD

Despite the absence of scientific knowledge about the causes of disease, there have been recorded attempts to employ biological weapons in warfare by poisoning the water supply or leaving diseased bodies in enemy areas.

600 BC

The two earliest recorded uses of biological weapons date back to the sixth century BC when the Assyrians poisoned enemy wells with rye ergot, and the Athenian lawgiver and poet Solon used the purgative herb, hellebore, during the siege of Krissa.

400 BC

Scythian archers infected their arrows by dipping them in decomposed bodies or in blood mixed with manure in 400 BC. Persian, Greek and Roman literature from 300 BC quotes examples of dead animals being used to contaminate wells and other sources of water.

184 BC

In the battle of Eurymedon in 184 BC, the Carthaginian leader Hannibal filled clay pots with poisonous snakes and instructed his soldiers to throw these pots onto the decks of enemy ships, which ensured a naval victory over King Eumenes II of Pergamon. There must have many such acts in this period, but they were not perceived as acts of bravery or valour.

MEDIEVAL PERIOD

Factual accounts of the use of disease in warfare during the Middle Ages are clear but not beyond doubt.

1155

During the battle of Tortona in the twelfth century AD, Barbarossa poisoned wells by contaminating them with corpses and decomposed bodies of soldiers. In 1155, in the battle of Tortona, he contaminated his enemy's water supply with corpses. Catapulting infected corpses into besieged cities was common place during the medieval period.

1340

In 1340, in Thun L'Eveque in Hainault (now northern France), the defenders reported that 'the stink in the air was so abominable that they no longer could endure it'. They negotiated a truce (and somewhat later abandoned the castle). The material used was carcasses of horses and other animals.

1346

In 1346–7, the Muslim Tatar, De Mussis, catapulted bubonic plague-infected corpses over the walls of Caffa on Russia's Black Sea in Crimea, causing an epidemic. The city surrendered and the defending Christian Genoese sailors fled to Italy. The attacking Tatar forces hurled plague-infected corpses into the city in an attempt to cause an epidemic in the enemy forces. Some historians believe that this was the cause of the plague epidemic that swept across medieval Europe claiming 25 million lives.

1422

During the siege of Karolstein in the Holy Roman Empire in 1422, soldiers' corpses and 2,000 cartloads of excrement were hurled at the enemy.

1485

Near Naples, the Spanish offered their French enemies wine laced with leprosy patients' blood. The objective was to transmit the disease.

In medieval medical theory, the stench of rotting organic material was believed to be a potent cause of disease. In the absence of scientific knowledge of disease however, their use was serendiptous. In two written records of these events, the victims interpreted the stench resulting from biological attack as the cause of subsequent disease. At least two (Thun L'Eveque and Caffa) instances of biological attacks appear to have been tactically successful. However, at times such techniques also failed. A case in point is that of Karolstein, where an outbreak of disease was attributed to a biological attack, but was more likely to be scurvy or some other deficiency disease. These three independent accounts attest to the medieval capacity to conceive of biological weaponry, and this form of warfare was occasionally employed.

MODERN TIMES

The modern history of biological warfare is well documented, though these agents were employed in a secretive manner. Smallpox is perhaps the most commonly and successfully used biological weapon in early modern times.

1500

Francisco Pizzaro of Spain is said to have presented variola contaminated clothing that led to the spread of smallpox among the South American natives.

1763

In retaliation against the attempt by native Indians to expel the British from Ottawa (popularly known as Pontiac's Rebellion), the commander-in-chief of the British forces, General Jeffrey Amherst, directed his subordinates to distribute smallpox infected blankets among the Indians as part of a peace offering. This led to the spread of smallpox among the Indian tribes, after which they no longer posed a threat to the British forces.

1863

During the US Civil War, biological agents were utilized by the Confederate forces during the Union campaign against Vicksburg by driving sick animals into ponds and shooting them. This polluted the water supply and provided some respite to the retreating armies.

1914–1918

The modern history of BW began in 1918 when Japanese set up a special section of its army (Unit 731) dedicated to BW. It was widely held at the time that 'Science and technology are the keys to winning the war and BW is the most cost effective.' The first modern attempt to use biological warfare was by the German army. Germany developed anthrax, glanders, cholera, and a wheat fungus specifically for use as biological weapons. They allegedly spread plague in St. Petersburg, Russia, infected mules with glanders in Mesopotamia, and attempted to infect the horses of the French Cavalry.

1925

After the First World War, the Geneva Protocol of 1925 was signed by 108 nations. This was the first multilateral agreement that extended the prohibition of chemical agents to biological agents. Unfortunately, no method for verification of compliance was addressed.

1931

Japan expanded its territory by annexing parts of Manchuria and Unit 731 moved in to secure 'an endless supply of human experiment materials'. Essentially all prisoners of war were available for Japan's BW experiments.

1939–1945

In 1941, Japanese planes sprayed bubonic plague over parts of China. At least five separate instances have been documented. In the following year, 'bacterial bombs' were deployed on mainland China, but these attacks were deemed to be ineffective. At this point, the United States became aware of the Japanese efforts and decided to launch its own programme. These acts were not the only atrocities committed. The Japanese released thousands of plague infested rats prior to their surrender, with unknown consequences. They also conducted tests on American POWs during the War. The US government was apparently aware of this but failed to take any action and did nothing (perhaps a worse atrocity).

Around this time Great Britain was engaged in developing a biological warfare programme. The reason for this was the fear that Germany and Japan would gain an advantage in this area. The programme focused on anthrax spores and their viability and 'range of spread' when delivered as a conventional bomb. The

Gruinard Island off the coast of Scotland was chosen as the site for testing. It was believed to be far away to prevent any contamination of the mainland; this later turned out to be false. The data obtained from these experiments was used by both Great Britain and the US to develop BWs that were better able to effectively disperse spores. A tragic consequence of this testing is that even today Gruinard Island is contaminated with *Bacillus anthracis* spores. The original method used for decontamination was to start a brush fire that burnt off the top of the soil and killed all traces of these organisms. Unfortunately, the spores had unexpectedly embedded themselves in the soil, so decontamination of the island was and still is impossible.

The US biological warfare programme started in 1942. With the acquisition of Japanese data and the increased tensions of the Cold War, the US programme accelerated and grew in size. In 1956 the former Soviet Union accused the US of using biological weapons in Korea, which led them to threaten the future use of chemical and biological weapons. This changed the focus of the US programme to a more defensive one. Before this, the bulk of the research was based at Ft. Detrick and used 'surrogate biological agents' to model more deadly organisms. Most of the offensive tests were based on 'secret spraying' of organisms over populated areas. This programme was terminated in 1969.

1950

The United States continued research on various offensive biological weapons during the 1950s and 1960s. From 1951 to 1954, harmless organisms were released off both coasts of the United States to demonstrate the vulnerability of American cities to biological attacks. This weakness was tested again in 1966 when a test substance was released into the New York City subway system.

1964

During the Vietnam War, Viet Cong guerrillas used needle-sharp punji sticks dipped in faeces to cause severe infections.

1972

The Biological and Toxic Weapons Convention opened for signature in 1972.

1974

The US finally ratified the 1928 Geneva Protocol.

1975

Indonesia annexed East Timor; planes spread herbicides on crop lands.

1978–1979

In 1978, the use of ricin as an assassination weapon in London was widely reported.

In 1979, an accidental release of anthrax from a weapons facility in Sverdlovsk, USSR, killed at least sixty-six people. The Russian government, however, claimed that these deaths were due to the consumption of infected meat, and steadfastly maintained this position till 1992, when Russian President Boris Yeltsin finally admitted to the accident.

Cuba accused the CIA of spreading swine fever virus that led to the death of 500,000 hogs. The *Washington Post* also reported on the US programme against Cuban agriculture since 1962, including the CIA biological warfare component.

A number of countries continued offensive biological weapons research. Since the 1980s, terrorist organizations have evinced an interest in using biological agents.

1981

The US accused Vietnam and its allies of using mycotoxins (fungal poisons) in Laos and Cambodia. Some refugees reported casualties; one analysis revealed 'yellow rain' to be faeces. Israel bombed the Iraqi nuclear reactor, leading to the Iraqi decision to develop chemical and biological weapons.

1984

In September and October 1984, 751 people were intentionally infected with *Salmonella*, an agent that causes food poisoning, when followers of Acharya Rajneesh contaminated restaurant salad bars in Oregon.

1985

Iraq launched an offensive biological weapons programme producing anthrax, botulinum toxin and aflatoxin. During Operation Desert Storm, the coalition of allied forces faced a threat from chemical and biological agents. Following the Persian Gulf War, Iraq disclosed that it had bombs, Scud missiles, 122-mm rockets and artillery shells armed with botulinum toxin, anthrax and aflatoxin. They also had spray tanks fitted to aircraft that could disperse agents over a specific target. Surprisingly, they did not use it during the second Gulf War.

1994

In 1994, a Japanese sect, Aum Shinrikyo cult, attempted an aerosolized release of anthrax from the tops of buildings in Tokyo and also from moving cars.

1995

Two members of a Minnesota militia group were convicted of being in possession of ricin, which they had produced for use in retaliation against local government officials.

1996

An Ohio man attempted to obtain bubonic plague cultures through the mail.

1997

Cuba accused the US of spraying crops with biological agents. These accusations were supported by the information provided by former US intelligence agents and various records made public under the Freedom of Information Act. The records revealed that the US launched biological warfare attacks against Cuba in 1962. According to William Blum, a former State Department official turned author, the US introduced a turkey virus on the island in 1962, killing thousands of birds and destroying Cuba's turkey industry. In 1971, the US allegedly unleashed an African swine fever epidemic forcing Cuba to destroy 500,000 pigs. In 1981, during the Reagan administration, Cuba was swept by a suspicious dengue fever epidemic, which quickly spread across the island, infecting over 300,000 people and killing 158, most of whom were children. All these accounts were made public in 1997.

Iraq expelled US citizens from the UN inspection teams which were allowed to continue their work without Americans. The US mobilized for military action. The Senate finally agreed to implement the Chemical Weapons Convention, with a provision that 'the President may deny a request to inspect any facility' on national security grounds.

1998

The US again mobilized for a bombing campaign against alleged Iraqi BC weapons sites, after Iraq questioned the role of a Gulf War veteran as UN inspector, and restricted inspectors access to presidential properties and security.

2001

Anthrax was delivered by mail to the US media and government offices. There were a total of 32 anthrax exposures, 4 deaths from inhalation infections, 3 cases of inhalation infections, and 7 cases of cutaneous anthrax.

2002

In December 2002, six terrorist suspects were arrested in Manchester, England; their apartment was used as a 'ricin laboratory'. Among them was a 27-year-old chemist who had produced the toxin. On 5 January 2003, British police raided two residences around London and found traces of ricin, which led to an investigation of a possible Chechen separatist plan to attack the Russian embassy with the toxin; this led to several arrests.

2004

On 3 February 2004, three US Senate office buildings were closed after ricin was found in the mailroom that serves as the office of the Senate Majority Leader Bill Frist.

MODERN BIO-WEAPONS: REAL WMDS?

Though the secret use of biological weapons to attack an adversary has been the purpose of biological weapons since times immemorial, there have been changes in the way these weapons are used and their ultimate result. First, many countries have undertaken systematic research to develop biological weapons and recent advances in microbiology and biotechnology have contributed to this process. Second, the systematic use of biological agents in a weapons system is a modern phenomenon which has aggravated the lethality of these weapons. The threat that biological agents could be used against military forces and civilian populations is more likely now than it was at any other time in history. The systemic delivery system has more or less resolved the dilemma of the attacker (employer of the weapons) being susceptible to the agents aimed at specific targets. Most importantly, the possibilities of non-state actors like terrorist organizations gaining access to these weapons as they are cheap and effective makes bio-weapons a real and potent weapon of mass destruction (WMD).

REFERENCES

Bhargava, Pushpa M., 'Biological Warfare, Bio-Terrorism, the World and Us', in *Terrorism in South Asia*, ed. A. Subramanyam Raju, New Delhi: India Research Press, 2004.

Bhushan, K. and G. Katyal, *Nuclear, Chemical and Biological Warfare*, New Delhi: A. P. H. Publishing Corporation, 2002.

Bioweapons: History. http://encyclopedia.thefreedictionary.com/Bioweapons accessed on 20 July 2004.

Chari, P.R. and Arpit Rajain, *Biological Weapons: Issues and Threats*, New Delhi: India Research Press, 2003.

Chronology of State Use and Biological and Chemical Weapons Control, Center for Non-proliferation Studies. http://cns.miis.edu/research/cbw/pastuse.htm accessed on 17 July 2004.

Couch, Dick, *The US Armed Forces Survival*, Manual, New York: Basic Books, 2003.

History of Biological Warfare. http://www.emedicinehealth.com/articles/15704-1.asp accessed on 18 July 2004.

Niman, Michael I., 'Is Cuba Evil?', *Art Voice*., http://mediastudy.com/articles/av5-23-2.html accessed on 17 July 2004.

Wheelis, Mark, *A Short History of Biological Warfare and Weapons*, University of California, Davis. http://microbiology.ucdavis.edu/faculty/mwheelis/BW_history.pdf accessed on 18 July 2004.

Bibliography

ARUN VISHWANATHAN

DOCUMENTS/TREATIES/AGREEMENTS

United Nations, *Convention on the Prohibition of the Development, Production and Stockpiling of Bacteriological (Biological) and Toxic Weapons and on Their Destruction*, General Assembly Resolution 2826 (XXVI), 16 December 1971. http://projects.sipri.se/cbw/docs/bw-btwc-text.html

———, *First Review Conference of the Parties to the Convention on the Prohibition of the Development, Production and Stockpiling of Bacteriological (Biological) and Toxin Weapons and on Their Destruction*, 3–21 March 1980, Final Declaration, BWC/CONF.I/10. http://projects.sipri.se/cbw/docs/bw-btwc-reviewconf-1.html.

———, *Ad hoc Group of the States Parties to the Convention on the Prohibition of the Development, Production and Stockpiling of Bacteriological (Biological) and Toxin Weapons and on Their Destruction: First Session*, 5 January 1995, Working Paper, BWC/AD HOC GROUP/WP. 2. http://www.bradford.ac.uk/acad/sbtwc/ahg28wp/wp002.pdf

———, *Ad hoc Group of the States Parties to the Convention on the Prohibition of the Development, Production and Stockpiling of Bacteriological (Biological) and Toxin Weapons and on Their Destruction: Second Session*, 6 January 1995, Report, BWC/AD HOC GROUP/3., http://www.bradford.ac.uk/acad/sbtwc/ahg27/doc03.pdf

———, *Procedural Report of the Ad hoc Group of the States Parties to the Convention on the Prohibition of the Development Production and Stockpiling of Bacteriological (Biological) and Toxin Weapons And on Their Destruction: Second Session*, BWC/AD HOC GROUP/28, 24 July 1995. http://www.bradford.ac.uk/acad/sbtwc/ahg28/doc28.pdf

———, *Ad hoc Group of the States Parties to the Convention on the Prohibition of the Development, Production and Stockpiling of Bacteriological (Biological) and Toxin Weapons and on Their Destruction: Second Session, Working Paper Submitted by* China: *Definitions for Some Terms Related to Measures Under Discussion for Strengthening the Convention on Biological Weapons*,

BWC/AD HOC GROUP/27, 20 July 1995. http://www.bradford.ac.uk/acad/sbtwc/2ndsesswp/doc27.pdf

United Nations, *Ad hoc Group of the States Parties to the Convention on the Prohibition of the Development, Production and Stockpiling of Bacteriological (Biological) and Toxin Weapons and on Their Destruction: Second Session, Working Paper Submitted by Brazil, France, Germany, Greece and the Russian Federation: Criteria for the Selection of Biological Agents to be Included in a List*, BWC/AD HOC GROUP/26, 19 July 1995. http://www.bradford.ac.uk/acad/sbtwc/2ndsesswp/doc26.pdf

———, *Ad hoc Group of the States Parties to the Convention on the Prohibition of the Development, Production and Stockpiling of Bacteriological (Biological) and Toxin Weapons and on Their Destruction: Second Session, Working Paper submitted by Sweden: Some Possible Elements in a Verification Protocol*, BWC/AD HOC GROUP/25, 14 July 1995. http://www.bradford.ac.uk/acad/sbtwc/2ndsesswp/doc25.pdf

———, *Ad hoc Group of the States Parties to the Convention on the Prohibition of the Development, Production and Stockpiling of Bacteriological (Biological) and Toxin Weapons and on Their Destruction: Second Session, Working Paper submitted by Japan: Japanese Cooperation in the Field of Biotechnology*, BWC/AD HOC GROUP/24, 13 July 1995. http://www.bradford.ac.uk/acad/sbtwc/2ndsesswp/doc24.pdf

———, *Ad hoc Group of the States Parties to the Convention on the Prohibition of the Development, Production and Stockpiling of Bacteriological (Biological) and Toxin Weapons and on Their Destruction: Second Session, Working Paper submitted by the United States of America: Discussion of Potential Article X Issues*, BWC/AD HOC GROUP/23, 13 July 1995. http://www.bradford.ac.uk/acad/sbtwc/2ndsesswp/doc23.pdf

———, *Ad hoc Group of the States Parties to the Convention on the Prohibition of the Development, Production and Stockpiling of Bacteriological (Biological) and Toxin Weapons and on Their Destruction: Second Session, Working Paper submitted by Brazil: Specific Measures for Implementation of Article X in the Context of a Compliance Regime for the BWC*, BWC/AD HOC GROUP/22, 13 July 1995. http://www.bradford.ac.uk/acad/sbtwc/2ndsesswp/doc22.pdf

———, *Ad hoc Group of the States Parties to the Convention on the Prohibition of the Development, Production and Stockpiling of Bacteriological (Biological) and Toxin Weapons and on Their Destruction: Second Session, Working Paper submitted by the United Kingdom: The Role and Objectives of Information Visits*, BWC/AD HOC GROUP/21, 13 July 1995. http://www.bradford.ac.uk/acad/sbtwc/2ndsesswp/doc21.pdf

———, *Ad hoc Group of the States Parties to the Convention on the Prohibition of the Development, Production and Stockpiling of Bacteriological (Biological) and Toxin Weapons and on Their Destruction: Second Session, Working*

Paper submitted by Portugal: Criteria and List of Animal Pathogens, BWC/AD HOC GROUP/20, 13 July 1995. http://www.bradford.ac.uk/acad/sbtwc/2ndsesswp/doc20.pdf

United Nations, *Ad hoc Group of the States Parties to the Convention on the Prohibition of the Development, Production and Stockpiling of Bacteriological (Biological) and Toxin Weapons and on Their Destruction: Second Session, Working Paper submitted by Brazil: List of Agents*, BWC/AD HOC GROUP/19, 17 July 1995. http://www.bradford.ac.uk/acad/sbtwc/2ndsesswp/doc19.pdf

———, *Ad hoc Group of the States Parties to the Convention on the Prohibition of the Development, Production and Stockpiling of Bacteriological (Biological) and Toxin Weapons and on Their Destruction: Second Session, Working Paper submitted by China: List of Biological Agents and Toxins*, BWC/AD HOC GROUP/18/Rev.1, 19 July 1995. http://www.bradford.ac.uk/acad/sbtwc/2ndsesswp/doc18r1.pdf

———, *Ad hoc Group of the States Parties to the Convention on the Prohibition of the Development, Production and Stockpiling of Bacteriological (Biological) and Toxin Weapons and on Their Destruction: Second Session, Working Paper submitted by China: List of Biological Agents and Toxins*, BWC/AD HOC GROUP/18, 17 July 1995, http://www.bradford.ac.uk/acad/sbtwc/2ndsesswp/doc18.pdf

———, *Ad hoc Group of the States Parties to the Convention on the Prohibition of the Development, Production and Stockpiling of Bacteriological (Biological) and Toxin Weapons and on Their Destruction: Second Session, Working Paper submitted by the Friend of the Chair on Compliance Measures: Declarations*, BWC/AD HOC GROUP/17, 13 July 1995. http://www.bradford.ac.uk/acad/sbtwc/2ndsesswp/doc17.pdf

———, *Ad hoc Group of the States Parties to the Convention on the Prohibition of the Development, Production and Stockpiling of Bacteriological (Biological) and Toxin Weapons and on Their Destruction: Second Session, Working Paper submitted by the Russian Federation: List of Biological Agents and Toxins*, BWC/AD HOC GROUP/16, 13 July 1995. http://www.bradford.ac.uk/acad/sbtwc/2ndsesswp/doc16.pdf

———, *Ad hoc Group of the States Parties to the Convention on the Prohibition of the Development, Production and Stockpiling of Bacteriological (Biological) and Toxin Weapons and on Their Destruction: Second Session, Working Paper submitted by the Russian Federation: Definition of Terms*, BWC/AD HOC GROUP/15, 11 July 1995. http://www.bradford.ac.uk/acad/sbtwc/2ndsesswp/doc15.pdf

———, *Ad hoc Group of the States Parties to the Convention on the Prohibition of the Development, Production and Stockpiling of Bacteriological (Biological) and Toxin Weapons and on Their Destruction: Second Session, Working Paper submitted by France and Germany: Working Document on Criteria and Lists of Agents to be Included in a Verification Protocol of the Convention on the Prohibition of Biological Weapons*, BWC/AD HOC GROUP/14, 17 July 1995. http://www.bradford.ac.uk/acad/sbtwc/2ndsesswp/doc14.pdf

United Nations, *Ad hoc Group of the States Parties to the Convention on the Prohibition of the Development, Production and Stockpiling of Bacteriological (Biological) and Toxin Weapons and on Their Destruction: Second Session, Working Paper submitted by France and Germany: Compilation of Questions for the Item 'Definitions of Terms and Objective Criteria'*, BWC/AD HOC GROUP/13, 10 July 1995. http://www.bradford.ac.uk/acad/sbtwc/2ndsesswp/doc13.pdf

———, *Ad hoc Group of the States Parties to the Convention on the Prohibition of the Development, Production and Stockpiling of Bacteriological (Biological) and Toxin Weapons and on Their Destruction: Second Session, Working Paper submitted by South Africa: The Application of Intrusive Measures On-site Inspections, Auditing, Sampling and Identification in Order to Strengthen the BWC*, BWC/AD HOC GROUP/12, 18 July 1995. http://www.bradford.ac.uk/acad/sbtwc/2ndsesswp/doc12.pdf

———, *Ad hoc Group of the States Parties to the Convention on the Prohibition of the Development, Production and Stockpiling of Bacteriological (Biological) and Toxin Weapons and on Their Destruction: Second Session, Working Paper submitted by South Africa: Investigation Alleged Use of Biological Weapons*, BWC/AD HOC GROUP/11/Add.1, 10 July 1995, http://www.bradford.ac.uk/acad/sbtwc/2ndsesswp/doc11a1.pdf

———, *Ad hoc Group of the States Parties to the Convention on the Prohibition of the Development, Production and Stockpiling of Bacteriological (Biological) and Toxin Weapons and on Their Destruction: Second Session, Working Paper submitted by Cuba: List of Equipment of Major Importance for the Convention*, BWC/AD HOC GROUP/10, 17 July 1995. http://www.bradford.ac.uk/acad/sbtwc/2ndsesswp/doc10.pdf

———, *Ad hoc Group of the States Parties to the Convention on the Prohibition of the Development, Production and Stockpiling of Bacteriological (Biological) and Toxin Weapons and on Their Destruction: Second Session, Working Paper submitted by Cuba: List of Biological and Toxin Agents of Major Importance for the Convention*, BWC/AD HOC GROUP/9, 17 July 1995. http://www.bradford.ac.uk/acad/sbtwc/2ndsesswp/doc09.pdf

———, *Ad hoc Group of the States Parties to the Convention on the Prohibition of the Development, Production and Stockpiling of Bacteriological (Biological) and Toxin Weapons and on Their Destruction: Second Session, Working Paper submitted by Cuba: Elements of a Possible Verification Regime in the Framework of the Convention on the Prohibition of the Development, Production and Stockpiling of Bacteriological (Biological) and Toxin Weapons and on Their Destruction (Convention on Biological Weapons)*, BWC/AD HOC GROUP/8, 9 July 1995. http://www.bradford.ac.uk/acad/sbtwc/2ndsesswp/doc08.pdf

United Nations, *Ad hoc Group of the States Parties to the Convention on the Prohibition of the Development, Production and Stockpiling of Bacteriological (Biological) and Toxin Weapons and on Their Destruction: Second Session, Working Paper submitted by United Kingdom, Programme of Work: Measures to Promote Compliance: Agenda*, BWC/AD HOC GROUP/7, 18 July 1995. http://www.bradford.ac.uk/acad/sbtwc/2ndsesswp/doc07.pdf

———, *Ad hoc Group of the States Parties to the Convention on the Prohibition of the Development, Production and Stockpiling of Bacteriological (Biological) and Toxin Weapons and on Their Destruction: Second Session, Working Paper submitted by The Netherlands: The Future Role of Confidence Building Measures (CBMs)*, BWC/AD HOC GROUP/6, 29 June 1995. http://www.bradford.ac.uk/acad/sbtwc/2ndsesswp/doc06.pdf

———, *Ad hoc Group of the States Parties to the Convention on the Prohibition of the Development, Production and Stockpiling of Bacteriological (Biological) and Toxin Weapons and on Their Destruction: Second Session, Working Paper submitted by The United Kingdom and Northern Ireland: Discussion Paper on Measures*, BWC/AD HOC GROUP/5, 29 June 1995. http://www.bradford.ac.uk/acad/sbtwc/2ndsesswp/doc05.pdf

———, *Ad hoc Group of the States Parties to the Convention on the Prohibition of the Development, Production and Stockpiling of Bacteriological (Biological) and Toxin Weapons and on Their Destruction: Second Session, Note submitted by the Secretariat*, BWC/AD HOC GROUP/4, 14 July 1995. http://www.bradford.ac.uk/acad/sbtwc/2ndsesswp/doc04.pdf

———, *Ad hoc Group of the States Parties to the Convention on the Prohibition of the Development, Production and Stockpiling of Bacteriological (Biological) and Toxin Weapons and on Their Destruction: Third Session, Working Paper submitted by Japan*, BWC/AD HOC GROUP/WP. 52, 8 December 1995. http://www.bradford.ac.uk/acad/sbtwc/ahg29wp/wp052.pdf

———, *Ad hoc Group of the States Parties to the Convention on the Prohibition of the Development, Production and Stockpiling of Bacteriological (Biological) and Toxin Weapons and on Their Destruction: Third Session, Working Paper submitted by Friend of the Chair on Definition and Objective Criteria*, BWC/AD HOC GROUP/WP. 51, 8 December 1995. http://www.bradford.ac.uk/acad/sbtwc/ahg29wp/wp051.pdf

———, *Ad hoc Group of the States Parties to the Convention on the Prohibition of the Development, Production and Stockpiling of Bacteriological (Biological) and Toxin Weapons and on Their Destruction: Third Session, Working Paper submitted by Friend of the Chair on Definition and Objective Criteria: Summary of Views on Definition and Threshold Quantities*, BWC/AD HOC GROUP/WP. 50/Rev.1, 8 December 1995. http://www.bradford.ac.uk/acad/sbtwc/ahg29wp/wp050r1.pdf

———, *Ad hoc Group of the States Parties to the Convention on the Prohibition of the Development, Production and Stockpiling of Bacteriological (Biological)*

and Toxin Weapons and on Their Destruction: Third Session, Working Paper submitted by Friend of the Chair on Definition and Objective Criteria: Summary of Views on Definition and Threshold Quantities, BWC/AD HOC GROUP/WP. 50, 8 December 1995. http://www.bradford.ac.uk/acad/sbtwc/ahg29wp/wp050.pdf

United Nations, *Ad hoc Group of the States Parties to the Convention on the Prohibition of the Development, Production and Stockpiling of Bacteriological (Biological) and Toxin Weapons and on Their Destruction: Third Session, Working Paper submitted by Friend of the Chair on Definition and Objective Criteria: Criteria for Plant Pathogens*, BWC/AD HOC GROUP/WP. 49, 7 December 1995. http://www.bradford.ac.uk/acad/sbtwc/ahg29wp/wp049.pdf

———, *Ad hoc Group of the States Parties to the Convention on the Prohibition of the Development, Production and Stockpiling of Bacteriological (Biological) and Toxin Weapons and on Their Destruction: Third Session, Working Paper submitted by Friend of the Chair on Definition and Objective Criteria: Criteria for Animal Pathogens*, BWC/AD HOC GROUP/WP. 48/Rev.1, 8 December 1995. http://www.bradford.ac.uk/acad/sbtwc/ahg29wp/wp048r1.pdf

———, *Ad hoc Group of the States Parties to the Convention on the Prohibition of the Development, Production and Stockpiling of Bacteriological (Biological) and Toxin Weapons and on Their Destruction: Third Session, Working Paper submitted by Friend of the Chair on Definition and Objective Criteria: Criteria for Animal Pathogens*, BWC/AD HOC GROUP/WP. 48, 7 December 1995. http://www.bradford.ac.uk/acad/sbtwc/ahg29wp/wp048.pdf

———, *Ad hoc Group of the States Parties to the Convention on the Prohibition of the Development, Production and Stockpiling of Bacteriological (Biological) and Toxin Weapons and on Their Destruction: Third Session, Working Paper submitted by Friend of the Chair on Article X*, BWC/AD HOC GROUP/WP. 47, 7 December 1995. http://www.bradford.ac.uk/acad/sbtwc/ahg29wp/wp047.pdf

———, *Ad hoc Group of the States Parties to the Convention on the Prohibition of the Development, Production and Stockpiling of Bacteriological (Biological) and Toxin Weapons and on Their Destruction: Third Session, Working Paper submitted by Japan: Protection of Intellectual Property Rights with Regard to Biotechnology*, BWC/AD HOC GROUP/WP. 46, 8 December 1995. http://www.bradford.ac.uk/acad/sbtwc/ahg29wp/wp046.pdf

———, *Ad hoc Group of the States Parties to the Convention on the Prohibition of the Development, Production and Stockpiling of Bacteriological (Biological) and Toxin Weapons and on Their Destruction: Third Session, Working Paper submitted by The Netherlands: Implementation of Article X of the BWTC*, BWC/AD HOC GROUP/WP. 45, 7 December 1995. http://www.bradford.ac.uk/acad/sbtwc/ahg29wp/wp045.pdf

United Nations, *Ad hoc Group of the States Parties to the Convention on the Prohibition of the Development, Production and Stockpiling of Bacteriological (Biological) and Toxin Weapons and on Their Destruction: Third Session, Working Paper submitted by The Islamic Republic of Iran: Animal Pathogens*, BWC/AD HOC GROUP/WP. 44, 7 December 1995. http://www.bradford.ac.uk/acad/sbtwc/ahg29wp/wp044.pdf

———, *Ad hoc Group of the States Parties to the Convention on the Prohibition of the Development, Production and Stockpiling of Bacteriological (Biological) and Toxin Weapons and on Their Destruction: Third Session, Working Paper submitted by* the *Friend of the Chair on Definitions and Objective Criteria: Types of Activity*, BWC/AD HOC GROUP/WP. 43, 6 December 1995. http://www.bradford.ac.uk/acad/sbtwc/ahg29wp/wp043.pdf

———, *Ad hoc Group of the States Parties to the Convention on the Prohibition of the Development, Production and Stockpiling of Bacteriological (Biological) and Toxin Weapons and on Their Destruction: Third Session, Working Paper submitted by The United Kingdom: The Role of Lists of Key Equipment in Measures*, BWC/AD HOC GROUP/WP. 42, 6 December 1995. http://www.bradford.ac.uk/acad/sbtwc/ahg29wp/wp042.pdf

———, *Ad hoc Group of the States Parties to the Convention on the Prohibition of the Development, Production and Stockpiling of Bacteriological (Biological) and Toxin Weapons and on Their Destruction: Third Session, Working Paper submitted by The United Kingdom: The Role of Quantitative Data in Measures to Promote Compliance with the BWTC*, BWC/A HOC GROUP/WP. 41, 5 December 1995. http://www.bradford.ac.uk/acad/sbtwc/ahg29wp/wp041.pdf

———, *Ad hoc Group of the States Parties to the Convention on the Prohibition of the Development, Production and Stockpiling of Bacteriological (Biological) and Toxin Weapons and on Their Destruction: Third Session, Working Paper submitted by The Islamic Republic of Iran: Threshold Quantities for Toxins*, BWC/AD HOC GROUP/WP. 40, 5 December 1995. http://www.bradford.ac.uk/acad/sbtwc/ahg29wp/wp040.pdf

———, *Ad hoc Group of the States Parties to the Convention on the Prohibition of the Development, Production and Stockpiling of Bacteriological (Biological) and Toxin Weapons and on Their Destruction: Third Session, Working Paper submitted by the Friend of the Chair on Definition of Terms and Objective Criteria: Human Pathogens*, BWC/AD HOC GROUP/WP. 39/Rev.l, 8 December 1995. http://www.bradford.ac.uk/acad/sbtwc/ahg29wp/wp039r1.pdf

———, *Ad hoc Group of the States Parties to the Convention on the Prohibition of the Development, Production and Stockpiling of Bacteriological (Biological) and Toxin Weapons and on Their Destruction: Third Session, Working Paper submitted by Friend of the Chair on Definition of Terms and Objective Criteria: Human Pathogens*, BWC/AD HOC GROUP/WP. 39, 5 December 1995. http://www.bradford.ac.uk/acad/sbtwc/ahg29wp/wp039.pdf

United Nations, *Ad hoc Group of the States Parties to the Convention on the Prohibition of the Development, Production and Stockpiling of Bacteriological (Biological) and Toxin Weapons and on Their Destruction: Third Session, Working Paper submitted by Friend of the Chair on Compliance Measures: Investigation of Alleged Use*, BWC/AD HOC GROUP/WP. 38, 5 December 1995. http://www.bradford.ac.uk/acad/sbtwc/ahg29wp/wp038.pdf

———, *Ad hoc Group of the States Parties to the Convention on the Prohibition of the Development, Production and Stockpiling of Bacteriological (Biological) and Toxin Weapons and on Their Destruction: Third Session, Working Paper submitted by Friend of the Chair on Compliance Measures: On-site Measures*, BWC/AD HOC GROUP/WP. 37, 5 December 1995. http://www.bradford.ac.uk/acad/sbtwc/ahg29wp/wp037.pdf

———, *Ad hoc Group of the States Parties to the Convention on the Prohibition of the Development, Production and Stockpiling of Bacteriological (Biological) and Toxin Weapons and on Their Destruction: Third Session, Working Paper submitted by Friend of the Chair on Compliance Measures: Declarations*, BWC/AD HOC GROUP/WP. 36, 5 December 1995, http://www.bradford.ac.uk/acad/sbtwc/ahg29wp/wp036.pdf

———, *Ad hoc Group of the States Parties to the Convention on the Prohibition of the Development, Production and Stockpiling of Bacteriological (Biological) and Toxin Weapons and on Their Destruction: Third Session, Working Paper submitted by Friend of the Chair on Confidence Building and Transparency Measures: Exchange Visits (Off-site)*, BWC/AD HOC GROUP/WP. 35/Rev. 2, 7 December 1995. http://www.bradford.ac.uk/acad/sbtwc/ahg29wp/wp035r2.pdf

———, *Ad hoc Group of the States Parties to the Convention on the Prohibition of the Development, Production and Stockpiling of Bacteriological (Biological) and Toxin Weapons and on Their Destruction: Third Session, Working Paper submitted by Friend of the Chair on Confidence Building and Transparency Measures: Exchange Visits (Off-site)*, BWC/AD HOC GROUP/WP. 35/Rev. 1, 5 December 1995. http://www.bradford.ac.uk/acad/sbtwc/ahg29wp/wp035r1.pdf

———, *Ad hoc Group of the States Parties to the Convention on the Prohibition of the Development, Production and Stockpiling of Bacteriological (Biological) and Toxin Weapons and on Their Destruction: Third Session, Working Paper submitted by Friend of the Chair on Confidence Building and Transparency Measures: Exchange Visits (Off-site)*, BWC/AD HOC GROUP/WP. 35, 5 December 1995. http://www.bradford.ac.uk/acad/sbtwc/ahg29wp/wp035.pdf

———, *Ad hoc Group of the States Parties to the Convention on the Prohibition of the Development, Production and Stockpiling of Bacteriological (Biological) and Toxin Weapons and on Their Destruction: Third Session, Proposal by Turkey: Definitions of Terms and Objective Criteria List of Biological Agents and Toxins*, BWC/AD HOC GROUP/WP, 5 December 1995. http://www.bradford.ac.uk/acad/sbtwc/ahg29wp/wp034.pdf

United Nations, *Ad hoc Group of the States Parties to the Convention on the Prohibition of the Development, Production and Stockpiling of Bacteriological (Biological) and Toxin Weapons and on Their Destruction: Third Session, Proposal by New Zealand: Criteria and Lists of Animal and Plant Pathogens to Support Specific Measures to Verify Compliance with the Biological Weapons Convention*, BWC/AD HOC GROUP/WP. 33, 4 December 1995. http://www.bradford.ac.uk/acad/sbtwc/ahg29wp/wp033.pdf

———, *Ad hoc Group of the States Parties to the Convention on the Prohibition of the Development, Production and Stockpiling of Bacteriological (Biological) and Toxin Weapons and on Their Destruction: Third Session, Working Paper submitted by Czech Republic: Czech Activities in the Field of Biotechnology*, BWC/AD HOC GROUP/WP. 32, 4 December 1995. http://www.bradford.ac.uk/acad/sbtwc/ahg29wp/wp032.pdf

———, *Ad hoc Group of the States Parties to the Convention on the Prohibition of the Development, Production and Stockpiling of Bacteriological (Biological) and Toxin Weapons and on Their Destruction: Third Session, Working Paper submitted by Friend of the Chair on Confidence Building and Transparency Measures: Exchange Visits—International Arrangements*, BWC/AD HOC GROUP/WP. 31/Rev. 3, 7 December 1995. http://www.bradford.ac.uk/acad/sbtwc/ahg29wp/wp031r3.pdf

———, *Ad hoc Group of the States Parties to the Convention on the Prohibition of the Development, Production and Stockpiling of Bacteriological (Biological) and Toxin Weapons and on Their Destruction: Third Session, Working Paper submitted by Friend of the Chair on Confidence Building and Transparency Measures: Exchange Visits—International Arrangements*, BWC/AD HOC GROUP/WP. 31/Rev.2, 5 December 1995. http://www.bradford.ac.uk/acad/sbtwc/ahg29wp/wp031r2.pdf

———, *Ad hoc Group of the States Parties to the Convention on the Prohibition of the Development, Production and Stockpiling of Bacteriological (Biological) and Toxin Weapons and on Their Destruction: Third Session, Working Paper submitted by Friend of the Chair on Confidence Building and Transparency Measures: Exchange Visits—International Arrangements*, BWC/AD HOC GROUP/WP. 31/Rev. 1, 5 December 1995. http://www.bradford.ac.uk/acad/sbtwc/ahg29wp/wp031r1.pdf

———, *Ad hoc Group of the States Parties to the Convention on the Prohibition of the Development, Production and Stockpiling of Bacteriological (Biological) and Toxin Weapons and on Their Destruction: Third Session, Working Paper submitted by Friend of the Chair on Confidence Building and Transparency Measures: Exchange Visits—International Arrangements*, BWC/AD HOC GROUP/WP. 31, 4 December 1995, http://www.bradford.ac.uk/acad/sbtwc/ahg29wp/wp031.pdf

United Nations, *Ad hoc Group of the States Parties to the Convention on the Prohibition of the Development, Production and Stockpiling of Bacteriological (Biological) and Toxin Weapons and on Their Destruction: Third Session, Working Paper submitted by Friend of the Chair on Confidence Building and Transparency Measures: Surveillance of Publications*, BWC/AD HOC GROUP/WP. 30/Rev. 2, 7 December 1995. http://www.bradford.ac.uk/acad/sbtwc/ahg29wp/wp030r2.pdf

———, *Ad hoc Group of the States Parties to the Convention on the Prohibition of the Development, Production and Stockpiling of Bacteriological (Biological) and Toxin Weapons and on Their Destruction: Third Session, Working Paper submitted by Friend of the Chair on Confidence Building and Transparency Measures: Surveillance of Publications*, BWC/AD HOC GROUP/WP. 30/Rev. 1, 5 December 1995. http://www.bradford.ac.uk/acad/sbtwc/ahg29wp/wp030r1.pdf

———, *Ad hoc Group of the States Parties to the Convention on the Prohibition of the Development, Production and Stockpiling of Bacteriological (Biological) and Toxin Weapons and on Their Destruction: Third Session, Working Paper submitted by Friend of the Chair on Confidence Building and Transparency Measures: Surveillance of Publications*, BWC/AD HOC GROUP/WP. 30, 4 December 1995. http://www.bradford.ac.uk/acad/sbtwc/ahg29wp/wp030.pdf

———, *Ad hoc Group of the States Parties to the Convention on the Prohibition of the Development, Production and Stockpiling of Bacteriological (Biological) and Toxin Weapons and on Their Destruction: Third Session, Working Paper submitted by Friend of the Chair on Confidence Building and Transparency Measures: Multilateral Information haring*, BWC/AD HOC GROUP/WP. 29, 4 December 1995. http://www.bradford.ac.uk/acad/sbtwc/ahg29wp/wp029.pdf

———, *Ad hoc Group of the States Parties to the Convention on the Prohibition of the Development, Production and Stockpiling of Bacteriological (Biological) and Toxin Weapons and on Their Destruction: Third Session, Working Paper submitted by Friend of the Chair on Confidence Building and Transparency Measures: Data on Transfers and Transfer Requests on Production*, BWC/AD HOC GROUP/WP. 28, 4 December 1995. http://www.bradford.ac.uk/acad/sbtwc/ahg29wp/wp028.pdf

———, *Ad hoc Group of the States Parties to the Convention on the Prohibition of the Development, Production and Stockpiling of Bacteriological (Biological) and Toxin Weapons and on Their Destruction: Third Session, Working Paper submitted by Friend of the Chair on Confidence Building and Transparency Measures: Surveillance of Legislation*, BWC/AD HOC GROUP/WP. 27, 4 December 1995. http://www.bradford.ac.uk/acad/sbtwc/ahg29wp/wp027.pdf

———, *Ad hoc Group of the States Parties to the Convention on the Prohibition of the Development, Production and Stockpiling of Bacteriological (Biological) and Toxin Weapons and on Their Destruction: Third Session, Working Paper submitted by Japan: BWC Definition: Lists of Biological Agents*, BWC/AD HOC GROUP/WP. 26, 4 December 1995. http://www.bradford.ac.uk/acad/sbtwc/ahg29wp/wp026.pdf

United Nations, *Ad hoc Group of the States Parties to the Convention on the Prohibition of the Development, Production and Stockpiling of Bacteriological (Biological) and Toxin Weapons and on Their Destruction: Third Session, Working Paper submitted by the United States: Computer Networking as a means of Strengthening the BWC*, BWC/AD HOC GROUP/WP. 25, 1 December 1995. http://www.bradford.ac.uk/acad/sbtwc/ahg29wp/wp025.pdf

———, *Ad hoc Group of the States Parties to the Convention on the Prohibition of the Development, Production and Stockpiling of Bacteriological (Biological) and Toxin Weapons and on Their Destruction: Third Session, Working Paper submitted by Brazil: Recent Trends in the Biology of Infectious Agents and Cooperation as an Element of the BWC Compliance Regime*, BWC/AD HOC GROUP/WP. 24, 1 December 1995. http://www.bradford.ac.uk/acad/sbtwc/ahg29wp/wp024.pdf

———, *Ad hoc Group of the States Parties to the Convention on the Prohibition of the Development, Production and Stockpiling of Bacteriological (Biological) and Toxin Weapons and on Their Destruction: Third Session, Working Paper submitted by Friend of the Chair on Article X: Informative Note Concerning Some Activities of Multilateral Cooperation in Areas Related to the BWC and Their Relevance for Cooperation under Article X of the BWC*, BWC/AD HOC GROUP/WP. 23, 30 November 1995. http://www.bradford.ac.uk/acad/sbtwc/ahg29wp/wp023.pdf

———, *Ad hoc Group of the States Parties to the Convention on the Prohibition of the Development, Production and Stockpiling of Bacteriological (Biological) and Toxin Weapons and on Their Destruction: Third Session, Working Paper submitted by Cuba: Elements for a Potential Verification Regime within the Framework of the BWC Convention*, BWC/AD HOC GROUP/WP. 22, 30 November 1995. http://www.bradford.ac.uk/acad/sbtwc/ahg29wp/wp022.pdf

———, *Ad hoc Group of the States Parties to the Convention on the Prohibition of the Development, Production and Stockpiling of Bacteriological (Biological) and Toxin Weapons and on Their Destruction: Third Session, Working Paper submitted by Cuba: Investigation on the Use or Alleged Use of Biological or Toxin Weapons Against a State Party to the Biological Weapons Convention*, BWC/AD HOC GROUP/WP. 21, 30 November 1995. http://www.bradford.ac.uk/acad/sbtwc/ahg29wp/wp021.pdf

———, *Ad hoc Group of the States Parties to the Convention on the Prohibition of the Development, Production and Stockpiling of Bacteriological (Biological)*

and Toxin Weapons and on Their Destruction: Third Session, Working Paper submitted by Friend of the Chair on Compliance Measures: Investigation of Alleged Use, BWC/AD HOC GROUP/WP. 20, 30 November 1995. http://www.bradford.ac.uk/acad/sbtwc/ahg29wp/wp020.pdf

United Nations, *Ad hoc Group of the States Parties to the Convention on the Prohibition of the Development, Production and Stockpiling of Bacteriological (Biological) and Toxin Weapons and on Their Destruction: Third Session, Working Paper submitted by France and Germany: Working Document on Genetically Modified Organisms (GMO)*, BWC/AD HOC GROUP/WP. 18, 30 November 1995. http://www.bradford.ac.uk/acad/sbtwc/ahg29wp/wp018.pdf

———, *Ad hoc Group of the States Parties to the Convention on the Prohibition of the Development, Production and Stockpiling of Bacteriological (Biological) and Toxin Weapons and on Their Destruction: Third Session, Working Paper submitted by Friend of the Chair for Compliance Measures: Proposed Revision of Paragraph 6 of FOC July Paper*, BWC/AD HOC GROUP/WP. 17, 30 November 1995. http://www.bradford.ac.uk/acad/sbtwc/ahg29wp/wp017.pdf

———, *Ad hoc Group of the States Parties to the Convention on the Prohibition of the Development, Production and Stockpiling of Bacteriological (Biological) and Toxin Weapons and on Their Destruction: Third Session, Working Paper submitted by South Africa: The Relationship Between Investigations of Alleged Use of BTW and Unusual Outbreaks of Disease and Challenge Inspections*, BWC/AD HOC GROUP/WP. 16, 29 November 1995. http://www.bradford.ac.uk/acad/sbtwc/ahg29wp/wp016.pdf

———, *Ad hoc Group of the States Parties to the Convention on the Prohibition of the Development, Production and Stockpiling of Bacteriological (Biological) and Toxin Weapons and on Their Destruction: Third Session, Working Paper submitted by Sweden: Short Notice On-site Information Visits and Inspections as Parts of a Verification Regime for the BTWC*, BWC/AD HOC GROUP/WP. 15, 29 November 1995. http://www.bradford.ac.uk/acad/sbtwc/ahg29wp/wp015.pdf

———, *Ad hoc Group of the States Parties to the Convention on the Prohibition of the Development, Production and Stockpiling of Bacteriological (Biological) and Toxin Weapons and on Their Destruction: Third Session, Discussion Paper submitted by Portugal: Overview of Some Epidemiological Factors Relevant to the Production and Use of Infectious Agents as Biological Weapons*, BWC/AD HOC GROUP/WP. 14, 29 November 1995. http://www.bradford.ac.uk/acad/sbtwc/ahg29wp/wp014.pdf

———, *Ad hoc Group of the States Parties to the Convention on the Prohibition of the Development, Production and Stockpiling of Bacteriological (Biological) and Toxin Weapons and on Their Destruction: Third Session, Working Paper submitted by Australia: Alleged Use Investigation—Authority to Trigger*,

BWC/AD HOC GROUP/WP. 13, 29 November 1995. http://www.bradford.ac.uk/acad/sbtwc/ahg29wp/wp013.pdf

United Nations, *Ad hoc Group of the States Parties to the Convention on the Prohibition of the Development, Production and Stockpiling of Bacteriological (Biological) and Toxin Weapons and on Their Destruction: Third Session, Working Paper submitted by Friend of the Chair on Compliance Measures: Declarations*, BWC/AD HOC GROUP/WP. 12, 29 November 1995. http://www.bradford.ac.uk/acad/sbtwc/ahg29wp/wp012.pdf

———, *Ad hoc Group of the States Parties to the Convention on the Prohibition of the Development, Production and Stockpiling of Bacteriological (Biological) and Toxin Weapons and on Their Destruction: Third Session, Working Paper submitted by South Africa: Use of Investigative Epidemiology as a Tool in the Investigation of Unusual Outbreak of Disease and Alleged Use of Biological Weapons*, BWC/AD HOC GROUP/WP. 11, 29 November 1995. http://www.bradford.ac.uk/acad/sbtwc/ahg29wp/wp011.pdf

———, *Ad hoc Group of the States Parties to the Convention on the Prohibition of the Development, Production and Stockpiling of Bacteriological (Biological) and Toxin Weapons and on Their Destruction: Third Session, Discussion Paper submitted by The Netherlands: The Relevance and Effectiveness of (Combinations of) Criteria for Declaration*, BWC/AD HOC GROUP/WP. 10, 28 November 1995. http://www.bradford.ac.uk/acad/sbtwc/ahg29wp/wp010.pdf

———, *Ad hoc Group of the States Parties to the Convention on the Prohibition of the Development, Production and Stockpiling of Bacteriological (Biological) and Toxin Weapons and on Their Destruction: Third Session, Discussion Paper submitted by France and Germany: Declarations in a BTWC-Verification Protocol*, BWC/AD HOC GROUP/WP. 9, 28 November 1995. http://www.bradford.ac.uk/acad/sbtwc/ahg29wp/wp009.pdf

———, *Ad hoc Group of the States Parties to the Convention on the Prohibition of the Development, Production and Stockpiling of Bacteriological (Biological) and Toxin Weapons and on Their Destruction: Third Session, Working Paper submitted by South Africa: Definition of Containment Facilities for Plant Pest Laboratories*, BWC/AD HOC GROUP/WP. 8/Corr.1, 29 November 1995. http://www.bradford.ac.uk/acad/sbtwc/ahg29wp/wp008c1.pdf

———, *Ad hoc Group of the States Parties to the Convention on the Prohibition of the Development, Production and Stockpiling of Bacteriological (Biological) and Toxin Weapons and on Their Destruction: Third Session, Working Paper submitted by South Africa: Definition of Containment Facilities for Plant Pest Laboratories*, BWC/AD HOC GROUP/WP. 8, 28 November 1995, http://www.bradford.ac.uk/acad/sbtwc/ahg29wp/wp008.pdf

———, *Ad hoc Group of the States Parties to the Convention on the Prohibition of the Development, Production and Stockpiling of Bacteriological (Biological)*

and Toxin Weapons and on Their Destruction: Third Session, Working Paper submitted by United Kingdom: BWC Article X: Areas of Biological Activity of Direct Relevance to the Convention, BWC/AD HOC GROUP/WP. 7, 28 November 1995. http://www.bradford.ac.uk/acad/sbtwc/ahg29wp/wp007.pdf

United Nations, *Ad hoc Group of the States Parties to the Convention on the Prohibition of the Development, Production and Stockpiling of Bacteriological (Biological) and Toxin Weapons and on Their Destruction: Third Session, Discussion Paper submitted by Canada: Declarations—List of Agents and Combinations of Criteria*, BWC/AD HOC GROUP/WP. 6, 28 November 1995. http://www.bradford.ac.uk/acad/sbtwc/ahg29wp/wp006.pdf

———, *Ad hoc Group of the States Parties to the Convention on the Prohibition of the Development, Production and Stockpiling of Bacteriological (Biological) and Toxin Weapons and on Their Destruction: Third Session, Ad Hoc Expert Group, Working Document submitted by Cuba: Rights and Obligations of the States Parties to the Convention on Biological and Toxinic Weapons within the Framework of the Economic and Technological Development and in the Field of International Cooperation and Assistance*, BWC/AD HOC GROUP/WP. 5, 28 November 1995. http://www.bradford.ac.uk/acad/sbtwc/ahg29wp/wp005.pdf

———, *Ad hoc Group of the States Parties to the Convention on the Prohibition of the Development, Production and Stockpiling of Bacteriological (Biological) and Toxin Weapons and on Their Destruction: Third Session, Ad Hoc Expert Group, Working Document submitted by Cuba: Some Elements Associated to the Promotion of Science and Technology with Peaceful Aims within the Framework of the Convention on Biological and Toxin Weapons*, BWC/AD HOC GROUP/WP. 4, 28 November 1995. http://www.bradford.ac.uk/acad/sbtwc/ahg29wp/wp004.pdf

———, *Ad hoc Group of the States Parties to the Convention on the Prohibition of the Development, Production and Stockpiling of Bacteriological (Biological) and Toxin Weapons and on Their Destruction: Third Session, Working Paper submitted by The United Kingdom: The Role of Containment in Facility Declarations Under the BTWC*, BWC/AD HOC GROUP/WP. 3, 27 November 1995. http://www.bradford.ac.uk/acad/sbtwc/ahg29wp/wp003.pdf

———, *Procedural Report and Rolling Text of the Ad hoc Group of the States Parties to the Convention on the Prohibition of the Development, Production and Stockpiling of Bacteriological (Biological) and Toxin Weapons and on Their Destruction: Third Session*, BWC/AD HOC GROUP/29*, 12 December 1995. http://www.bradford.ac.uk/acad/sbtwc/ahg29/doc29.pdf

———, *Ad hoc Group of the States Parties to the Convention on the Prohibition of the Development, Production and Stockpiling of Bacteriological (Biological)*

and Toxin Weapons and on Their Destruction: Fourth Session Working Papers 53–90, 15–26 July 1996. http://www.bradford.ac.uk/acad/sbtwc/adhocgrp/bw-adhocgrp. htm

United Nations, *Procedural Report and Rolling Text of the Ad hoc Group of the States Parties to the Convention on the Prohibition of the Development, Production and Stockpiling of Bacteriological (Biological) and Toxin Weapons and on Their Destruction: Fourth Session*, BWC/AD HOC GROUP/31, 26 July 1996. http://www.bradford.ac.uk/acad/sbtwc/ahg31/doc31.pdf

———, *Ad hoc Group of the States Parties to the Convention on the Prohibition of the Development, Production and Stockpiling of Bacteriological (Biological) and Toxin Weapons and on Their Destruction: Fifth Session, Working Papers 91–113*, 16–27 September 1996. http://www.bradford.ac.uk/acad/sbtwc/ahg32wp/ahg32wp. htm

———, *Procedural Report and Rolling Text of the Ad hoc Group of the States Parties to the Convention on the Prohibition of the Development, Production and Stockpiling of Bacteriological (Biological) and Toxin Weapons and on Their Destruction: Fifth Session*, BWC/AD HOC GROUP/32, 27 September 1996. http://www.bradford.ac.uk/acad/sbtwc/ahg32/doc32.pdf

———, *Ad hoc Group of the States Parties to the Convention on the Prohibition of the Development, Production and Stockpiling of Bacteriological (Biological) and Toxin Weapons and on Their Destruction: Sixth Session Working Papers 151–114*, 3–21 March 1997. http://www.bradford.ac.uk/acad/sbtwc/ahg34wp/ahg34wp. htm

———, *Procedural Report and Rolling Text of the Ad hoc Group of the States Parties to the Convention on the Prohibition of the Development, Production and Stockpiling of Bacteriological (Biological) and Toxin Weapons and on Their Destruction: Sixth Session*, BWC/AD HOC GROUP/34, 27 March 1997. http://www.bradford.ac.uk/acad/sbtwc/ahg34/doc34.pdf

———, *Ad hoc Group of the States Parties to the Convention on the Prohibition of the Development, Production and Stockpiling of Bacteriological (Biological) and Toxin Weapons and on Their Destruction: Seventh Session Working Papers 197–134*, 14 July–1 August 1997. http://www.bradford.ac.uk/acad/sbtwc/ahg36wp/ahg36wp. htm

———, *Procedural Report and Rolling Text of the Ad hoc Group of the States Parties to the Convention on the Prohibition of the Development, Production and Stockpiling of Bacteriological (Biological) and Toxin Weapons and on Their Destruction: Seventh Session*, BWC/AD HOC GROUP/36, 4 August 1997. http://www.bradford.ac.uk/acad/sbtwc/ahg36/doc36.pdf

———, *Ad hoc Group of the States Parties to the Convention on the Prohibition of the Development, Production and Stockpiling of Bacteriological (Biological) and Toxin Weapons and on Their Destruction: Eighth Session, Working Papers 232–182*, 15 September–3 October 1997. http://www.bradford.ac.uk/acad/sbtwc/ahg38wp/ahg38wp. htm

———, *Procedural Report of the Ad hoc Group of the States Parties to the*

Convention on the Prohibition of the Development, Production and Stockpiling of Bacteriological (Biological) and Toxin Weapons and on Their Destruction: Eighth Session, BWC/AD HOC GROUP/38, 6 October 1997. http://www.bradford.ac.uk/acad/sbtwc/ahg38/procrep. htm

United Nations, *List of Documents submitted at the Eighth Session of the Ad hoc Group of the States Parties to the Convention on the Prohibition of the Development, Production and Stockpiling of Bacteriological (Biological) and Toxin Weapons and on Their Destruction*. http://www.bradford.ac.uk/acad/sbtwc/ahg38/annex-3.htm

———, *Ad hoc Group of the States Parties to the Convention on the Prohibition of the Development, Production and Stockpiling of Bacteriological (Biological) and Toxin Weapons and on Their Destruction: Ninth Session, Working Papers 233–265*, 5–23 January 1998. http://www.bradford.ac.uk/acad/sbtwc/ahg39wp/ahg39wp. htm

———, *Procedural Report of the Ad hoc Group of the States Parties to the Convention on the Prohibition of the Development, Production and Stockpiling of Bacteriological (Biological) and Toxin Weapons and on Their Destruction: Ninth Session*, BWC/AD HOC GROUP/39, 2 February 1998. http://www.bradford.ac.uk/acad/sbtwc/ahg39/procrep. htm

———, *Ad hoc Group of the States Parties to the Convention on the Prohibition of the Development, Production and Stockpiling of Bacteriological (Biological) and Toxin Weapons and on Their Destruction: Tenth Session, Working Papers 237–274*, 9–13 March 1998. http://www.bradford.ac.uk/acad/sbtwc/ahg40wp/ahg40wp. htm

———, *Procedural Report and Outcome of Discussions of the Ad hoc Group of the States Parties to the Convention on the Prohibition of the Development, Production and Stockpiling of Bacteriological (Biological) and Toxin Weapons and on Their Destruction: Tenth Session*, BWC/AD HOC GROUP/40, 17 March 1998. http://www.bradford.ac.uk/acad/sbtwc/ahg40/1-15.htm

———, *Ad hoc Group of the States Parties to the Convention on the Prohibition of the Development, Production and Stockpiling of Bacteriological (Biological) and Toxin Weapons and on Their Destruction: Eleventh Session, Working Papers 275-296*, 22 June–10 July 1998. http://www.bradford.ac.uk/acad/sbtwc/ahg41wp/ahg41wp. htm

———, *Procedural Report of the Ad hoc Group of the States Parties to the Convention on the Prohibition of the Development, Production and Stockpiling of Bacteriological (Biological) and Toxin Weapons and on Their Destruction: Eleventh Session*, BWC/AD HOC GROUP/41, 16 July 1998. http://www.bradford.ac.uk/acad/sbtwc/ahg41/procrp41.htm

———, *Ad hoc Group of the States Parties to the Convention on the Prohibition of the Development, Production and Stockpiling of Bacteriological (Biological) and Toxin Weapons and on Their Destruction: Twelfth Session, Working*

Papers 297–324, 14 September–9 October 1998. http://www.bradford.ac.uk/acad/sbtwc/ahg43wp/ahg43wp. htm

United Nations, *Procedural Report of the Ad hoc Group of the States Parties to the Convention on the Prohibition of the Development, Production and Stockpiling of Bacteriological (Biological) and Toxin Weapons and on Their Destruction: Twelfth Session*, BWC/AD HOC GROUP/43, 15 October 1998. http://www.bradford.ac.uk/acad/sbtwc/ahg43/431-4.htm

———, *Ad hoc Group of the States Parties to the Convention on the Prohibition of the Development, Production and Stockpiling of Bacteriological (Biological) and Toxin Weapons and on Their Destruction: Thirteenth Session, Working Papers 325–352*, 4–22 January 1999. http://www.bradford.ac.uk/acad/sbtwc/ahg44wp/ahg44wp.htm

———, *Procedural Report of the Ad hoc Group of the States Parties to the Convention on the Prohibition of the Development, Production and Stockpiling of Bacteriological (Biological) and Toxin Weapons and on Their Destruction: Thirteenth Session*, BWC/AD HOC GROUP/44, 29 January 1999. http://www.bradford.ac.uk/acad/sbtwc/ahg44/doc44-1.pdf

———, *Ad hoc Group of the States Parties to the Convention on the Prohibition of the Development, Production and Stockpiling of Bacteriological (Biological) and Toxin Weapons and on Their Destruction: Fourteenth Session, Working Papers 353–365*, 29 March–9 April 1999. http://www.bradford.ac.uk/acad/sbtwc/adhocgrp/bw-adhocgrp. htm

———, *Procedural Report of the Ad hoc Group of the States Parties to the Convention on the Prohibition of the Development, Production and Stockpiling of Bacteriological (Biological) and Toxin Weapons and on Their Destruction: Fourteenth Session*, BWC/AD HOC GROUP/45, 14 April 1999. http://www.bradford.ac.uk/acad/sbtwc/ahg45/doc45-1.pdf

———, *Ad hoc Group of the States Parties to the Convention on the Prohibition of the Development, Production and Stockpiling of Bacteriological (Biological) and Toxin Weapons and on Their Destruction: Fifteenth Session Working Papers 356–396*, 28 June–23 July 1999. http://www.bradford.ac.uk/acad/sbtwc/ahg46wp/ahg46wp. htm

———, *Procedural Report of the Ad hoc Group of the States Parties to the Convention on the Prohibition of the Development, Production and Stockpiling of Bacteriological (Biological) and Toxin Weapons and on Their Destruction: Fifteenth Session*, BWC/AD HOC GROUP/46, 30 July 1999. http://www.bradford.ac.uk/acad/sbtwc/ahg46/doc46 1.pdf

———, *Ad hoc Group of the States Parties to the Convention on the Prohibition of the Development, Production and Stockpiling of Bacteriological (Biological) and Toxin Weapons and on Their Destruction: Sixteenth Session, Working Papers 397–407*, 13 September–8 October 1999. http://www.bradford.ac.uk/acad/sbtwc/ahg47wp/ahg47wp. htm

———, *Procedural Report of the Ad hoc Group of the States Parties to the*

Convention on the Prohibition of the Development, Production and Stockpiling of Bacteriological (Biological) and Toxin Weapons and on Their Destruction: Sixteenth Session, BWC/AD HOC GROUP/47, 20 October 1999. http://www.bradford.ac.uk/acad/sbtwc/ahg47/doc47-1.pdf

United Nations, *Ad hoc Group of the States Parties to the Convention on the Prohibition of the Development, Production and Stockpiling of Bacteriological (Biological) and Toxin Weapons and on Their Destruction: Seventeenth Session, Working Paper submitted by Norway: Explanations*, BWC/AD HOC GROUP/WP. 408, 30 November 1999. http://www.bradford.ac.uk/acad/sbtwc/ahg49wp/wp408.pdf

———, *Ad hoc Group of the States Parties to the Convention on the Prohibition of the Development, Production and Stockpiling of Bacteriological (Biological) and Toxin Weapons and on Their Destruction: Seventeenth Session, Working Paper submitted by Ukraine: Article III, Section D, Subsection I*, BWC/AD HOC GROUP/WP. 409, 6 December 1999. http://www.bradford.ac.uk/acad/sbtwc/ahg49wp/wp409.pdf

———, *Procedural Report of the Ad hoc Group of the States Parties to the Convention on the Prohibition of the Development, Production and Stockpiling of Bacteriological (Biological) and Toxin Weapons and on Their Destruction: Seventeenth Session*, BWC/AD HOC GROUP/49/Add.1, 10 December 1999. http://www.brad.ac.uk/acad/sbtwc/ahg49/ahg49add1.pdf

———, *Ad hoc Group of the States Parties to the Convention on the Prohibition of the Development, Production and Stockpiling of Bacteriological (Biological) and Toxin Weapons and on Their Destruction: Eighteenth Session, Working Paper submitted by Japan: Provisions Relating to Host State Party*, BWC/AD HOC GROUP/WP. 412, 20 January 2000. http://www.bradford.ac.uk/acad/sbtwc/ahg50wp/wp412.pdf

———, *Ad hoc Group of the States Parties to the Convention on the Prohibition of the Development, Production and Stockpiling of Bacteriological (Biological) and Toxin Weapons and on Their Destruction: Eighteenth Session, Working Paper submitted by Ukaraine: Proposal: Article II–Definitions*, BWC/AD HOC GROUP/WP. 411, 20 January 2000. http://www.bradford.ac.uk/acad/sbtwc/ahg50wp/wp411.pdf

———, *Procedural Report of the Ad hoc Group of the States Parties to the Convention on the Prohibition of the Development, Production and Stockpiling of Bacteriological (Biological) and Toxin Weapons and on Their Destruction: Eighteenth Session*, BWC/AD HOC GROUP/50, 11 February 2000. http://www.bradford.ac.uk/acad/sbtwc/ahg50/doc50-1.pdf

———, *Ad hoc Group of the States Parties to the Convention on the Prohibition of the Development, Production and Stockpiling of Bacteriological (Biological) and Toxin Weapons and on Their Destruction: Nineteenth Session Working Papers 413–415*, 13–31 March 2000. http://www.bradford.ac.uk/acad/sbtwc/ahg51wp/ahg51wp. htm

United Nations, *Procedural Report of the Ad hoc Group of the States Parties to the Convention on the Prohibition of the Development, Production and Stockpiling of Bacteriological (Biological) and Toxin Weapons and on Their Destruction: Nineteenth Session*, BWC/AD HOC GROUP/51, 6 April 2000. http://www.bradford.ac.uk/acad/sbtwc/ahg51/doc51-1.pdf

———, *Ad hoc Group of the States Parties to the Convention on the Prohibition of the Development, Production and Stockpiling of Bacteriological (Biological) and Toxin Weapons and on Their Destruction: Twentieth Session Working Papers 416–427*, 10 July–4 August 2000. http://www.bradford.ac.uk/acad/sbtwc/ahg52wp/ahg52wp. htm

———, *Procedural Report of the Ad hoc Group of the States Parties to the Convention on the Prohibition of the Development, Production and Stockpiling of Bacteriological (Biological) and Toxin Weapons and on Their Destruction: Twentieth Session*, BWC/AD HOC GROUP/52, 11 August 2000. http://www.bradford.ac.uk/acad/sbtwc/ahg52/doc52-1.pdf

———, *Ad hoc Group of the States Parties to the Convention on the Prohibition of the Development, Production and Stockpiling of Bacteriological (Biological) and Toxin Weapons and on Their Destruction: Twenty First Session, Working Papers 428–437*, 20 November–8 December 2000. http://www.bradford.ac.uk/acad/sbtwc/ahg54wp/ahg54wp. htm

———, *Procedural Report of the Ad hoc Group of the States Parties to the Convention on the Prohibition of the Development, Production and Stockpiling of Bacteriological (Biological) and Toxin Weapons and on Their Destruction: Twenty First Session*, BWC/AD HOC GROUP/54, 18 December 2000. http://www.bradford.ac.uk/acad/sbtwc/ahg54/doc54-1.pdf

———, *Ad hoc Group of the States Parties to the Convention on the Prohibition of the Development, Production and Stockpiling of Bacteriological (Biological) and Toxin Weapons and on Their Destruction: Twenty Second Session, Working Papers 438–444*, 12–23 February 2001. http://www.bradford.ac.uk/acad/sbtwc/ahg55wp/ahg55wp. htm

———, *Procedural Report of the Ad hoc Group of the States Parties to the Convention on the Prohibition of the Development, Production and Stockpiling of Bacteriological (Biological) and Toxin Weapons and on Their Destruction: Twenty Second Session*, BWC/AD HOC GROUP/55–1, 1 March 2001. http://www.bradford.ac.uk/acad/sbtwc/ahg55/doc55-1.pdf

———, *Ad hoc Group of the States Parties to the Convention on the Prohibition of the Development, Production and Stockpiling of Bacteriological (Biological) and Toxin Weapons and on Their Destruction: Twenty Third Session, Working Papers 445–454*, 23 April–11 May 2001. http://www.bradford.ac.uk/acad/sbtwc/ahg56wp/ahg56wp. htm

———, *Procedural Report of the Ad hoc Group of the States Parties to the Convention on the Prohibition of the Development, Production and Stockpiling of Bacteriological (Biological) and Toxin Weapons and on Their Destruction:*

Twenty Third Session, 18 May 2001. http://www.bradford.ac.uk/acad/sbtwc/ahg56/doc56-1.pdf

United Nations, Second *Review Conference of the Parties to the Convention on the Prohibition of the Development, Production and Stockpiling of Bacteriological (Biological) and Toxin Weapons and on Their Destruction*, 8–26 September 1986, Conference Documents. http://www.opbw.org/rev_cons/2rc.htm

———, Second *Review Conference of the Parties to the Convention on the Prohibition of the Development, Production and Stockpiling of Bacteriological (Biological) and Toxin Weapons and on Their Destruction*, 8–26 September 1986, Final Declaration, BWC/CONF.II/13/II. http://www.opbw.org/rev_cons/2rc/docs/final_dec/2RC%20Final%20Doc.pdf

———, *Third Review Conference of the Parties to the Convention on the Prohibition of the Development, Production and Stockpiling of Bacteriological (Biological) and Toxin Weapons and on Their Destruction*, 9–27 September 1991, Conference Documents. http://www.opbw.org/rev_cons/3rc.htm

———, *Third Review Conference of the Parties to the Convention on the Prohibition of the Development, Production and Stockpiling of Bacteriological (Biological) and Toxin Weapons and on Their Destruction*, 8–26 September 1986, Final Declaration, BWC/CONF.III/23. http://www.opbw.org/rev_cons/3rc/docs/final_dec/3RC%20Final%20Doc.pdf

———, *Fourth Review Conference of the Parties to the Convention on the Prohibition of the Development, Production, and Stockpiling of Bacteriological (Biological) and Toxin Weapons and on Their Destruction*, 25 November–6 December 1996, Conference Documents. http://www.opbw.org/rev_cons/4rc.htm

———, *Preparatory Committee for the Fourth Review Conference of the States Parties to the Convention on the Prohibition of the Development, Production and Stockpiling of Bacteriological (Biological) and Toxin Weapons and on Their Destruction*, BWC/CONF. IV/PC/2, 18 April 1996. http://www.opbw.org/rev_cons/4rc/docs/prep_com/IV-PC-3.pdf

———, *Report of the Preparatory Committee for the Fourth Review Conference of the Parties to the Convention on the Prohibition of the Development, Production and Stockpiling of Bacteriological (Biological) and Toxin Weapons and on Their Destruction*, BWC/CONF.IV/1, 1 November 1996. http://www.unog.ch/disarm/review/bannex42.htm.

———, *Fourth Review Conference of the Parties to the Convention on the Prohibition of the Development, Production and Stockpiling of Bacteriological (Biological) and Toxin Weapons and on Their Destruction*, 25 November–6 December 1996, Final Declaration, BWC/CONF.IV/9. http://www.unog/ch/disarm/review/biointro.htm

———, *Fifth Review Conference of the Parties to the Convention on the Prohibition of the Development, Production, and Stockpiling of Bacteriological (Biological)*

and Toxin Weapons and on Their Destruction, 7 December 2001–11–22 November 2002, Conference Documents. http://www.opbw.org/rev_cons/5rc.htm

United Nations, *Fifth Review Conference of the Parties to the Convention on the Prohibition of the Development, Production and Stockpiling of Bacteriological (Biological) and Toxin Weapons and on Their Destruction*, 7 December 2001–11–22 November 2002, Final Document, BWC/CONF.V/17. http://www.opbw.org/rev_cons/5rc/docs/final_dec/BWC-CONF.V-17-(final_doc).pdf

BOOKS

Alibek, Ken and Stephen Handelman, *Biohazard: The Chilling True Story of the Largest Covert Biological Weapons Program in the World—Told from Inside by the Man Who Ran It*, New York: Random House, 1990.

Atkinson, Rick, *Crusade: The Untold Story of the Persian Gulf War*, Boston: Houghton, Mifflin, 1993.

Bowman, Steve, ed., *Biological Weapons: A Primer*, New York: Novinka Books, 2001.

Bull, Hedley, *The Control of the Arms Race*, New York: Praeger for the Institute for Strategic Studies, 1961.

Bush, Vannevar, *Modern Arms and Free Men*, New York: Simon and Schuster, 1949.

Butler, Thomas, *Plague and Other Yersinia Infections*, New York: Plenum, 1983.

Cameron, Gavin, *Nuclear Terrorism: A Threat Assessment for the 21st Century*, New York: St. Martin's, 1999.

Carnegie Endowment for International Peace, *The Control of Chemical and Biological Weapons*, New York: Carnegie Endowment for International Peace, 1971.

Chari, P.R. and Arpit Rajain, eds., *Working Towards a Verification Protocol for Biological Weapons*, New Delhi: IPCS, 2001.

———, *Biological Weapons: Issues and Threats*, New Delhi: India Research Press, 2003.

Cole, Leonard A., *The Eleventh Plague: The Politics of Biological and Chemical Warfare*, New York: W.H. Freeman, 1996.

Cordesman, Anthony H., *Weapons of Mass Destruction in Iraq: A Summary of Biological, Chemical, Nuclear and Delivery Efforts and Capabilities*, Washington DC: Center for Strategic and International Studies, 1996.

Endicott, Stephen and Edward Hagerman, *The United States and Biological Warfare: Secrets from the Cold War and Korea*, Bloomington, IN: Indiana University Press, 1999.

Falkenrath, Richard A., Robert D. Newman and Bradley A. Thayer, *America's Achilles Heel: Nuclear, Biological, and Chemical Terrorism and Covert Attack*, Cambridge: MIT Press, 1998.

Fenner, Frank, Donald A. Henderson, Isao Arita, Zdnek Jezek and Ivan D. Ladnyi, *Smallpox and Its Eradication*, Geneva: World Health Organization, 1988.

Garrett, Laurie, *The Coming Plague: Newly Emerging Diseases in a World Out of Balance*, New York: Farrar, Strauss and Giroux, 1994.

Graham, L.R., *Science in Russia and the Soviet Union: A Short History*, Cambridge: Cambridge University Press, 1993.

Gurr, Nadine and Benjamin Cole, *The New Face of Terrorism: Threats from Weapons of Mass Destruction*, New York: I.B. Tauris & Co., 2000.

Haber, Fritz F., *The Poisonous Cloud: Chemical Warfare in the First World War*, Oxford: Clarendon Press, 1986.

Harris, Robert and Jeremy Paxman, *A Higher Form of Killing*, New York: Hill and Wang, 1982.

Harris, Sheldon H., *Factories of Death: Japanese Biological Warfare*, New York: Routledge, 1994.

Kaplan, David E. and Andrew Marshall, *The Cult at the End of the World*, New York: Crown Publishing, 1996.

Lavoy, Peter R., Scott D. Sagan and James J. Wirtz, eds., *Planning the Unthinkable: How New Powers will Use Nuclear, Biological, and Chemical Weapons*, Ithaca: Cornell University Press, 2000.

Lederberg, Joshua, ed., *Biological Weapons: Limiting the Threat*, Cambridge: MIT Press, 1999.

Manwaring, Max G., ed., *Deterrence in the 21st Century*, Portland: Frank Cass, 2001.

Miller, Judith, Stephen Engelberg and William Broad, *Germs: Biological Weapons and American Secret War*, New York: Simon and Schuster, 2001.

Mortimer, Edward A. Jr, *Vaccines*, Philadelphia: W.B. Saunders, 1994.

Murray, Williamson and Alan R. Millett, eds., *Military Innovation in the Interwar Period*, Cambridge: Cambridge University Press, 1996.

Pearson, Graham S. and Malcolm R. Dando, eds., *Strengthening the biological Weapons Convention: Key Points for the Fourth Review Conference*, University of Bradford, Department of Peace Studies, 1996. http://www.brad.ac.uk/acad/sbwtc

Pearson, Graham S. and Malcolm R. Dando, *The Fourth Review Conference of the Biological and Toxin Weapons Convention: Issues, Outcomes, and Unfinished Business*, March 1997.

Roberts, Brad, and Michael Moodie, *Combatting NBC Terrorism: An Agenda for Enhancing International Cooperation*, Alexandria, VA: Chemical and Biological Arms Control Institute, 1998.

Roberts, Brad ed., *Biological Weapons: Weapons of the Future?* Washington DC: Center for Strategic and International Studies, 1993.

———, *Hype or Reality: The 'New Terrorism' and Mass Casualty Attacks*, Alexandria, VA: Chemical and Biological Arms Control Institute, 2000.

———, *Terrorism with Chemical and Biological Weapons: Calibrating Risks and Responses*, Alexandria, VA: Chemical and Biological Arms Control Institute, 1997.

Robinson, Julian, Jeanne Gillemin and Matthew Meselson, 'Yellow Rain in Southeast Asia: The Story Collapses', in *Preventing a Biological Arms Race*, ed. Susan Wright, Cambridge: MIT Press, 1990.

Seagrave, Sterling, *Yellow Rain: A Journey Through the Terror of Chemical Warfare*, New York: M. Evans and Co., 1981.

Sims, Nicholas A., *The Diplomacy of Biological Disarmament*, New York: Plenum, 1983.

Stockholm International Peace Research Institute (SIPRI), *The Problem of Chemical and Biological Warfare: The Rise of CB Weapons*, 1, New York: Humanities Press, 1971.

Thranert, Oliver, ed., *Preventing the Proliferation of Weapons of Mass Destruction: What Role for Arms Control?*, Bonn: Friedrich-Ebert-Stiftung, 1999.

Tucker, Jonathan B., ed., *Toxic Terror: Assessing Terrorist Use of Chemical and Biological Weapons*, Cambridge: MIT Press, 2000.

———, *The Conduct of Challenge Inspections under the Chemical Weapons Convention*, Proceedings of an Expert Workshop, 29–31 May 2002, Washington DC: Monterey Institute of International Studies, 2002.

US Congress, Senate Committee on Human Resources, Subcommittee on Health and Scientific Research, *Biological Testing Involving Human Subjects by the Department of Defense, 1977: Hearings Before the Subcommittee on Health and Science Research of the United States Senate, 8 March and 23 May 1977*, 95th Congress, 1st Session, 1977, Washington DC: US Government Printing Office, 1977.

US Department of the Army, *US Army activity in the US Biological Warfare Programs, II, Annexes*, Washington DC: US Department of Army Publication, DTIC, B 193427 L, 1977.

Williams, Peter and David Wallace, *Unit 731: Japan's Secret Biological Warfare in World War II*, New York: Free Press, 1989.

Weiming, Zhu, ed., *Big Dictionary of Nuclear, Chemical and Biological Protection*, Shanghai: Shanghai Dictionary Publishing, 2000.

Witcover, Jules, *Sabotage at Black Tom: Imperial Germany's Secret War in America 1914–1917*, Chapel Hill, NC: Algonquin Books, 1989.

Wright, Susan, ed., *Biological Warfare and Disarmament: New Problems New Perspectives*, New Delhi: Vision Books, 2003.

Zilinskas, Ray, *Biological Warfare: Modern Offence and Defence*, Boulder: Lynne Rienner, 1999.

REPORTS

Abramova, Faina A., Lev M. Grinberg, Olga V. Yamposkaya and David H. Walker, '*Pathology of Inhalation Anthrax in 42 Cases from the Sverdlovsk Outbreak of 1979, Proceedings of the National Academy of Sciences of the United States of America*', 90, March 1993.

Cordesman, Anthony H., '*Defending America: Asymmetric and Terrorist Attacks with Radiological and Nuclear Weapons*', Center for Strategic and International Studies, 23 September 2001.

———, '*Defending America: Asymmetric and Terrorist Attacks with Chemical Weapons*', Center for Strategic and International Studies, 24 September 2001.

———, '*Defending America: Asymmetric and Terrorist Attacks with Biological Weapons*', Center for Strategic and International Studies, 24 September 2001.

Danzig, Richard, '*Biological Warfare: A Nation at Risk—A Time to Act,*' INSS Strategic Forum 58, Washington DC: National Defence University, Institute for National Strategic Studies, January 1996.

Ford, James L., '*Radiological Dispersal Devices: Assessing the Transnational Threat*', INSS Strategic Forum, 136, Washington DC: National Defense University, Institute for National Strategic Studies, March 1998.

Gill, Bates, '*Case Study 6: People's Republic of China, The Deterrence Series: Chemical and Biological Weapons and Deterrence*', Alexandria VA, Chemical and Biological Arms Control Institute, 1998.

Leitenberg, Milton, '*An Assessment of the Biological Weapons Threat to the United States*', White Paper prepared for Conference on Emerging Threats Assessment, Dartmouth College, Institute for Security Technology Studies, 7–9 July 2000.

Livingstone, Neil C. and Joseph D. Douglass, '*CBW: The Poor Man's Atom Bomb*', National Security Paper No. 1, Cambridge MA, Washington DC: Institute for Foreign Policy Analysis, 1984.

McCloud, Kimberly and Matthew Osborne, '*WMD Terrorism and Usama bin Laden*', Center for Non-proliferation Studies, 20 November 2001, http://cns.miis.edu/pubs/reports/binladen.htm

Moodie, Michael, Jonathan Ban, Catherine Manzi and Michael J. Powers, '*Bioterrorism in the United States: Threat, Preparedness, and Response*', Alexandria VA: Chemical and Biological Arms Control Institute, 2001.

Pate, Jason, Gary Ackerman and Kimberly McCloud, '*2000 WMD Terrorism Chronology: Incidents Involving Sub-national Actors and Chemical, Biological, Radiological, or Nuclear Materials*', Center for Non-proliferation Studies, 13 August 2001. http://cns.miis.edu/pubs/reports/cbrn2k.htm

Pearson, Graham S., '*Strengthening the Biological and Toxin Weapons Convention, Progress in Geneva*', *Quarterly Review*, no. 12, CBW Conventions Bulletin, no. 49, September 2000.

Smithson, Amy E. and Leslie-Anne Levy, '*Ataxia: The Chemical and Biological Threat and the US Response*', Report no. 35, Henry L. Stimson Center, October 2000.

Taylor, Henry H. and Jesse Orlansky, '*The Effects of Wearing Protective Chemical Warfare Combat Clothing on Human Performance*', Report no. P-2433, Alexandria, VA, Institute for Defence Analyses, 1991.

World Health Organization (WHO), *Health Aspects of Chemical and Biological Weapons*, Geneva, WHO, 1970.

ARTICLES

Adams, James, 'The Red Death: The Untold Story of Russia's Secret Biological Weapons', *Sunday Times*, 27 March 1994, Section 4, pp. 1–2.

Barletta, Michael, Amy Sands and Jonathan B. Trucker, 'Keeping track of Anthrax: The case for a Biosecurity Convention', *Bulletin of Atomic Scientists*, vol. 58, no. 3, May–June 2002, p. 61.

Baxter, R.R., Thomas Buergenthal, 'Legal Aspects of the Geneva Protocol of 1925', in *The Control of Chemical and Biological Weapons*, Carnegie Endowment for International Peace, New York: Carnegie Endowment for International Peace, 1971.

Betts, Richard K., 'The Threat of Mass Destruction', *Foreign Affairs*, vol. 77, no. 1, Jan.–Feb. 1998, pp. 26–41.

Beres, Louis Rene, 'Israel, the 'Peace Process', and Nuclear Terrorism; Recognising the Linkages', *Studies on Conflict and Terrorism*, vol. 21, no. 1, Jan.–Mar. 1998, pp. 59–86.

'Biological Weapons Convention Chronology', *Arms Control Reporter*, 30 March 1992, p. 701, B. 89.

'Bioweapons in the Former Soviet Union: An Interview with Dr. Kenneth Alibek', *Nonproliferation Review*, vol. 6, Spring–Summer 1999, pp. 2–3.

Black, Stephen, 'Investigating Iraq's Biological Weapons Program', *Biological Weapons—Limiting the Threat*, ed. Joshua Lederberg, Cambridge: MIT Press, 2001.

———, 'UNSCOM and the Iraqi Biological Weapons Program: Technical Success, Political Failure', in *Biological Warfare and Disarmament—New Problems and New Perspectives*, ed. Susan Wright, New Delhi: Vision Books, 2003.

Boyd, Kerry, 'US Army Obtains Patent for Bio-Weapons Launcher', *Arms Control Today*, vol. 33, no. 5, June 2003.

Bojtzov, Valentin and Erhard Geissler, 'Military Biology in the USSR, 1920-

1945', in *Biological and Toxic Weapons: Research, Development and Use from the Middle Ages to 1945*, ed. Erhard Geissler and John Ellis van Courtland Moon, Oxford: Oxford University Press for the Stockholm International Peace Research Institute, 1999.

Brachman, Philip S., 'Inhalation Anthrax', *Annals of the New York Academy of Science*, vol. 167, 1980, pp. 82-93.

Brachman, Philip S. and Arthur M. Friedlander, 'Anthrax', in *Vaccines*, ed. Stanley A. Mortimer Jr., Philadelphia: Saunders, 1994, pp. 729-39.

'Briefing Paper on the Status of Biological Weapons Proliferation: Fact Sheet', *Arms Control Today*, vol. 33, no. 4, May 2003.

Broad, William J., 'How Japan Germ Terror Alerted the World,' *New York Times*, 26 May 1998, pp. A1, A10.

Brugger, Seth, 'US Presents Alternatives to the BWC Protocol at Review Conference', *Arms Control Today*, vol. 31, no. 10, December 2001.

———, 'US says Cuba has Limited Germ Weapons Effort', *Arms Control Today*, vol. 32, no. 5, June 2002.

———, 'Tóth Issues Draft BWC Protocol, Reactions in Geneva Mixed', *Arms Control Today*, vol. 31, no. 4, May 2001.

———, 'No Breakthroughs at BWC Ad hoc Group Meeting', *Arms Control Today*, vol. 30, no. 2, March 2000.

———, 'US Names Countries Thought to be Violating BWC', *Arms Control Today*, vol. 31, no. 10, December 2001.

———, 'International Reaction to Secret US Bio-Weapons Research Muted', *Arms Control Today*, vol. 31, no. 8, October 2001.

Bunn, George and Fritz Steinhausler, 'Guarding Nuclear Reactors and Material from Terrorists and Thieves', *Arms Control Today*, vol. 31, no. 8, October 2001, pp. 8–12.

Cameron Gavin, 'WMD Terrorism in the United States: The Threat and Possible Countermeasures', *Nonproliferation Review*, vol. 7, no. 1, Spring 2000, pp. 162–79.

———, 'Multi-track Microproliferation: Lessons from Aum Shinrikyo and Al Qaida', *Studies in Conflict and Terrorism*, vol. 22, no. 4, November 1999, pp. 277–309.

Cameron, Gavin and Jason Pate, 'Covert Biological Weapons Attacks against Agricultural Targets: Assessing the Impact against US Agriculture', *Terrorism and Political Violence*, vol. 13, no. 3, Autumn 2001, pp. 61–82.

Cameron, Gavin, Jason Pate, Diana McCauley and Lindsay DeFazio, '1999 WMD Terrorism Chronology: Incidents involving Sub-national Actors and Chemical, Biological, Radiological, and Nuclear Materials', *Nonproliferation Review*, vol. 7, no. 2, Summer 2000, pp. 157–74.

Carus, W. Seth, 'Biological Warfare Threats in Perspective', *Critical Reviews in Microbiology*, vol. 24, no. 3, September 1998, pp. 149–55.

Carus, W. Seth, 'Unlawful Acquisition and Use of Biological Agents', in *Biological Weapons—Limiting the Threat*, ed. Joshua Lederberg, Cambridge: MIT Press, 2001.

Carter, Ashton, John Deutch and Philip Zelikow, 'Catastrophic Terrorism: Tackling the New Danger', *Foreign Affairs*, vol. 77, no. 6, November–December 1998, pp. 80–94.

Casagrande, Rocco, 'Biological Terrorism Targeted at Agriculture: The Threat to US National Security', *Nonproliferation Review*, vol. 7, no. 3, Fall–Winter 2000, pp. 92–105.

Cavanaugh, Dan C., et al., 'Plague Immunisation', *Journal of Infectious Diseases*, vol. 129, 1974, pp. S37–S40.

Chari, P.R. and Giri Deshingkar, 'India: Straddling East and West', in *Biological Warfare and Disarmament—New Problems and New Perspectives*, ed. Susan Wright, New Delhi: Vision Books, 2003.

Chester, C.V. and G.P. Zimmerman, 'Civil Defence Implications of Biological Weapons', *Journal of Civil Defence*, vol. 17, no. 6, December 1984, pp. 6–12.

Chittaranjan, Kalpana, 'Biological Weapons: An Insidious WMD', *Strategic Analysis*, vol. 22, no. 9, December 1998, pp. 1428–31.

———, 'The BWC: A Status Report,' *Strategic Analysis*, vol. 25, no. 2, May 2001, pp. 215–25.

———, 'Verification Protocol: A must for BWC Effectiveness', *Strategic Analysis*, vol. 23, no. 6, September 1999, pp. 947–65.

Christopher, George W., et al., 'Biological Warfare: A Historical Perspective', in *Biological Weapons—Limiting the Threat*, ed. Joshua Lederberg, Cambridge: MIT Press, 2001.

Chyba, Christopher F., 'Biological Terrorism and Public Health', *Survival* vol. 43, no. 1, Spring 2001, pp. 93–106.

Cohen, Anver, 'Israel: Reconstructing a Black Box', in *Biological Warfare and Disarmament—New Problems and New Perspectives*, ed. Susan Wright, New Delhi: Vision Books, 2003.

Cohen, William S., 'Foreword', in *Biological Weapons—Limiting the Threat*, ed. Joshua Lederberg, Cambridge: MIT Press, 2001.

Danzig, Richard and Pamela B. Berkowsky, 'Why Should we be Concerned about Biological Warfare', in *Biological Weapons—Limiting the Threat*, ed. Joshua Lederberg, Cambridge: MIT Press, 2001.

Dashiell, Thomas, 'A Review of US Biological Warfare Policies', in *Biological Weapons: Weapons of the Future?* ed. Roberts Brad, Washington DC: Center for Strategic and International Studies, 1993.

Derbes, Vincent J., 'De Mussi and the Great Plague of 1348: A Forgotten Episode of Bacteriological War', *Journal of American Medical Association (JAMA)*, vol. 196, no. 1, 4 April 1966, pp. 59–62.

Dhar, Biswajit, 'The Global Patent Regime: Implementing Article X', in

Biological Warfare and Disarmament—New Problems and New Perspectives, ed. Susan Wright, New Delhi: Vision Books, 2003.

Dixon, M.F., 'Smallpox Vaccination', *British Medical Journal*, vol. 2, no. 708, 30 May 1970, p. 539.

Drake, Laura, 'The Middle East: Integrated Regional Approaches to Arms Control and Disarmament', in *Biological Warfare and Disarmament—New Problems and New Perspectives*, ed. Susan Wright, New Delhi: Vision Books, 2003.

Dutz, Werner and Elfriede Kohout, 'Anthrax', *Pathology Annual*, vol. 6, 1971, pp. 209–48.

Falk, Richard, 'The Challenges of Biological Weaponry: A Twenty-First Century Assessment', in *Biological Warfare and Disarmament—New Problems and New Perspectives*, ed. Susan Wright, New Delhi: Vision Books, 2003.

Falkenrath, Richard A., 'Confronting Nuclear, Biological and Chemical Terrorism', *Survival*, vol. 40, no. 3, Autumn 1998, pp. 43–65.

Farmer III, J.J., Betty R. Davis, P.A.D. Grimot and F. Grimont, 'Source of American *Serratia*', *Lancet*, vol. 2, 27 August 1977, p. 459.

Ferguson, James R., 'Biological Weapons and US Law', in *Biological Weapons—Limiting the Threat*, ed. Joshua Lederberg, Cambridge: MIT Press, 2001.

Ferrante, Mark A. and Mathew J. Dolan, 'Q fever Meningoecephalitis in a Soldier returning from the Persian Gulf War', *Clinical Infectious Diseases*, vol. 16, 1993, pp. 489–96.

Ford, Peter, 'US Diplomatic Might Irks Nations', *Christian Science Monitor*, 24 April 2002.

Foxell, Joseph W., 'Current Trends in Agroterrorism, Antilivestock, Anticrop, and Antisoil Bioagricultural Terrorism and Their Potential Impact on Food Security', *Studies in Conflict and Terrorism*, vol. 24, no. 2, April 2001, pp. 107–29.

———, 'The Debate on the Potential for Mass-Casualty Terrorism: The Challenge to US Security', *Terrorism and Political Violence*, vol. 11, no. 1, Spring 1999 pp. 94–109.

Franz, David R., et al., 'Clinical Recognition and Management of Patients Exposed to Biological Warfare Agents', in *Biological Weapons—Limiting the Threat*, ed. Joshua Lederberg, Cambridge: MIT Press, 2001.

Friedlander, Arthur M., Susan L. Welkos and Louise M. Pitt, 'Postexposure Prophylaxis against Experimental Inhalation Anthrax', *Journal of Infectious Diseases*, vol. 167, 1993, pp. 1239–43.

Franz, David R., Cheryl D. Parrott and Ernest T. Takafuji, 'The US Biological Warfare and Biological Defense Programs', in Zajtchuk, *Textbook of Military Medicine*, pp. 425–36.

Garrett, Laurie, 'The Nightmare of Bioterrorism', *Foreign Affairs*, vol. 80, no. 1, January–February 2001, pp. 76–89.

Gill, D.M., 'Bacterial Toxins: A Table of Lethal Amounts', *Microbiology Review*, March 1982, pp. 86–94.

Goldstein, Lyle, 'Saddam's Biological Warfare Card', *The Washington Post*, 11 October 1966, p. A24.

Gotuzzo, Eduardo, Graciela S. Alarcon and Tomas S. Bocanegra, 'Articular Involvement in Human Brucellosis', *Seminars in Arthritis and Rheumatism*, vol. 12, 1982, pp. 245–55.

Gressang, Daniel S., 'Audience and Message: Assessing Terrorist WMD Potential', *Terrorism and Political Violence*, vol. 13, no. 3, Autumn 2001, pp. 83–106.

Graham, Bradley, 'Military Chiefs Back Anthrax Inoculations: Initiative would Affect All of Nation's Forces', *The Washington Post*, 2 October 1996, p. A1.

Harris, Sheldon H., 'Japanese Biological Warfare Research on Humans: A Case Study of Microbiology and Ethics', in *The Microbiologist and Biological Defence Research: Ethics, Politics, and International Security*, ed. Raymond A. Zilinskas, *Annals of the New York Academy of Science*, no. 666, 31 December 1992, pp. 21–52.

Holloway, Harry C., et al., 'The Threat of Biological Weapons: Prophylaxis and Mitigation of Psychological and Social Consequences', in *Biological Weapons—Limiting the Threat*, ed. Joshua Lederberg, Cambridge: MIT Press, 2001.

Hugh-Jones, Martin, 'Wickham Steed and German Biological Warfare Research', *Intelligence and National Security*, vol. 7, no. 4, October 1992, pp. 379–402.

Huxsoll, David L., Cheryl D. Parrott and William C. Patrick III, 'Medicine in Defence against Biological Warfare', *Journal of the American Medical Association (JAMA)*, vol. 262, no. 5, 4 August 1989, pp. 677–9.

Jacobs, Stanley S., 'The Nuclear Threat as a Terrorist Option', *Terrorism and Political Violence*, vol. 10, no. 4, Winter 1998, pp. 149–63.

Jenkins, Brian, 'The Limits of Terror: Constraints on the Escalation of Violence', *Harvard International Review*, vol. 17, no. 3, Summer 1995, pp. 44–6.

Kaplan, David E., 'Terrorism's Next Wave: Nerve Gas and Germs are the New Weapons of Choice', *US New and World Report*, 17 November 1997, p. 28.

Kadivar, H. and S.C. Adams, 'Treatement of Chemical and Biological Warfare Injuries: Insights Derived from the 1984 Iraqi Attack on Majnoon Island', *Military Medicine*, vol. 156, 1991, pp. 171–7.

Kadlec, Robert P., Allan P. Zelicoff and Ann M. Vrtis, 'Biological Weapons Control: Prospects and Implications for the Future', in *Biological Weapons—Limiting the Threat*, ed. Joshua Lederberg, Cambridge: MIT Press, 2001.

Kadlec, Robert P., 'First, do No Harm', *Arms Control Today*, vol. 31 no. 4, May 2001.

Kamp, Karl-Heinz, et al., 'WMD Terrorism: An Exchange,' *Survival*, 40, no. 4, Winter 1998-99, pp. 168–83.

Keeney, Spurgeon M., 'Tokyo Terror and Chemical Arms Control', *Arms Control Today*, 25 April 1995.

Kolavic, Shellie A., et al., 'An Outbreak of *Shigella Dysenteriae* Type 2 Among Laboratory Workers due to Intentional Food Contamination', in *Biological Weapons—Limiting the Threat*, ed. Joshua Lederberg, Cambridge: MIT Press, 2001.

Kupperman, Robert H., 'A Dangerous Future: The Destructive Potential of Criminal Arsenals', *Harvard International Review*, vol. 17, no. 3, Summer 1995, pp. 46–8.

Laquer, Walter, 'Postmodern Terrorism', *Foreign Affairs*, vol. 75, no. 5, 1996, pp. 23–34.

Lazowski, E.S. and S. Matulewicz, 'Serendipitous Discovery of Artificial Weil-Felix Reaction Used in "Private Immunological War"', *American Society for Microbiology News*, vol. 43 no. 6, June 1977, pp. 690–1.

Lederberg, Joshua, 'Infection Emergent', *Journal of the American Medical Association (JAMA)*, vol. 275 no. 3, 17 January 1996, pp. 243–5.

———, 'Introdution', in *Biological Weapons—Limiting the Threat*, ed. Joshua Lederberg, Cambridge: MIT Press, 2001.

———, 'Epilogue', in *Biological Weapons—Limiting the Threat*, ed. Joshua Lederberg, Cambridge: MIT Press, 2001.

———, 'The Control of Chemical and Biological Weapons', *Stanford Journal of International Studies*, vol. 7, 1972, pp. 22–44.

Leitenberg, Milton, 'The Biological Weapons Program of the Former Soviet Union', *Biologicals*, vol. 21, 1993, pp. 187–91.

———, 'Biological Weapons, International Sanctions and Proliferation', *Asian Perspective*, Winter 1997, p. 11.

———, 'An Assessment of the Biological Weapons Threat to the United States', *The Journal of Homeland Security*, January 2001, http://www.homelandsecurity.org/journal/Articles/Leitenberg.htm

———, 'Aum Shinrikyo's Efforts to Produce Biological Weapons: A Case Study in the Serial Propagation of Misinformation', *Terrorism and Political Violence*, vol. 11, no. 4, Winter 1999, pp. 149–58.

Letts, M., et al., 'The Conclusion of the Chemical Weapons Convention: An Australian Perspective', *Arms Control*, vol. 14, no. 3, December 1993, pp. 311–32.

Long, James, 'Rajneesh Dies in Indian Commune', *Oregonian*, 20 January 1990.

Lowe, Karl, Graham S. Peterson and Victor Utgoff, 'Potential Values of a Simple Biological Warfare Mask', in *Biological Weapons—Limiting the Threat*, ed. Joshua Lederberg, Cambridge: MIT Press, 2001.

Maerli, Morten Bremer, 'Relearning the ABCs: Terrorists and "Weapons of Mass Destruction"', *Nonproliferation Review*, vol. 7, no. 2, Summer 2000, pp. 108–19.

Marlo, Francis H., 'WMD Terrorism and US Intelligence Collection', *Terrorism and Political Violence*, vol. 11, no. 3, Autumn 1999, pp. 53–71.

Mayer, Jean-François, 'Cults, Violence and Religious Terrorism: An International Perspective', *Studies in Conflict and Terrorism*, vol. 24, no. 5, September 2001, pp. 361–76.

McGlinchey, David, 'International Response: Biological Security Convention Needed Experts Says', *Global Security Newswire*, 27 September 2002.

McNaugher, Thomas, 'Ballistic Missiles and Chemical Weapons: The Legacy of Iran-Iraq War', *International Security*, Fall 1990, pp. 5–34.

Miller, Judith et al., 'US Germ Warfare Research Pushes Treaty Limits', *New York Times*, 4 February 2001, p. A1.

Miller, Judith, 'When Is a Bomb Not a Bomb?', *New York Times*, 5 February 2001.

Miller, Judith and William J. Broad, 'Clinton Expected to Back Plan to Deter Terrorist Attack', *New York Times*, 26 April 1998, p. 1.

Meier, Oliver, 'Bare Bones Multilateralism at the BWC Review Conference', *Arms Control Today*, vol. 32, no. 10, December 2002.

Meselson Matthew, et al., 'The Sverdlovsk Anthrax Outbreak of 1979', in *Biological Weapons—Limiting the Threat*, ed. Joshua Lederberg, Cambridge: MIT Press, 2001.

Moon, John Ellis van Courtland, 'The Korean War Case', in *The Microbiologist and Biological Defense Research*, ed. Zilinskas, pp. 53–83.

Morganthau, Tom, 'A Shadow over the Olympics', *Newsweek*, 6 May 1996, p. 34.

Mueller, John and Karl Mueller, 'The Methodology of Mass Destruction: Assessing Threats in the New World Order', *Journal of Strategic Studies*, vol. 23, no. 1, March 2000, pp. 163–87.

Nye, Joseph S. and R. James Woolsey, 'Heed the Nuclear, Biological and Chemical Terrorist Threat', *International Herald Tribune*, 5 June 1997, p. 8.

Olle-Goig, Jaime E. and Jaume Canela-Soler, 'An Outbreak of *Brucella Melitensis* Infection by Airborne Transmission Among Laboratory Workers', *American Journal of Public Health*, vol. 77, 1987, pp. 335–8.

Olson, K.B., 'Biological Weapons and the Terror in Japan', *Terrorism*, 1, August 1997, p. 1.

Orient, Jane M., 'Chemical and Biological Warfare: Should Defences be Researched and Deployed?', *Journal of the American Medical Association (JAMA)*, vol. 262, no. 5, 4 August 1989, pp. 644–8.

Parachini, John V., 'Comparing Motives and Outcomes of Mass Casualty Terrorism Involving Conventional and Unconventional Weapons',

Studies in Conflict and Terrorism, vol. 24, no. 5, September 2001, pp. 389–406.

Parachini, John V., 'Non-Proliferation Policy and the War on Terrorism', *Arms Control Today*, vol. 31, no. 8, October 2001, pp. 13–15.

Pearson, Graham S. and Marie Isabelle Chevrier, 'An Effective prohibition of Biological Weapons', in *Biological Weapons—Limiting the Threat*, ed. Joshua Lederberg, Cambridge: MIT Press, 2001.

Pearson, Graham S., 'The Fourth BWC Review Conference: An Important Step Forward', *Arms Control Today*, vol. 27 no. 1, January–February 1997.

———, 'The Protocol to the Biological Weapons Convention is Within Reach', *Arms Control Today*, vol. 30, no. 5, June 2000.

———, 'Prospects for Chemical and Biological Arms Control: The Web of Deterrence', *The Washington Quarterly*, Spring 1993, pp. 145–62.

Pecha, Ann Marie, 'US Response: BWC Protocol, Proposed Alternatives Both Fall Short', *Global Security Newswire*, 1 October 2002.

Perry, William J., 'Preparing for the Next Attack', *Foreign Affairs*, vol. 80, no. 6, November–December 2001, pp. 31–45.

Pike, John, 'Taiwan, Chemical Weapons', *Federation of American Scientists*, (*FAS*), 24 August 1999. http://www.fas.org/nuke/guide/taiwan/cw

Pomerantsev A.P., et al., 'Expression of Cereolysine Ab Genes in Bacillus Anthracis Vaccine Strain Ensures Protection against Experimental Hemolytic Anthrax Infection', *Vaccine*, vol. 15, 1997, pp. 1846–50.

'Prospects for Progress, Drafting the Protocol to the BWC: Interview with Ambassador Tibor Tóth, Hungary's Permanent Representative to the UN Office in Vienna', *Arms Control Today*, vol. 30, no. 4, May 2000.

Rahman, Abdul et al., 'The Nature of Human Brucellosis in Kuwait: Study of 379 Cases', *Review of Infectious Diseases*, vol. 10, 1988, pp. 211–17.

——— et al., 'Brucellosis in Kuwait', *Transactions of the Royal Society for Tropical Medicine and Hygiene*, vol. 81, 1987, pp. 1019–21.

Reed, Laura and Seth Shulman, 'A Perilious Path to Security? Weighing US "Biodefence" against Qualitative Proliferation', in *Biological Warfare and Disarmament—New Problems and New Perspectives*, ed. Susan Wright, New Delhi: Vision Books, 2003.

Rich, Vera, 'Russia: Anthrax in the Urals', *Lancet*, vol. 339, 15 February 1992, pp. 419–20.

Rimmington, Anthony, 'The Soviet Union's Offensive Program: The Implications for Contemporary Arms Control', in *Biological Warfare and Disarmament—New Problems and New Perspectives*, ed. Susan Wright, New Delhi: Vision Books, 2003.

Risanen, Jenni, 'Hurdles Cleared, Obstacles Remaining: the Ad hoc Group Prepares for the Final Challenge', *Disarmament Diplomacy*, no. 56, April 2001.

Risanen, Jenni, 'A Turning Point to Nowhere? BWC in Trouble as US Turns its Back on Verification Protocol', *Disarmament Diplomacy*, no. 59, July–August 2001.

———, 'Left in Limbo: Review Conference Suspended—On Edge of Collapse', *Disarmament Diplomacy*, no. 6, December–January 2002.

———, 'Anger after the Ambush: Review Conference Suspended after US Asks for AHG's Termination', *BWC Review Conference Bulletin*, 9 December 2001. http://www. Acronym.org.uk/bwc/revcon8.htm

Roberts, Brad, 'Implementing the Biological Weapons Convention: Looking beyond the Verification Issue', in *The Verification of the Biological Weapons Convention: Problems and Perspectives*, ed. Oliver Thraenert, Bonn: Friedrich Ebert Stiftung, 1992.

———, 'New Challenges and New Policy Priorities for the 1990s', in *Biological Weapons: Weapons of the Future?* ed. Brad Roberts, Washington DC: Center for Strategic and International Studies, 1993.

Robertson, Andrew G. and Laura J. Robertson, 'From Asps to Allegations: Biological Warfare in History', *Military Medicine*, vol. 160, no. 8, August 1995, pp. 369–73.

Robinson, Julian P. Perry, 'Chemical and Biological Weapons Proliferation and Export Control', in *Proliferation and Export Controls*, eds. E. Clegg, P., Eavis, and J. Thurlow, London: Deltac and Saferworld, 1995, pp. 29–53.

Rolicka, Mary, 'New Studies Disputing Allegations of Bacteriological Warfare during the Korean War', *Military Medicine*, vol. 160, no. 3, March 1995, pp. 97–100.

Rosenau, William, 'Aum Shinrikyo's Biological Weapons Program: Why did it Fail?', *Studies in Conflict and Terrorism*, vol. 24, no. 4, July 2001, pp. 289–310.

Rosenberg, Barbara H., 'Allergic Reaction: Washington's Response to the BWC Protocol', *Arms Control Today*, vol. 31, no. 6, July–August 2001.

Rosenberg, Barbara H. and Milton Leitenberg, 'Who's Afraid of a Germ Warfare Treaty?', *Los Angeles Times*, 6 September 2001.

'Roundtable on the Implications of the 11 September 2001, Terrorist Attacks for Nonproliferation and Arms Control', *Nonproliferation Review*, vol. 8, no. 3, Fall–Winter 2001, pp. 11–26.

Roy, Olivier, et al., 'In America and the New Terrorism: An Exchange', *Survival*, vol. 42, no. 2, Summer 2000, pp. 165–72.

Russell, Philip K., 'Biological Terrorism—Responding to the Threat', *Emerging Infectious Diseases*, vol. 3, no. 2, April–June 1997, pp. 203–4.

Saikal, Amin, 'The Coercive Disarmament of Iraq', in *Biological Warfare and Disarmament—New Problems and New Perspectives*, ed. Susan Wright, New Delhi: Vision Books, 2003.

Salmon, M.M., et al., 'Q Fever in an Urban Area', *Lancet*, vol. 1, 1982, pp. 1002–4.

Schaap, Bill, 'US Biological Warfare: The 1981 Cuban Dengue Epidemic', *Covert Action*, no. 17, Summer 1982, pp. 28–31.

Schmid, Alex P., 'Terrorism and the Use of Weapons of Mass Destruction: From Where the Risk?', *Terrorism and Political Violence*, vol. 11, no. 4, Winter 1999, pp. 106–32.

Seeley, Thomas D., et al., 'Yellow Rain', *Scientific American*, vol. 253, no. 3, March 1985, pp. 128–37.

Selvin, Peter, 'US Drops Bid to Strengthen Germ Warfare Accord', *The Washington Post*, 19 September 2002, p. A01.

Shoham, Dany, 'Chemical and Biological Weapons in Egypt', *Nonproliferation Review*, Spring–Summer 1998, pp. 48–58.

Sidel, Victor W., 'Defence against Biological Weapons: Can Immunization and Secondary Prevention Succeed?', in *Biological Warfare and Disarmament—New Problems and New Perspectives*, ed. Susan Wright, New Delhi: Vision Books, 2003.

———, 'Weapons of Mass Detruction: The Greatest Threat to Public Health', *Journal of the American Medical Association (JAMA)*, vol. 262, no. 5, 4 August 1989, pp. 680–2.

Siegrist, David W., 'The Threat of Biological Attack: Why Concern Now?', *Emerging Infectious Diseases*, vol. 5, no. 4, July–August 1999, pp. 505–8.

Simon, Jeffrey D., 'Biological Terrorism: Preparing to Meet the Threat', in *Biological Weapons—Limiting the Threat*, ed. Joshua Lederberg, Cambridge: MIT Press, 2001.

Simon, Steven and Daniel Benjamin, 'The Terror', *Survival*, vol. 43, no. 4, Winter 2001–2, pp. 5–18.

Smith, D.L., et al., 'A Large Q Fever Outbreak in the West Midlands: Clinical Aspects', *Respiratory Medicine*, vol. 87, 1993, pp. 509–16.

Smith, Jeffrey R., 'Japanese Cult had Network of Front Companies, Investigators Say', *The Washington Post*, 1 November 1995, p. A8.

———, 'Yelstin Blames '79 Anthrax on Germ Warfare Efforts', *The Washington Post*, 16 June 1992, p. A1.

Sopko John F., 'The Changing Proliferation Threat', *Foreign Affairs*, vol. 105, Winter 1996–7, pp. 6–16.

Spicer, A.J., 'Military Significance of Q Fever: A Review', *Journal of the Royal Society of Medicine*, vol. 71, 1978, pp. 762–7.

Steinbruner, John D., 'Biological Weapons: A Plague Upon All Houses', *Foreign Policy*, vol. 109, Winter 1997–8, pp. 85–96.

Stephenson, Joan, 'Confronting a Biological Armageddon: Experts Tackle Prospect of Bioterrorism', *Journal of the American Medical Association (JAMA)*, vol. 276, no. 5, 7 August 1996, pp. 349–51.

'Sverdlovsk Outbreak: A Portent of Disaster', *Jane's Intelligence Review*, May 1998, p. 37.

Taylor, Robert, 'Bioterrorism Special Report: All Fall Down', *New Scientist*, vol. 150, no. 2029, 11 May 1996, p. 32.

Terril, Andrew W., 'The Chemical Warfare Legacy of the Yemen War', *Comparative Strategy*, vol. 10, no. 2, 1991, pp. 48–58.

Thanert, Oliver, 'The Compliance Protocol and the Three Depository Powers', in *Biological Warfare and Disarmament—New Problems and New Perspectives*, ed. Susan Wright, New Delhi: Vision Books, 2003.

'The Biological Weapons Convention at a Glance: Fact Sheet', *Arms Control Today*, vol. 34, no. 1, February 2004.

Tigerett, William D. and A.S. Benenson, 'Studies of Q Fever in Man', *Transactions of the Association of American Physicians*, 69, 1956, pp. 98-104.

Toner, Mike, 'Backgrounder: Germ Sharing: A Necessary Risk', *Atlanta Journal-Constitution*, 2 October 2002.

Torok, Thomas J., et al., 'A Large Community Outbreak of Salmonellosis Caused by Intentional Contamination of Restaurant Salad Bars', in *Biological Weapons—Limiting the Threat*, ed. Joshua Lederberg, Cambridge: MIT Press, 2001.

Tucker, David, 'What is New about the New Terrorism and How Dangerous is It?', *Terrorism and Political Violence*, vol. 13, no. 3, Autumn 2001, pp. 1–14.

Tucker, Johathan B., 'Bioterrorism: Threats and Responses', in *Biological Weapons—Limiting the Threat*, ed. Joshua Lederberg, Cambridge: MIT Press, 2001.

———, 'Strengthening the BWC: Moving Towards a Compliance Protocol,' *Arms Control Today*, vol. 28, no. 1, January–February 1998.

———, 'Historical Trends Related to Bioterrorism: An Empirical Analysis', *Emerging Infectious Diseases*, vol. 5, no. 4, July–August 1999, pp. 498–504.

———, 'In the Shadow of Anthrax: Strengthening the Biological Disarmament Regime', *The Nonproliferation Review*, vol. 9, no. 1, Spring 2002, pp. 114–20.

———, 'National Health and Medical Services Response to Incidents of Chemical and Biological Terrorism', *Journal of the American Medical Association (JAMA)*, vol. 278, no. 5, 6 August 1997, pp. 362–8.

———, 'Preventing Terrorist Access to Dangerous Pathogens: The Need for International Biosecurity Standards', *Disarmament Diplomacy*, no. 66, September 2002.

Tucker, Jonathan B. and Ziliinakas, Raymond A., 'Assessing U S Proposal to Strengthen the Biological Weapons Convention', *Arms Control Today*, vol. 32, no. 3, April 2002.

Turner, Douglas, 'US Sent Iraq Germs in Mid-80s', *The Buffalo News*, 23 September 2002.

Vick, Karl, 'Plea Bargain Rejected in Bubonic Plague Case', *Washington Post*, 3 April 1996, p. A8.

Vegar, Jose, 'Terrorism's New Breed', *Bulletin of the Atomic Scientists*, vol. 54, no. 2, March–April 1998, pp. 50–5.

Watanabe, Manabu, 'Religion and Violence in Japan Today: A Chronological and Doctrinal Analysis of Aum Shinrikyo', *Terrorism and Political Violence*, vol. 10, no. 4, Winter 1998, pp. 80–100.

Wheat, Richard P., Anne Zuckerman and Lowell A. Rantz, 'Infection Due to Chromobactiria: Report of Eleven Cases', *Archives of Internal Medicine*, vol. 88, no. 4, October 1951, pp. 461–6.

Whitehair, Rebecca, 'US under Anthrax Attack; Bioterror Source Unknown', *Arms Control Today*, vol. 31, no. 9, November 2001.

Wright, Susan, 'Introduction: In search of a New Paradigm of Biological Disarmament', in *Biological Warfare and Disarmament—New Problems and New Perspectives*, ed. Susan Wright, New Delhi: Vision Books, 2003.

———, 'Geopolitical Origins', in *Biological Warfare and Disarmament —New Problems and New Perspectives*, ed. Susan Wright, New Delhi: Vision Books, 2003.

———, 'Proposals for the Future: Strengthening Global Commitments to Biological Disarment', in *Biological Warfare and Disarmament—New Problems and New Perspectives*, ed. Susan Wright, New Delhi: Vision Books, 2003.

Wright, Susan and David A. Wallace, 'Secrecy in the Biolotechnology Industry: Implications for the Biological Weapons Convention', in *Biological Warfare and Disarmament—New Problems and New Perspectives*, ed. Susan Wright, New Delhi: Vision Books, 2003.

Wright, Susan and Richard Falk, 'Rethinking Biological Disarmament', in *Biological Warfare and Disarmament—New Problems and New Perspectives*, ed. Susan Wright, New Delhi: Vision Books, 2003.

Yang, Jonathan, 'US Biodefence Plans Worry Nonproliferation Advocates', *Arms Control Today*, vol. 33 no. 7, September 2003.

Young, Edward J., 'An Overview of Human Brucellosis', *Clinical Infections and Diseases*, vol. 21, 1995, pp. 283–9.

Yu, Victor L., '*Serratia Marcescens*: Historical Perspective and Clinical Review', *New England Journal of Medicine*, vol. 300, no. 16, 19 April 1979, p. 889.

Yunhua, Zou, 'China: Balancing Disarmament and Development', in *Biological Warfare and Disarmament—New Problems and New Perspectives*, ed. Susan Wright, New Delhi: Vision Books, 2003.

Zanders, Jean Pascal, 'Assessing the Risk of Chemical and Biological Weapons Proliferation to Terrorists', *Nonproliferation Review*, vol. 6, no. 4, Fall 1999, pp. 17–34.

Zelicoff, Alan P., 'An Impractical Protocol', *Arms Control Today*, vol. 31, no. 4, May 2001.

Zilinskas, Raymond A., 'Bioethics and Biological Weapons', Science, vol. 279, 30 January 1998, p. 635.

———, 'Iraq's Biological Warfare Program: The Past as Future?', in *Biological Weapons—Limiting the Threat*, ed. Joshua Lederberg, Cambridge: MIT Press, 2001.

———, 'Terrorism and Biological Weapons: Inevitable Alliance?', *Perspectives in Biology and Medicine*, vol. 34, no. 1, Autumn 1990, pp. 44–72.

———, 'The Other Biological-Weapons Worry', *New York Times*, 28 November 1997, p. A39.

Contributors

P.R. CHARI is a former member of the Indian Administrative Service. He served in several senior positions at the Central and State level. He was an Additional Secretary in the Ministry of Defence. His last position in the Government was as Chief Executive of the Narmada Valley Development Authority. On the academic side he was Director of the Institute for Defence Studies and Analyses, New Delhi (1975-80), International Fellow, Center for International Affairs, Harvard University (1983-84), Research Professor, Centre for Policy Research (1992-96), Co-Director and Director, Institute of Peace and Conflict Studies (1996-2003). Currently he is Research Professor at the Institute of Peace and Conflict Studies.

His books include *Indo-Pak Nuclear Stand off: Role of the United States* (1995); Co-author, *Brasstacks and Beyond: Perception and Management of Crisis* (1995); Co-author and Co-editor, *Nuclear Non-Proliferation in India and Pakistan: South Asian Perspectives* (1996); Editor, *Perspectives on National Security in South Asia: In Search of a New Paradigm* (1999); Co-editor, *Kargil: The Tables Turned* (2001); Co-editor, *Working towards a Verification Protocol for Biological Weapons* (2001); Co-author, *The Spring 1990 Crisis in Indo-Pak Relations* (2003). Co-editor, *Nuclear Stability in Southern Asia* (2003); Co-editor, *Biological Weapons: Issues and Threats* (2003).

SUBA CHANDRAN is Assistant Director at the Institute of Peace and Conflict Studies, New Delhi. He is currently a Visiting Fellow at the South Asian Strategic Stability Unit (SASSU), Department of Peace Studies, University of Bradford. His research interests include Pakistan, Kashmir, Indo-Pak relations and terrorism. He is currently working on a study titled *India's Security Problematique*; and another joint study titled *Indo-Pak Conflicts: Ripe to Resolve?* along with a Pakistani scholar.

Some of his recent research works include *Limited War: Revisiting Kargil in Indo-Pak Conflict* (2005). He has also contributed articles to journals. He can be contacted at suba@ipcs.org

KALPANA CHITTARANJAN received her doctorate from the School of International Studies, Pondicherry University. Before joining ORF Chennai in 2003, she was in New Delhi for almost seven years, working as a Research Officer in the Institute of Defence Studies and Analyses, where her areas of interest included arms control issues in nuclear and biological weapons. Her present area of interest is Sri Lanka on which she brings out a weekly newsletter. She has contributed articles to newspapers, research journals and books and has authored two items for the world's first comprehensive encyclopedia on weapons of mass destruction. She can be contacted at kalpana@orfonline.org

COL. P.K. GAUTAM was commissioned in the Regiment of Artillery in 1970 after training at the National Defence Academy and the Indian Military Academy. He was a gun position officer with 24 Medium Regiment in the 1971 Indo-Pakistan war in Bangladesh and also an observation post officer with the infantry.

He has authored two books *Environmental Security: Internal and External Dimensions and Response* (2003) and *National Security: A Primer* (2004). His articles have featured in well-known journals. He has presented papers at various seminars on environment. At present he is with the USI of India on their Editorial Staff.

COL. V.M. KALIA was commissioned in the Regiment of Artillery in 1976. He is an alumnus of National Defence Academy and Indian Military Academy. He has held various appointments in staff, instructional and command tenures. He has done M.Sc (Defence Studies) from Madras University, Defence Services Staff College and the Higher Command course. The officer has specialized in NBC warfare and is presently holding the appointment of Director Perspective Planning and deals with the aspects of threat assessment strategy and operations pertaining to NBC warfare at Army Headquarters.

BRIGADIER GURMEET KANWAL, commanded an infantry brigade in the high-altitude Gurez Sector on the Line of Control with Pakistan (Operation Parakaram, 2001-03) and an artillery field regiment in counter-insurgency operations in Kashmir Valley (Operation Rakshak, 1993-94). He has served as Deputy Assistant Chief of Integrated Defence Staff at HQ Integrated Defence Staff, New Delhi; as Director MO-5 in the Directorate General of Military Operations at Army Headquarters (dealing with threat, strategy and force structure); United Nations Military Observer Group in UNTAG, Namibia; Brigade Major of an infantry brigade and, as an Instructor-in-Gunnery at the School of Artillery, Devlali.

A former Senior Fellow at the Institute for Defence Studies and Analyses (IDSA), New Delhi, Brigadier Kanwal has authored several books including *Nuclear Defence: Shaping the Arsenal*; *Pakistan's Proxy War*; *Heroes of Kargil*; *Kargil '99: Blood, Guts and Firepower and Artillery: Honour and Glory*. He has contributed extensively to journals of repute as well as leading national newspapers. He is Senior Fellow, Institute of Security Studies at the Observer Research Foundation, New Delhi. He can be contacted at gurmeetkanwal@hotmail.com.

RESHMI KAZI is presently working as a Research Officer in the Institute of Peace and Conflict Studies, New Delhi. She is doing her doctorate from the Centre for International Politics, Organization and Disarmament, School of International Studies, JNU, New Delhi. Her M.Phil. was on 'The Rationale of India's Nuclear Deterrence'. Her articles have been published on the IPCS web-site and leading research journals like *Mainstream*. Her areas of interest include WMD nonproliferation and India's nuclear policy. She can be contacted at reshmi@ipcs.org

PRAFULLA KETKAR has been working as a Research Officer at the Institute of Peace and Conflict Studies. His M.Phil. dissertation was on 'New Regionalism and its impact on Globalisation'.

His research interests include energy security, cyber terrorism, bio-terrorism, environmental security, organized crime, criminalization of politics and globalization. He has written extensively for the IPCS website. He can be contacted at prafulla@ipcs.org

SQN LDR AJEY LELE is an Indian Air Force Officer from Meteorological Branch and is currently working as a Research Fellow at Institute for Defence Studies and Analyses (IDSA), New Delhi. He works on issues related to Weapons of Mass Destruction (WMD), Environmental Security and Space Tech-nologies. Author of many articles, he has published *Bio-Weapons: The Genie in the Bottle*. He can be contacted at ajeylele@yahoo.co.in

ASHOK RATTAN (MD, MAMS) is a medical microbiologist currently Director of Microbiology in Ranbaxy's New Drug Discovery Research at Gurgaon, Haryana. At present his laboratory is involved in identification and development of new anti-infective, antibacterials and antifungals to meet the unmet medical needs of the society. He can be contacted at ashok.rattan@ranbaxy.com

ANIMESH ROUL is presently working with the Society for the Study of Peace and Conflict (SSPC), New Delhi where he specializes in WMD terrorism and security issues. He writes frequently on issues related to arms control and proliferations, terrorism, and on his latest interest, emerging and reemerging infectious diseases (ERIDs). He is also a correspondent for International Security Network (ISN), Switzerland. He can be contacted at officemail @sspconline.org.

ARUN VISHWANATHAN is presently a Research Scholar at the Disarmament Division of the Centre for International Politics, Organisation and Disarmament (CIPOD), at the School of International Studies, JNU. His interest areas include Arms Control and Disarmament issues and Nuclear Issues in Southern Asia. He has written articles for the IPCS website and the *Hindustan Times*. He can be contacted at arun_summerhill@ yahoo.com